It's Not Just Another Cover-Up!

Pam Bono Designs, Inc.

It's Not Just Another Cover-Up!

Published by

the art of everyday living

LEISURE ARTS
5701 Ranch Drive
Little Rock, AR 72212
www.leisurearts.com

EDITORIAL STAFF

Editor-in-Chief:
Pam Bono
Editorial Assistants
Susan Clark and Nora Smith, Claire Walker
Editors
Robert Bono, Susan Clark, Nora Smith
Art Director and Book Design
Pam Bono
Graphic Illustrations
Pam Bono
Photographer For Pam Bono Designs
Christopher Marona

Photographer For Zelda Wisdom
Shane Young
Photo Stylists
Christopher Marona, Pam and Robert Bono,
and Susan Clark
Photo Stylists for Zelda Wisdom
Carol Gardner and Shane Young

Produced by

Pam Bono Designs, Inc.

P.O. Box 659
Pagosa Springs, CO 81147
www.pambonodesigns.com

Quilts shown on page 1 are from this book, and other Leisure Arts/Pam Bono Designs books. The Baltimore Album quilt can be found in "Pieces Of Baltimore, The Ultimate Collection". The Irish Chain and Heart Throw can be found in "The Big Book Of Rotary Cutter Quilts", and the Butterfly quilt may be found in the "Dear Pam.....Teach Me" book.

The information in this publication is presented in good faith, but no warranty is given, nor results guaranteed. Since we have no control over physical conditions surrounding the application of information herein contained, Leisure Arts, Inc. disclaims any liability for untoward results.

* Some products mentioned in this book may be trademarked, but not to be acknowledged as so.

Made in the United States of America.

Softcover ISBN 1-57486-440-8

10 9 8 7 6 5 4 3 2 1

Dedication:

This book is dedicated to the memory of Darla. I know you can see the beautiful things your sister is doing.

Credits

Designs by Mindy Kettner: Staffordshire dog and cat beds, Palm tree, and Shoe Boutique.

Designs by Susan Clark: In The Pines, and Pastel Spring.

Window treatment and pillow designs: Susan Clark

Designs by Susan Clark, Pam and Robert Bono: Log Cabin Duvet Cover, Spring At Dusk Tablecloth, and Forget Me Not

Designs by Pam Bono: Circling Tulips, Folk Flowers, and Buttons & Bows.

Quilting by: Mary Nordeng

Piecing by Susan Clark, Nora Smith, Tara Coronado, and Kim Zenk,

Binding by: Carolyn Matson

Special Thanks To:

Sandra Case and the art department team at Leisure Arts for being so great to work with.

Valorie Green, owner of Canyon Crest Lodge Bed and Breakfast. Phone: (877) 731-1377. www..canyoncrestlodge.com. Thank you for your hospitality and for allowing us to shoot in such beautiful surroundings.

Whispering Pines Homes. P.O. Box 4896 • Pagosa Springs, CO. 81147. Phone: (970)731-3093. Thank you for allowing us to shoot our duvet cover in your beautiful home.

Linda Love, owner of "The Hideout." Thanks for the loan of your wagon wheel bench. Visit this great shop at 117 Navajo Trail Drive, Suite C. • Pagosa Springs, CO. 81147

Cherron Adair owner of Adair Kennels, Aztec, NM. (505) 334-9834. Thanks for driving so far to share those adore-a-bull puppies!

Husqvarna Viking Sewing Machine Company for the loan of our Designer 1 machines.

RJR Fabrics, Benartex Fabrics, and Robert Kaufman Fabrics for your supply of lovely fabrics.

Carol Gardener, Shane Young and the fabulous "Ms. Zelda" for your participation in this book to add joy and laughter. www.zeldawisdom.com

The designs in this book bring new concepts for you to consider to make your surroundings beautiful in many ways, even for your best loved animal friend! Toaster covers, tea cozies, and sewing machine covers were deliberately left out of our plans as they are available in many other places. The window treatments in this book may be accomplished without a huge investment, and are simple to do. It's amazing what can be done with a small investment and a little ingenuity and creativity.

With the large number of pillow top mattress covers now in use, the ordinary queen sized quilt becomes a bit too small to meet the needs of these new and comfortable additions. As sheet manufacturers have made adjustments for the pillow tops, we also decided to enlarge our quilts a bit. They not only cover the top of the bed properly, but hang down far enough to make the quilts and coordinating borders more attractive. Many of you have gone into your favorite quilt shops asking for suggestions to add more borders to accommodate the new depth of the pillow top mattresses. We hope that we have solved the problem with the designs in this book.

Our move to Pagosa Springs, Colorado over a year ago has not only brought new inspiration because of the beauty of the majestic mountains, lovely valleys, stately pines and wildlife, but the challenge of developing a new team in a small town.

This book is a collaboration of old and new. In March, my friend, and old design partner, Mindy Kettner, who now lives in Canada, joined me for a week of working together once again, along with our usual fun and laughter. When we are fortunate enough to get together, it seems as though we have never been apart. This kind of friendship is a gift to be found only a few times in our lives.

It has been exciting for me to find someone who possesses a great deal of talent that has not been used to its best advantage. When we reviewed the work of people to piece our designs before our move, an interesting lady presented her work to me. I saw immediately that it was anything but ordinary, and I was impressed by her extraordinary color sense. I knew that if I dug a little deeper, there was a lot more to be brought out. It is with great pleasure that we introduce the work of Susan Clark in this book, both in a collaborative and individual design presentation. Her contributions are numerous. Not only is she a fun and joyful soul, with a great sense of humor, but a terrific creative talent and friend.

Enjoy, and Happy Quilting!
Pam Bono

4

Table of Contents

Log Cabin duvet cover. Pages 90-97

Spring At Dusk tablecloth. Pages 25-33

Staffordshire cat bed Pages 72-73

Pastel Spring Pages 13-24

5

Learning Our Techniques

**The techniques shown on the following pages are used in projects throughout the book. Please refer to these techniques frequently and practice them with scraps.

STRIP PIECING

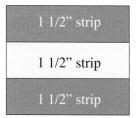

Strip Set 1. Make 2. Cut into fifty - 1 1/2" segments.

Strip piecing.

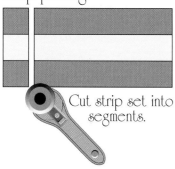

Cut strip set into segments.

For some projects, you'll join strips of different fabrics to make what is called a strip set. Project directions not only show illustrations of each strip set, but specify how many strip sets to make, how many segments are to be cut from each strip set, and the specific size of each strip and segment. In each project where strip sets are used, you are also shown exactly where to place them in the project diagrams and instructions. To sew a strip set, match each pair of strips with right sides facing. Stitch through both layers along one long edge. When sewing multiple strips in a set, practice "antidirectional" stitching to keep strips straight. As you add strips, sew each new seam in the *opposite direction* from the last one. This distributes tension evenly in both directions, and keeps your strip set from getting warped and wobbly.

DIAGONAL CORNERS

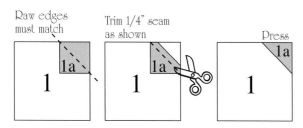

Raw edges must match   Trim 1/4" seam as shown   Press

This technique turns squares into sewn triangles. It is especially helpful if the corner triangle is very small. It's easier to cut and handle a square than a small triangle. The best thing about this technique is that it completely eliminates templates! By sewing squares,

to squares, you don't have to guess where the seam allowance meets, which is difficult with triangles. Project instructions give the size of the fabric pieces needed. The sizes given in the cutting instructions *include* seam allowance. The base is either a square or rectangle, but the contrasting corner is <u>always</u> a square.

1. To make a diagonal corner, with right sides facing match the small square to one corner of the base fabric. It is important that raw edges match perfectly and do not shift during sewing.

2. As a seam guide, you may wish to draw or press a diagonal line from corner to corner. For a quick solution to this time consuming task, refer to our instructions on the following pages for The Angler 2.

3. Stitch the small square diagonally from corner to corner. Trim the seam allowance as shown on the diagonal corner square only, leaving the base fabric untrimmed for stability and keeping the corner square. Press the diagonal corner square over as shown.

4. Many units in the projects have multiple diagonal corners or ends. When these are the same size, and cut from the same fabric, the identifying unit letter is the same. But, if the unit has multiple diagonal pieces that are different in size and/or color, the unit letters are different. These pieces are joined to the main unit in alphabetical order.

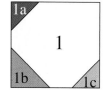

5. Many of our projects utilize diagonal corners on diagonal corners as

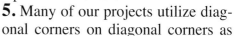
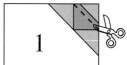
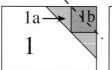

shown above. Diagonal corners are also added in alphabetical order. Join the first diagonal corner, trim, and press it out. Next add the second diagonal corner, trim and press it out as shown.

6. Our designs also utilize diagonal corners on joined units such as strip sets. In this case, the joined units will have one unit number in the center of the unit as shown at right. The diagonal corner will have its own unit number.

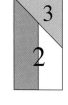

7. We have discovered many ways in which our quick piecing techniques can be used, especially with diagonal corners.

See diagrams on the following page. Practicing these techniques so they become second nature to you, speeds you through a project, and will save a great deal of time.

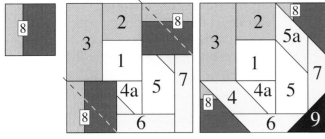

Strip sets used as diagonal corners.

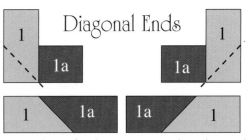

Diagonal Ends

Diagonal End - Left Slant   Diagonal End - Right Slant

We have discovered how quickly units can be made by sewing together two strips of specified dimensions, then using these units as diagonal corners. This technique is very effective. To end up with horizontal stripes, Unit 8 is placed on the main unit with the stripes going vertically. To end up with vertical stripes, place Unit 8 on the main unit with the stripes going horizontally. Raw edges must match. Accuracy in piecing is critical to the final dimensions of a block. Stitch a diagonal seam as shown for both. Trim center seam and press.

IMPORTANT: If your diagonal corner is a light color on top of a darker fabric, DO NOT trim the center seam, or the darker fabric will show through!

DIAGONAL CORNERS USING THE ANGLER 2™

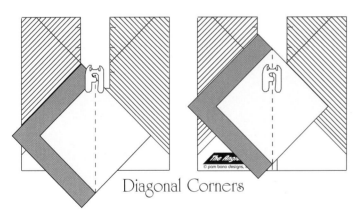

Diagonal Corners

When using the Angler 2, watch the point of your fabric on the center line - NOT the needle!

1. Align the diagonal corners with raw edges matching. Line the fabric up so the right side of the square is aligned with the first 45° line on the right of the Angler 2. Have the tip of the fabric under the needle. No seam guide lines will need to be drawn unless the square is larger than 7 3/4". As the feed dogs pull the fabric through the machine, keep the fabric aligned with the diagonal lines on the right until the center line of the Angler 2 bottom is visible.

2. Keep the tip of the square on this line as the diagonal corner is fed through the machine. Trim the seam as shown on page 6.

1. This method joins two rectangles on the diagonal and eliminates the difficulty of measuring and cutting a trapezoid. It is similar to the diagonal corner technique, but here you work with two rectangles. Our project cutting instructions specify the size of each rectangle, and identify the unit numbers and letters.

2. To sew diagonal ends, place rectangles perpendicular to each other with right sides facing, matching corners to be sewn. Before you sew, mark or press the diagonal stitching line, and check the right side to see if the line is angled in the desired direction.

3. Position the rectangles under the needle, leading with the top edge. Sew a diagonal seam to the opposite edge. Check the right side to see that the seam is angled correctly. Press the seam and trim the excess fabric from the seam allowance.

4. As shown above, the direction of the seam makes a difference. Make mirror-image units with this in mind, or you can put different ends on the same strip.

5. This technique is wonderful for making *continuous* binding strips. On the diagrams below, diagonal ends are made first. Diagonal corners may then be added in alphabetical order.

6. Diagonal ends may be added to joined units in the same manner as shown in the diagram on page 8.

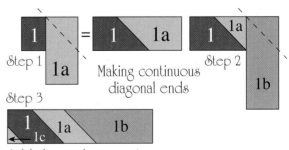

Making continuous diagonal ends

Add diagonal corner 1c

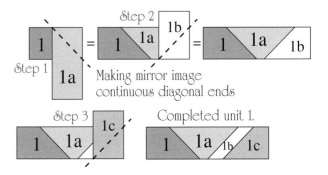

Making mirror image continuous diagonal ends

Completed unit 1.

Making mirror image combined unit diagonal ends.

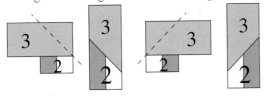

Strip sets used as diagonal ends.

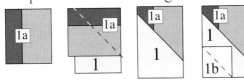

Please note:

This technique is the same as for strip set diagonal corners, only this time the strip set is not square and is used as a diagonal end as shown above. Diagonal corners may be added after the diagonal end is trimmed and pressed.

DIAGONAL ENDS USING THE ANGLER 2™

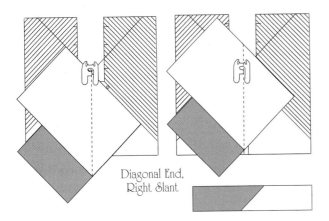

Diagonal End, Right Slant

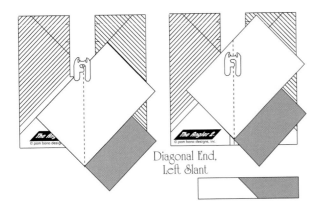

Diagonal End, Left Slant

1. For both slants, prepare rectangles with raw edges matching. For the right slant, align the top rectangle with the first 45° line on right side of The Angler 2.

2. The bottom rectangle should align on the first 45° left line as shown. As feed dogs pull fabric through machine, keep fabric aligned with the diagonal lines on the right until center line on the Angler 2 bottom is visible. Keep the top of the rectangle on this line as it is fed through the machine. Trim seam and press.

3. For the left slant, align the top rectangle with the first 45° line on left side of The Angler 2 as shown. As rectangles are fed through the machine, keep top rectangle aligned with left diagonal lines on The Angler 2. This technique is great for joining binding strips.

TRIANGLE SQUARES

1. Many patchwork designs are made by joining two contrasting triangles to make a square. Many people use the grid method when dozens of triangles are required in a design. However, for the designs in this book we use a simple way to make one or more triangle-squares. To do so, draw or press a diagonal line from corner to corner on the back of the lightest colored square.

2. As an extra tip, we have found that spraying the fabric with spray starch before cutting the squares to be used keeps them from distorting. A bit more fabric may be used; however, it is a quick and easy technique.

3. Place squares right sides together and stitch on the line. Trim the seam as shown and press. When you begin stitching these units, your needle may have a tendency to pull the tip of the square down in the hole. This is maddening! Our remedy is to use a small piece of stabilizer as a "leader", then follow with the diagonal seam. This technique may be done easily by using The Angler 2.

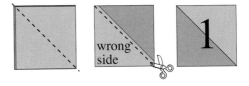

4. The illustration at right shows how triangle-square units are marked in the book. A diagonal line is always shown, separating the two fabric colors. The unit number is always shown in the center of the square.

MACHINE PIECING

An accurate, consistent 1/4" seam allowance is essential for good piecing. If each seam varies by the tiniest bit, the difference multiplies greatly by the time the block is completed. Before you start a project, be sure that you can sew a precise 1/4" seam allowance. Refer to instructions and illustrations for use of The Angler 2 in this section to aid with accurate seams.

1. Set your sewing machine to 12-14 stitches per inch. Use 100%-cotton or cotton/polyester sewing thread.

2. Match pieces to be sewn with right sides facing. Sew each seam from cut edge to cut edge of the fabric piece. It is not necessary to backstitch, because most seams will be crossed and held by another seam. We do stay stitch the ends on the outer borders.

COMBINING THE TECHNIQUES

Multiple units sewn together into a square to be used as a diagonal corner.

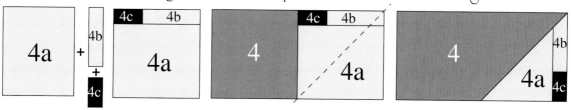

We discovered how well this new technique worked when we were working on one of the quilt designs. As we wanted all of the 4a, 4b, and 4c units sewn into the triangle, we noticed that by piecing the 4b and 4c units; then adding them to the 4a unit, it became a square, which was usable as a diagonal corner making it much easier to sew into the corner triangle instead of trying to piece these units as a diagonal. The step-by-step diagram above shows how it is done.

Multiple units using the diagonal corner and triangle-square techniques.

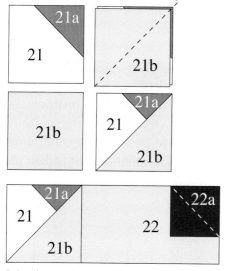

Join diagonal corner 21a onto 3 1/2" square, Unit 21. Place 3 1/2" square, Unit 21b right sides facing, and raw edges matching as shown. Stitch diagonal. Trim seam and press.

When you want two different 45° angles in the same unit, this technique works like a dream. First a diagonal corner is sewn as shown above; then our triangle-square technique is used to make this multiple unit.

SEWING AN "X"

1. When triangles are pieced with other units, seams should cross in an "X" on the back. If the joining seam goes precisely through the center of the "X", the triangle will have a nice sharp point on the front.

PRESS AND PIN

1. To make neat corners and points, seams must meet precisely. Pressing and pinning can help achieve matched seams.

2. To press, set your iron on cotton. Use an up-and-down motion, lifting the iron from spot to spot. Sliding the iron back and forth can push seams out of shape. First press the seam flat on the wrong side; then open the piece and press the right side.

3. Press patchwork seam allowance to one side, not open as in dressmaking. If possible, press toward the darker fabric to avoid seam allowance showing through light fabric. Press seam allowances in opposite directions from row to row. By offsetting seam allowances at each intersection, you reduce the bulk under the patchwork. This is more important than pressing seam allowances toward dark fabric.

4. Use pins to match seam lines. With right sides facing, align opposing seams, nesting seam allowances. On the top piece, push a pin through the seam line 1/4" from the edge. Then push the pin through the bottom seam and set it. Pin all matching seams; then stitch the joining seams, removing pins as you sew.

EASING FULLNESS

1. Sometimes two units that should be the same size are slightly different. When joining such units, pin-match opposing seams. Sew the seam with the shorter piece on top. As you sew, the feed dogs ease the fullness on the bottom piece. This is called "sewing with a baggy bottom."

2. If units are too dissimilar to ease without puckering, check each one to see if the pieces were correctly cut and that the seams are 1/4" wide. Remake the unit that varies the most from the desired size.

CHAIN PIECING

1. Chain piecing is an efficient way to sew many units in one operation, saving time and thread. Line up several units to be sewn. Sew the first unit as usual, but at the end of the seam do not backstitch, clip the thread, or lift the presser foot. Instead, feed the next unit right on the heels of the first. There will be a little twist of thread between each unit. Sew as many seams as you like on a chain. Keep the chain intact to carry to the ironing board and clip the threads as you press.

Using Our Instructions..

The following points explain how the instructions in our book are organized. You will find that all projects are made easier if you read this section thoroughly and follow each tip.

• Yardage is based on 40-42" wide fabric, allowing for up to 4% shrinkage. 100% cotton fabric is recommended for the quilt top and backing.

• At the beginning of each project, we tell you which techniques are used so you can practice them before beginning. Seam allowances *are included* in all stated measurements and cutting.

• The materials list provides you with yardage requirements for the project. We have included the exact number of inches needed to make the project, with Yardage given to the nearest 1/8 yard. By doing this, we are giving you the option to purchase extra yardage if you feel you may need more.

• A color key accompanies each materials list, matching each fabric with the color-coded illustrations given with the project directions. We have made an effort to match the colors in the graphics to the actual fabric colors used in the project.

• Cutting instructions are given for each fabric, the first cut, indicated by a •, is usually a specific number of cross grain strips. The second cut, indicated by *, specifies how to cut those strips into smaller pieces, or "segments." The identification of each piece follows in parenthesis, consisting of the block letter and unit number that corresponds to the assembly diagram. For pieces used in more than one unit, several unit numbers are given.

• Every project has one or more block designs. Instructions include block illustrations that show the fabric color, and the numbered units.

• Organize all cut pieces in zip top bags, and label each bag with the appropriate unit numbers. We use masking tape on the bags to label them. This avoids confusion and keeps the pieces stored safely until they are needed. Arrange all fabric colors, in their individual bags with like fabrics together, making it easy to find a specific unit and fabric color.

• In order to conserve fabric, we have carefully calculated the number of units that can be cut from specified strips. In doing this, units may be cut in two or three different places in the cutting instructions, from a variety of strips. So that cut units may be organized efficiently, the units that appear in more than one strip are shown in red on the cutting list. This immediately tells you that there will be more of that specific unit. Additional cuts are not only shown in red, but the words "add to" are shown within the parenthesis so you may keep that zip top bag open, knowing in advance there will be more units to add. "Stack this cut" will appear frequently in the cutting instructions. Refer to the drawing below. We utilize the width of the strip with the first unit to be cut; then other units can be stacked on top of each other to best utilize the strips.

"Stack this cut......."

2"	Cut #1 two 1" x 2"	Cut #2 stacked. four 1" x 3"	Cut #3 two 1 3/4" squares

2" wide strip. Do not cut strips down unless directed.

• Large pieces such as sashing and borders are generally cut first to assure you have enough fabric. To reduce further waste of fabric, you may be instructed to cut some pieces from a first-cut strip, and then cut that strip down to a narrower width to cut additional pieces.

• Cutting and piecing instructions are given in a logical step-by-step progression. Follow this order always to avoid having to rip out in some cases. Although there are many assembly graphics, we strongly suggest reading the written instructions along with looking at the graphics.

• Individual units are assembled first. Use one or

more of the "quick piecing" techniques described on pages 6-8.

- Strip set illustrations show the size of the segments to be cut from that strip set. The illustration also designates how many strip sets are to be made, and the size of the strips. The strip set segments are then labeled as units within the block illustration. Keep strip set segments in their own labeled zip top bag.

- Each unit in the assembly diagram is numbered. The main part of the unit is indicated with a number only. A diagonal line represents a seam where a diagonal corner or end is attached. Each diagonal piece is numbered with the main unit number plus a letter: Example: (1a).

- Many extra illustrations are given throughout the projects for assembly of unusual or multiple units for more clarity.

QUILTING TIP

The finished measurements for all projects in the book are given for the PIECED TOP. Quilting can take up anywhere from 1" - 3".
Be sure to take this into consideration.

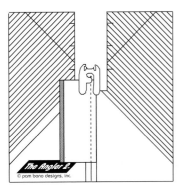

Fabric is lined up on the computer generated 1/4" seam line on The Angler 2, and stitching is along center guide line. To take a full 1/4" seam, line fabric up on 1/4" seam line. If you want a "scant" 1/4" seam, line fabric up so that the seam guide line shows. **We recommend a "scant" 1/4" seam as your seams end up being more accurate after they are pressed.**

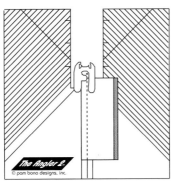

EMBROIDERY CHAIN STITCH

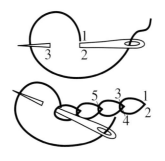

We have used this stitch in a few of the blocks in this book. Follow the diagrams at left. This is a looped stitch with each loop or link being secured to the fabric by the next link. It can be worked along a straight line or in a circle. Come up at 1 and swing thread in a counterclockwise direction under the needle tip. Insert the needle at 2, one or two threads away from 1. Come up at 3 and pull thread through, keeping loop beneath point of needle. Pull until loop is desired fullness. Continue down at r and up at 5 until desired number of loops is completed. Anchor end of chain by inserting needle over top of loop, close to previous exit point.

HOW TO MAKE ONE BLOCK

Cutting instructions are given for making the project as shown. There may be times that you want to make just one block for a project of your own design. All you have to do is count, or divide if preferred.

With each cutting list there is an illustration for the block (s). Unit numbers in the cutting list correspond with the units in the illustration. Count how many of each unit are in the block illustration. Instead of cutting the number shown on the cutting list, cut the number you need for one block. Should you wish to make two or more blocks, multiply the number of units X the number of blocks you wish to make.

HELPFUL TIPS

For all strip set diagonal corners, if you want your strip set to end up horizontally, it must be placed vertically. If you want it to end up vertically, it must be placed horizontally.

All "Q" units in cutting instructions stand for "quilt top". These units are not incorporated into any specific block, however they are part of the quilt top.

11

Straight-grain, French Fold binding.

Diagram 1
Joining binding strips.

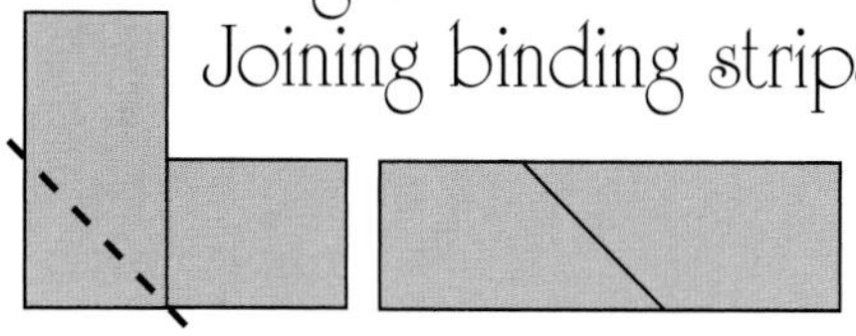

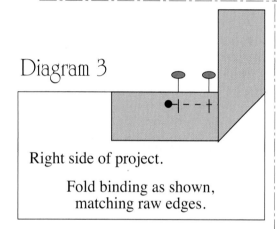

Continuous Binding
Bias or straight-grain.

Diagram 2

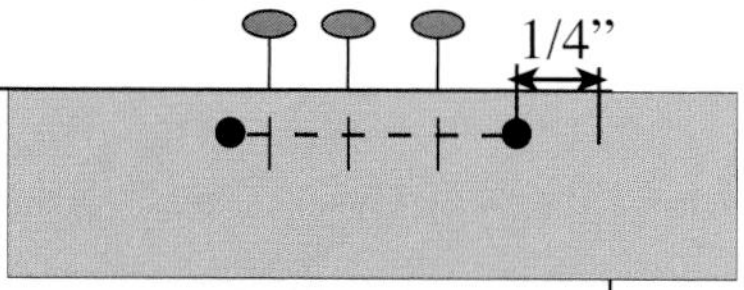

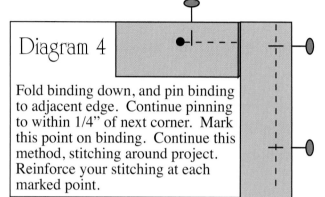

1/4"

Fold binding in half lengthwise and press. Matching right sides, and beginning at lower edge of project, pin raw edges of binding to project, (dot) leaving a 6" tail. Continue pinning to within 1/4" of corner. Mark this point on binding. Use a 1/4" seam allowance and stitch to your mark. Backstitch at beginning of stitching and again when you reach your mark. Lift needle out of fabric and clip thread.

Diagram 3

Right side of project.

Fold binding as shown,
matching raw edges.

Diagram 4

Fold binding down, and pin binding to adjacent edge. Continue pinning to within 1/4" of next corner. Mark this point on binding. Continue this method, stitching around project. Reinforce your stitching at each marked point.

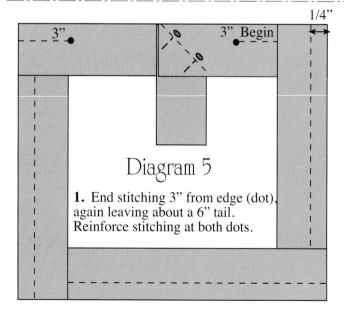

3"   3" Begin   1/4"

Diagram 5

1. End stitching 3" from edge (dot), again leaving about a 6" tail. Reinforce stitching at both dots.

2. Fold left tail down at a 45° angle (perpendicular to top). Bring other tail straight across on top of folded bottom tail. Draw a 45° line from top left to bottom right where they meet, and pin in place as shown.
3. As there is plenty of room that is unsewn between the dots, pull the pinned binding out, and stitch the diagonal as shown on dashed 45° line. Trim seam 1/4" from stitching.
4. Complete sewing binding to project between dots, 1/4" from edge.

5. Trim batting and backing even with the seam allowance. Fold the binding over the seam allowance to the back. Blind stitch the folded edge to backing fabric. Fold and mitre into the binding at back corners

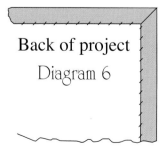

Back of project
Diagram 6

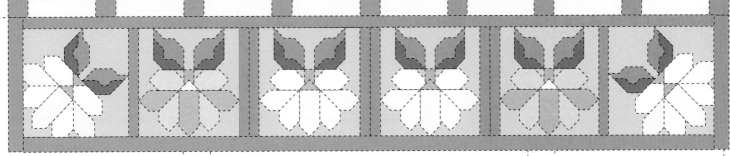

Pastel Spring

This gorgeous ensemble by Susan Clark is a true breath of spring! Easy piecing with large open areas to fill with your own creative quilting ideas. The lovely trapunto quilting by Mary Nordeng sets this aside as an exquisite art piece. Quick to make decorative pillows, coordinating pillow cases, and a simple window treatment turn any bedroom into a garden in full bloom!

Quilt finishes to: 90 1/4" x 106".

Techniques Used: Diagonal corners, diagonal ends, and strip sets used as diagonal corners.

MATERIALS

Fabric I (light green print)
Need 258 5/8"   7 3/8 yards

Fabric II (medium green print)
Need 30"   1 yard

Fabric III (medium green solid)
Need 6 1/4"   3/8 yard

Fabric IV (dark green print)
Need 77"   2 1/4 yards

Fabric V (light pink print)
Need 18 3/8"   5/8 yard

Fabric VI (dark pink print)
Need 17 1/2"   5/8 yard

Fabric VII (light yellow solid)
Need 22 1/8"   3/4 yard

Fabric VIII (medium yellow print)
Need 18 5/8   5/8 yards

Fabric IX (dark yellow print)
Need 5 1/8"   1/4 yard

Backing   8 1/4 yards

CUTTING

FROM FABRIC I, CUT: (LT. GREEN PRINT)
- **One 11" wide strip. From this, cut:**
  * Four - 7 1/2" x 11" (Q13)
  * Two - 4 7/8" x 10 1/2" (Q11)
- **One 10 1/2" wide strip. From this, cut:**
  * Four - 5 3/4" x 10 1/2" (Q10)
  * Four - 2 3/4" x 10 1/2" (Q3)
  * Four - 1 1/2" x 10" (Q26)
- **Two 10 1/8" wide strips. From these, cut:**
  * Four - 10 1/8" x 19 1/4" (Q14)
- **Three 10" wide strips. From these, cut:**
  * Four - 10" x 17" (Q24)
  * Four - 10" squares (Q25)
  * Four - 2 1/2" x 10" (Q23)
- **Two 8 1/2" wide strips. From these, cut:**
  * Four - 4" x 8 1/2" (Q29)
  * Four - 3 1/4" x 8 1/2" (Q21)
  * Four - 2 1/8" x 8 1/2" (Q28)
  * Four - 2" x 8 1/2" (Q20)
  Stack these, cuts:
  * Eight - 1 1/4" x 4 1/4" (F3)
  * Four - 1 1/8" x 4 1/4" (E3)
  * Two - 4 1/8" x 20 1/2" (Q27)
  * Twelve - 1 3/8" squares (E10a, F10a)
- **Three 6 1/2" wide strips. From these, cut:**
  * Eight - 6 1/2" x 12" (Q4)
  Stack these cuts:
  * Sixteen - 1 1/8" x 3 1/4" (E5, E7, E23, E26)
  * Sixteen - 1 1/8" x 3 1/8" (F7, F23)
  * Eight - 1 1/8" x 2 1/2" (E9, E25)
- **Two 5 3/4" wide strips. From these, cut:**
  * Four - 5 3/4" x 16 3/4" (Q16)
  * Four - 1 3/4" x 5 3/8" (E20)
  Stack this cut:
  * Eight - 1" squares (C18a, D18a)
- **Two 5" wide strips. From these, cut:**
  * Four - 5" x 11" (Q15)
  * Twenty-four - 1 1/2" x 4 1/2" (A6, B6, G6)
- **One 4 3/8" wide strip. From this, cut:**
  * Eight - 4 3/8" squares (C20, D20)
- **One 4 1/8" wide strip. From this, cut:**
  * Two - 4 1/8" x 20 1/2" (add to Q27 above)
- **Three 3 1/2" wide strips. From these, cut:**
  * Four - 3 1/2" x 12 3/4" (Q19)
  * Thirty-two - 1 1/2" x 3 1/2" (A4, B4)
  * Four - 3 3/8" x 3 7/8" (E16)
- **One 3 3/8" wide strip. From this, cut:**
  * Eight - 3 3/8" x 4 1/8" (F16)
  * Ten - 1 1/2" squares (A1a, A3b, A7a, A11b, A12a, A15a, B1a, B3b, B7a, B11b, B12a, B15a, C11a, D11a, G1b, G3a, G7a, G10a)
- **Two 3 1/8" wide strips. From these, cut:**
  * Sixteen - 3 1/8" x 4 5/8" (C2, C25, D2, D25)
- **Two 2 7/8" wide strips. From these, cut:**
  * Eight - 2 7/8" x 3 5/8" (F29)
  * Four - 2 7/8" x 3 1/4" (E29)
  * Eight - 2 7/8" squares (F2)
  * Four - 2 5/8" x 2 7/8" (E2)

- **Three 2 5/8" wide strips. From these, cut:**
  * Twelve - 2 5/8" squares (E17, F17)
  * Eight - 1 7/8" x 2 5/8" (F28a)
  * Twenty-eight - 1 1/4" x 2 5/8" (C4, C23, D4, D23, E18, F18)
  * Two - 2 1/2" x 19" (Q18)
- **Seven 2 1/2" wide strips. From these, cut:**
  * Thirty-two - 2 1/2" x 3" (A14, B14)
  * Eight - 2 1/2" squares (F11)
  * Four - 1 7/8" x 2 1/2" (E28b)
  * Forty-eight - 1 1/2" x 2 1/2" (A10, B10, G4)
  * Twenty-four - 1 3/8" x 2 1/2" (C8, D8, G11)
  * Thirty-two - 1" x 2 1/2" (A13, B13)
- **One 2 3/8" wide strip. From this, cut:**
  * Four - 2 3/8" squares (E11)
  * Sixteen - 1" x 2 3/8" (F9, F25)
  Stack this cut:
  * Twenty-six - 1 1/8" squares (C3b, C7a, C10b, C22a, D3b, D7a, D10b, D22a, E13a, E21a, F15a, F19a)
- **Four 2 1/4" wide strips. From these, cut:**
  * Eight - 2 1/4" x 11" (Q12)
  * Twenty-four - 1 3/4" x 2 1/4" (E6, E27, F6, F27)
  * Sixteen - 1 1/8" x 2 1/8" (C12, D12)
  * Thirteen - 1 1/8" squares (add to 1 1/8" sq. above)
- **Six 2" wide strips. From these and scrap, cut:**
  * Eight - 2" x 5 1/2" (F20)
  * Thirty-two - 2" x 4 1/2" (A5, B5)
  * Twenty-four - 1 1/8" x 2" (C5b, C21b, D5b, D21b, F14)
  * Twelve - 1 7/8" squares (E1a, F1a)
  * Four - 1 1/4" x 1 3/4" (E14)
  * Four - 1 1/4" squares (C3a, C6b, D3a, D6b, E15a, E19a, F13a, F21a)
- **One 1 5/8" wide strip. From this, cut:**
  * Eight - 1 5/8" x 2 1/8" (C14, D14)
  * Twelve - 1 5/8" squares (E12a, F12a)
- **Twenty-four 1 1/2" wide strips. From these, cut:**
  * One - 1 1/2" x 22 1/2" (Q2)
  * Two - 1 1/2" x 19" (Q17)
  * Four - 1 1/2" x 12 3/4" (Q22)
  * Four - 1 1/2" x 12" (Q7)
  * Six - 1 1/2" x 11" (Q1, Q6)
  * 470 - 1 1/2" squares (add to 1 1/2" sq. above)
- **Two 1 3/8" wide strips. From these, cut:**
  * Eight - 1 3/8" x 3 3/8" (C9, D9)
  * Sixteen - 1 3/8" x 2 3/8" (C1, C24, D1, D24)
- **One 1 1/4" wide strip. From this and scrap, cut:**
  * Thirty-six - 1 1/4" sq. (add to 1 1/4" sq. above)
- **One 1 1/8" wide strip. From this and scrap, cut:**
  * Thirty-three - 1 1/8" sq. (add to 1 1/8" sq. above)
- **Three 1" wide strips. From these and scrap, cut:**
  * Sixteen - 1" x 4 1/2" (G2)
  * Sixteen - 1" x 3 1/8" (F5, F26)

FROM FABRIC II, CUT: (MED. GREEN PRINT)
- **Four 2 1/2" wide strips. From these, cut:**
  * Forty-eight - 2 1/2" squares (A1, B1, G3)
  * Sixteen - 1 1/2" x 2 1/2" (G1a)
  * Sixteen - 1" x 2 1/8" (C11, D11)
- **Two 2" wide strips. From these, cut:**

* Sixteen - 2" x 2 1/8" (C13, D13)
  * Sixteen - 1 1/4" x 2" (F13, F21)
  * Eight - 1 1/8" x 1 3/4" (E13, E21)
  * Eight - 1 1/4" x 1 5/8" (C18, D18)
- **Four 1 7/8" wide strips. From these, cut:**
  * Twenty-four - 1 7/8" x 2 5/8" (E15, E19, F15, F19)
  * Twenty-four - 1 7/8" squares (E17a, F17a)
  * Eight - 1 5/8" x 1 7/8" (C14a, D14a)
  * Twenty-four - 1 1/2" squares (A2a, A3a, A4a, B2a, B3a, B4a, G5a)
- **Four 1 1/2" wide strips. From these and scrap, cut:**
  * Eighty-eight - 1 1/2" sq. (add to 1 1/2" sq. above)
  * Twenty-four - 1 1/8" squares (C12a, C14b, D12a, D14b)
- **Two 1 1/4" wide strips. From these, cut:**
  * Forty-eight - 1 1/4" squares (E1b, E9a, E25a, E28a, F1b, F9a, F25a, F28b)

FROM FABRIC III, CUT: (MED. GREEN SOLID)
- **Two 2 1/2" wide strips. From these, cut:**
  * Forty-eight - 1" x 2 1/2" (A8, B8, G8)
  * Eight - 1 7/8" squares (C17, D17)
- **One 1 1/4" wide strip. From this and scrap, cut:**
  * Thirty-six - 1 1/4" squares (E8, E17b, E24, F8, F17b, F24)

FROM FABRIC IV, CUT: (DK. GREEN PRINT)
- **Two 3 1/2" wide strips. From these, cut:**
  * Forty-eight - 1 1/2" x 3 1/2" (A3, B3, G1)
- **Fourteen 2 1/2" wide strips. Eleven for straight-grain binding. From remaining strips, cut**
  * Eight - 1 7/8" x 2 1/2" (E9, E25)
  * Forty-eight - 1 1/2" x 2 1/2" (A2, B2, G5)
  * Sixteen - 1 3/8" x 2 1/8" (C1a, C24a, D1a, D24a)
- **One 2 3/8" wide strip. From this, cut:**
  * Sixteen - 1 7/8" x 2 3/8" (F9, F25)
- **Two 1 7/8" wide strips. From these, cut:**
  * Sixteen - 1 7/8" x 2 7/8" (F1, F28)
  * Eight - 1 7/8" x 2 5/8" (E1, E28)
  * Eight - 1" x 1 1/4" (C19, D19)
- **Fourteen 1 3/4" wide strips. From these, cut:**
  * Four - 1 3/4" x 40" (Q30, Q31)
  * Four - 1 3/4" x 32 1/2" (Q30) Piece two on opposite sides of one 40" strip to = two 104" lengths.
  * Four - 1 3/4" x 25 7/8" (Q31) Piece two on opposite sides of one 40" strip to = two 90 3/4" lengths.
  * Four - 1 3/4" x 13 1/4" (Q9)
  * Four - 1 3/4" x 12" (Q8)
  * Eight - 1 3/4" x 6 1/2" (Q5)
- **One 1 3/8" wide strip. From this, cut:**
  * Sixteen - 1 3/8" x 2" (C5b, C21b, D5b, D21b)
- **Three 1" wide strips. From these, cut:**
  * Eight - 1" x 2 7/8" (C16, D16)
  * Sixteen - 1" x 2 1/8" (C11, D11)
  * Eight - 1" x 1 5/8" (C15, D15)
  * Thirty-two - 1" squares (C13a, D13a)

FROM FABRIC V, CUT: (LT. PINK PRINT)
- **One 3 3/8" wide strip. From this, cut:**
  * Eight - 3 3/8" squares (C5, C21)
  * Four - 2 5/8" x 3 3/8" (C10)
- **One 2 5/8" wide strip. From this, cut:**
  * Four - 2 5/8" x 4 1/8" (C6)
  * Four - 2 3/8" x 4 1/4" (E12)
- **Four 2 1/2" wide strips. From these, cut:**
  * Twenty-four - 2 1/2" x 4" (A7, G7)
  * Sixteen - 2 1/2" squares (A11a, A12)
  * Four 1 1/4" squares (C6d)
- **One 2 3/8" wide strip. From this, cut:**
  * Four - 2 3/8" squares (E10)
  * Eight - 1" x 2 1/4" (E6, E27)

FROM FABRIC VI, CUT: (DK. PINK PRINT)
- **One 3" wide strip. From this, cut:**
  * Eight - 3" x 3 1/4" (E4, E22)
  * Eighteen - 1 1/2" squares (B9)
- **One 2 5/8" wide strip. From this, cut:**
  * Four - 2 5/8" x 4" (C6a)
  * Eight - 2 5/8" squares (C3, C22)
- **Four 2 1/2" wide strips. From these, cut:**
  * Four - 2 1/2" x 5" (A15)
  * Eight - 2 1/2" x 4 1/2" (A11)
  * Sixteen - 2 1/2" x 3 5/8" (G10)
  * Four - 2 1/2" squares (C7)
  * Sixteen - 2" squares (C5a, C21a, F12b)
- **One 1 7/8" wide strip. From this, cut:**
  * Eight - 1 7/8" squares (C10a, D6c)
  * Six - 1 1/2" squares (add to 1 1/2" sq. above)

FROM FABRIC VII, CUT: (LT. YELLOW SOLID)
- **One 3 3/8" wide strip. From this, cut:**
  * Eight - 3 3/8" squares (D5, D21)
  * Four - 2 5/8" x 3 3/8" (D10)
- **Two 3 1/8" wide strips. From these, cut:**
  * Sixteen - 3 1/8" squares (F4, F22)
  * Four - 2 5/8" x 4 1/8" (D6)
  * Four - 1 1/4" squares (D6d)
- **Five 2 1/2" wide strips. From these, cut:**
  * Twenty-four - 2 1/2" x 4" (B7)
  * Forty-eight - 2 1/2" squares (B11a, B12)

FROM FABRIC VIII, CUT: (MED. YELLOW PRINT)
- **Five 2 1/2" wide strips. From these, cut:**
  * Twelve - 2 1/2" x 5" (B15)
  * Twenty-four - 2 1/2" x 4 1/2" (B11)
  * Eight - 2 1/4" x 2 1/2" (F10)
  * Four - 2" squares (E12b)
- **Two 2 1/4" wide strips. From these, cut:**
  * Eight - 2 1/4" x 4 1/4" (F12)
  * Sixteen - 1" x 2 1/4" (F6, F27)
  * Four - 1 7/8" squares (C6c)
  * Eight - 1 1/2" squares (A9)
- **One 1 5/8" wide strip. From this, cut:**
  * Sixteen - 1 5/8" squares (G9)

FROM FABRIC IX, CUT: (DK. YELLOW PRINT)
- **One 2 5/8" wide strip. From this, cut:**
  * Four - 2 5/8" x 4" (D6a)
  * Eight - 2 5/8" squares (D3, D22)
- **One 2 1/2" wide strip. From this, cut:**
  * Four - 2 1/2" squares (D7)
  * Eight - 2" squares (D5a, D21a)
  * Four - 1 7/8" squares (D10a)

BLOCKS A and B ASSEMBLY

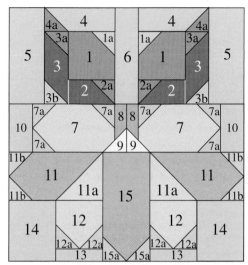

Block A. Make 4. When completed, block should measure 10 1/2" x 11".

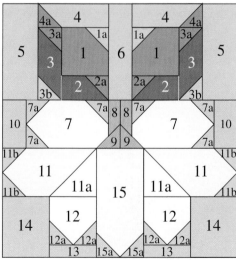

Block B. Make 12. When completed, block should measure 10 1/2" x 11".

1. Refer to pages 6-9 to learn our techniques. Blocks A and B are constructed exactly the same. The only difference is the color. These instructions are for both blocks.
2. Use diagonal corner technique to make two each of mirror image units 1, 2, 3, 4, 7, and 11. Make two of Unit 12, and one of Unit 15. To make combined units 7-8, refer to diagrams above for correct placement of mirror image units. Join Unit 7 to Unit 8; then add diagonal corner, Unit 9 as shown.

3. To assemble the blocks, begin by joining mirror image units 1 and 2. Add Unit 3 to the sides as shown; then add Unit 4 to the top, matching leaf seams. Join Unit 5 to sides as shown. Join these two combined unit sections to opposite sides of Unit 6 to complete the leaf section of the block.
4. Join mirror image combined units 7-9 together as shown, matching Unit 9 seams. Join Unit 10 to opposite sides; then join this to bottom of leaf section. Join units 12 and 13 as shown; then add Unit 14 to the sides. Refer to block diagrams and join these combined units to the bottoms of Unit 11, matching petal seams. Join these combined units to opposite sides of Unit 15 as shown to complete the flower.
5. Join bottom of flower to bottom of combined units 7-10 to complete the block.

BLOCKS C and D ASSEMBLY

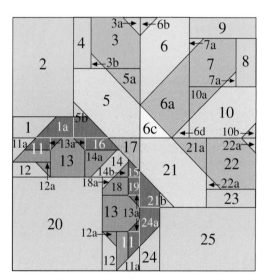

Block C. Make 4. When completed, block should measure 11" square.

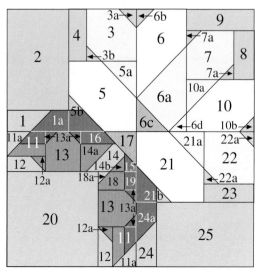

Block D. Make 4. When completed, block should measure 11" square.

1. Blocks C and D are constructed exactly the same. The only difference is the color. These instructions are for both blocks.

2. Use diagonal corner technique to make two each of mirror image units 11 and 12. Make two of Unit 13. Make one each of units 3, 5, 7, 10, 21, and 22.

3. Use diagonal end technique to make one each of units 1, 6, 14, and 24. Refer to diagrams below for making these units. Note that diagonal end for Unit 6 is made first; then diagonal corners are added.

4. Units C11 and D11 are made by joining 1" x 2 1/8" strips of fabrics II and IV, making a small strip set. Diagonal corner 11a is then added.

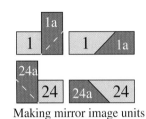

Making mirror image units
C1, C24, D1, and D24

Making mirror image
units C11 and D11

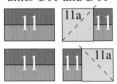

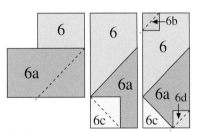

Making units C6, and D6. Refer to
Block D diagram for color changes.

Making mirror image units C5, C21, D5, and D21.
Refer to block D diagram for color changes.

Join 1 1/8"
x 2" strip
of Fabric I
with 1 3/8"
x 2" strip
of Fabric
IV.

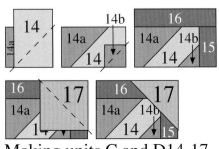

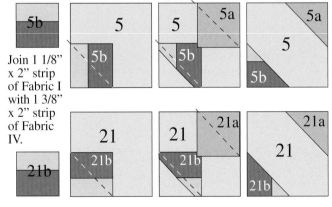

Making units C and D14-17

5. Units 5 and 21 are shown. Here we have used a small strip set as a diagonal corner. Follow the instructions given for the strip set. Refer to the diagram for correct placement for both units 5b and 21b. Stitch diagonal, trim seam and press; then add diagonal corners 5a and 21a. Refer to Block D diagram frequently for color change.

6. To make combined units 14-17, refer to diagram below. Join diagonal end, Unit 14 first; then add diagonal corner 14b. Trim seam and press. Join Unit 15 to right side; then add Unit 16 across the top. Join diagonal corner, Unit 17. Trim seam and press.

7. To assemble the blocks, begin by joining units 1 and 2. Join units 3 and 4; then add Unit 5 to bottom of 3-4 combination, matching seams. Join Unit 6 to right side of the 3-5 combined units, and combined units 1-2 to the left side. Join units 7 and 8; then add Unit 9 to top of these combined units and Unit 10 to the bottom, matching seams. Join this section to the right side of flower to complete the top section.

8. Refer to block diagrams for correct placement of mirror image units. Join mirror image units 11 and 12; then add Unit 13 to the sides as shown. Make 2. Join combined units 14-17 to right side of horizontally placed combined units 11-13. Join units 18 and 19; then add the remaining combined units 11-13 to the bottom of 18-19. Join Unit 20 to the left side of these combined units; then add combined units 11-17 to the top as shown.

9. Join units 22 and 23; then add Unit 21 to left side of these combined units, matching seams. Join units 24 and 25; then add these units to the bottom of combined units 21-23. Join this section to the right side of the other combined bottom units to complete the bottom of the flower. Join the top and bottom together, matching seams, to complete the block. Make 4 of each block.

BLOCKS E and F ASSEMBLY

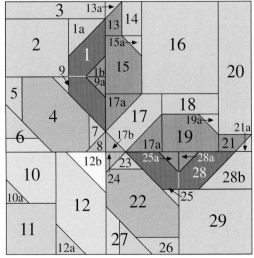

Block E. Make 4. When completed,
block should measure 9 3/4" square.

18

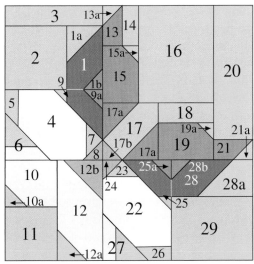

Block F. Make 8. When completed,
block should measure 10" square.

1. Blocks E and F are constructed exactly the same except for the color difference. Refer to Block F diagram frequently for the color change.

2. Use diagonal corner technique to make one of units 1, 10, 12, 13, 15, 17, 19, and 21. Use diagonal end technique to make one of Unit 28.

3. Refer to the step-by-step diagram below for making combined units 4-9 and 22-27. Make these combined units, again referring to Block F diagram for color changes.

4. To assemble the blocks, begin by joining units 1 and 2; then add Unit 3 to top of the combined 1-2 units. Join combined units 4-9 to bottom of combined 1-3 units, matching leaf seam.

5. Join units 10 and 11; then add Unit 12 to the side of the 10-11 combined units. Join these units to the bottom of the 1-9 combined units to complete the left side of the block.

6. For the right side of the block, join units 13 and 14; then add Unit 15 to bottom of these combined units. Join Unit 16 to the right side of combined 13-15 units. Join units 18 and 19; then add Unit 17 to left side of these combined units. Join the two combined unit sections together, matching leaf seams. Join units 20 and 21; then add these units to the right side of combined 13-19 units, again matching leaf seam.

7. For both blocks, join units 28 and 29; then add combined units 22-27 to left side of these combined units. Join the bottom combined units to the top combined units, matching seams where necessary.

8. Join the left side of the flower to the right side of the flower, carefully matching seams to complete the blocks.

Making units E4-E9, E22-E27. For F4-F9, and F22-F27, refer to Block F diagram for color changes.

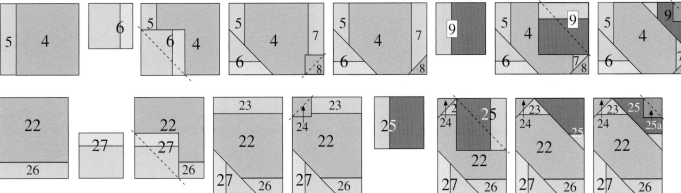

For Block E, combined units 4-9, join units 4 and 5. For combined units 22-27, join units 22 and 26. Join 1" x 2 1/4" strip of Fabric V with 1 3/4" x 2 1/4" strip of Fabric I for units 6 and 27. These will now be used as diagonal corners. Place these units as shown, with raw edges matching. Stitch diagonal seam, trim and press. Join Unit 7 to right side of Unit 4; then add diagonal corner, Unit 8. For combined 22-27 units, join Unit 23 to Unit 22; then add diagonal corner, Unit 24. Join 1 1/8" x 2 1/2" strip of Fabric I with 1 7/8" x 2 1/2" strip of Fabric IV for units 9 and 25. These will now be used as diagonal corners. Place these units as shown, with raw edges matching. Stitch diagonal seam, trim and press. Add diagonal corners 9a and 25a as shown.

For Block F, Units 6 and 27, join 1 3/4" x 2 1/4" strip of Fabric I with 1" x 2 1/4" strip of Fabric VIII. For Block F, Units 9 and 25, join 1" x 2 3/8" strip of Fabric I with 1 7/8" x 2 3/8" strip of Fabric IV. Assembly instructions are the same as for Block E.

BLOCK G ASSEMBLY

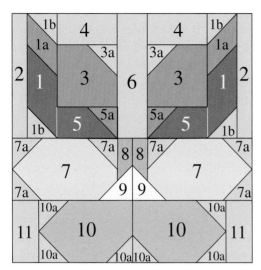

Block G. Make 8. When completed, block should measure 8 1/2" square.

1. Use diagonal corner technique to make two each of mirror image units 3, 5, 7, and 10. Use diagonal end technique to make two of mirror image Unit 1, shown below. For Unit 1, make diagonal end first; then add diagonal corners 1b.

2. To assemble the block, begin by joining units 1 and 2, referring to block diagram for correct position of mirror image units. Join units 4, 3, and 5 in a vertical row, and add this row to the sides of 1-2 combined units, matching leaf seams. Join these mirror image combined units to opposite sides of Unit 6 to complete the top of the block.

Making mirror image Unit G1

3. Join Unit 8 to side of Unit 7; then add Unit 9 diagonal corners as shown. Join these two combined unit sections together. Join units 11, 10, 10, and 11 in a horizontal row as shown. Join this row to bottom of combined 7-9 units.

4. Join the top of the block to the bottom of the block, matching stem and leaf seams to complete the block.

QUILT CENTER ASSEMBLY

1. The quilt is assembled in sections. The following instructions are for the center section. To begin, refer to the quilt diagram at right for the correct placement of the blocks. Begin by joining Block D to opposite sides of Unit Q1. Make two. Join the two Block D sections to top and bottom of Unit Q2, forming the center.

2. Join Unit Q3 to the leaf side of all four Block A's as shown. Join units Q4 and Q5. Make 8. Join these combined units to opposite sides of Block A-Q3 combination as shown. Make 4. Join two of these combined Block A units to the top and bottom of center section as shown.

3. For the corners, refer to the Block C combination at top left corner of center section. With this as a starting point, join Unit Q6 to left side of Block C; then add Unit Q7 to the top as shown. Join Unit Q8 to the top; then add Unit Q9 to the left side. Make 4. These combined Block C units will be turned as you assemble the sides. Join two of the Block C combinations to opposite sides of the Block A combination, matching border seams. Refer to quilt diagram for correct position of Block C. Make two of these sections; then join them to opposite sides of center section.

QUILT SIDE ASSEMBLY

1. Join Unit Q10 to flower side of one Block B, and Unit Q11 to the leaf side as shown. Refer to diagram for correct position of Unit Q12, as the following will be mirror imaged, and correct placement is important. Join Unit Q12 to the sides of Block B's. Join Unit Q13 to the opposite sides; then add Unit Q14. Join these sections to opposite sides of the Q10-Block B-Q11 combined sections to complete the sides. Make 2. Join the side sections to opposite sides of the center section.

QUILT TOP AND BOTTOM ASSEMBLY

1. Join Unit Q10 to the flower side of one Block B. Referring to diagram, join Unit 12 to sides of two Block B's. Refer to diagram for correct position of Unit Q12, as the following will be mirror imaged, and correct placement is important. Join Unit Q15 to opposite sides of the Unit Q12-Block B combination; then add Unit Q16 to the leaf side as shown. Join these combined Block B sections to opposite sides of Unit Q10-Block B combination.

2. Referring to quilt diagram, join two Block E's matching leaf tips as shown. Join Unit Q17 to the top of the combined E blocks, and Unit Q18 to the bottom. Join Unit Q19 to opposite sides of the Block E combination. Join Unit Q20 to the top of Block G, and Unit Q21 to the bottom. Make 2. Again referring to the diagram join Unit 22 to the side of each Block G combination, keeping in mind that they will be mirror images when pieced into the quilt. Join these Block G combinations to opposite sides of the Block E combined units. Join this row to Block B combined units as shown.

3. For the corners, begin by joining Unit Q23 to the top of Block F; then add Unit Q24 to the bottom. Join Unit Q26 to the bottom of another Block F; then add Unit Q25 to the top. Join Unit Q27 to the side of this Block F combination. Join Unit Q28 to the flower side of Block G; then add Unit 29 to the leaf side. Join this Block G combination to the bottom of

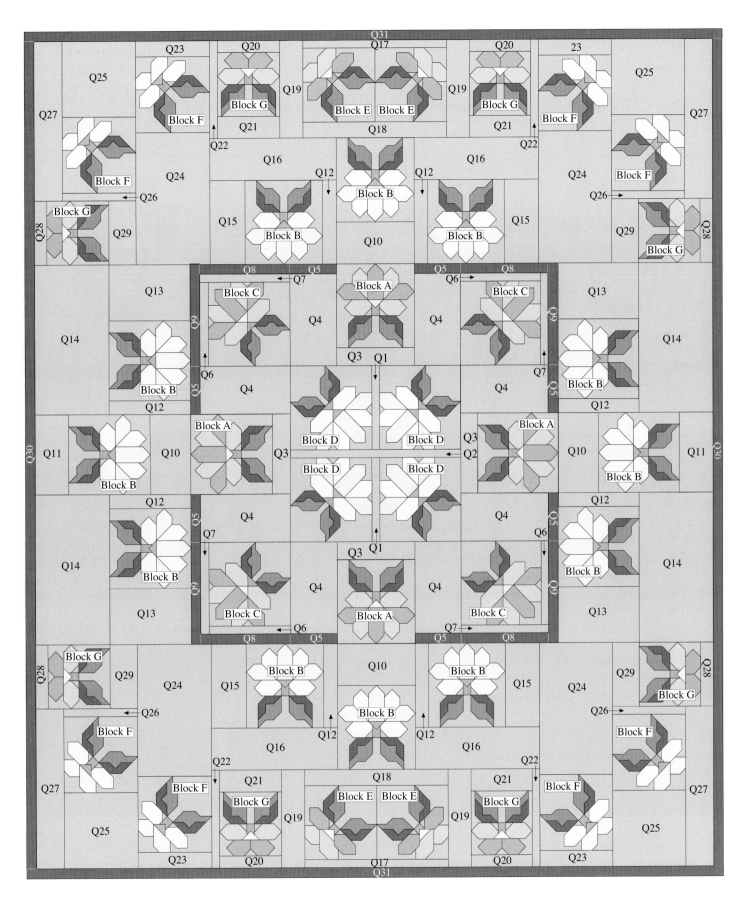

the Q26-Block F-Q25-Q27 combination, referring to diagram for correct placement. Join the remaining Block F combination to the side to complete the corner. Make two mirror image corners, and join them to opposite sides of the center flowers. Make two of these sections. Join one to the top and one to the bottom of quilt, matching Unit Q10 to center section Block A.

4. Join border Q30 (previously pieced) to opposite sides of the quilt. Trim to fit. Join border Q31 (previously pieced) to top and bottom of quilt.

21

QUILTING AND FINISHING

Mary quilted swirling feather designs and crest motifs with feathers. She worked a very small stipple between the feather designs, giving the illusion of trapunto.
Join eleven 2 1/2" strips of Fabric IV for straight-grain binding and bind your quilt.

VALANCE

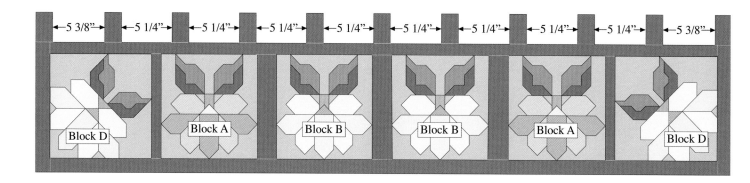

1. For the valance, measure the space needed in your window. We needed 72" for our double window. Refer to the quilt blocks. Each block is 10" wide, and 10 1/2" long when sewn into the borders. The corner blocks that we used are 11" square finished. Follow the instructions on page 11 for making one or two blocks, and refer to the assembly instructions for the quilt blocks.
2. When calculating the size and the number of blocks that you will need, don't forget to add 1/2" to the blocks, sashing and borders for seam allowance. We spaced the sashing so that it would give a nice appearance. Add the *finished* inches of your blocks; then space them as evenly as possible with the sashing between the blocks and the outer short borders to establish your length. The top and bottom borders may be the width that you desire. After the top is pieced, cut a piece of batting and muslin 2" wider and longer than the valance top. Sandwich the batting between the muslin back and valance top. Pin in place securely. We quilted all of the patchwork in the ditch, and quilted along the sashing and border seams. Trim the batting and muslin even with the valance top.
3. Measure the size of the valance, and piece a backing to the same size. Our loops were cut 4" x 6 1/2". Fold the loops in half lengthwise, right sides together and stitch the long edge. Turn right side out and press so that seam is in the center back. Space the loops evenly. Place the outer loops 1/4" in from the edge with the finished loop facing downward and the raw edge against the raw edge of the valance top and pin. Pin the backing, right sides facing on top of the valance top. Stitch around the edges, leaving a space to turn on one short side. Turn right side out and pull the loops up. Slip stitch the opening closed.

COVER FOR CURTAIN ROD

For the rod, use a shower curtain rod that is expandable. With a tape measure, measure around the widest point of the rod, such as the ends. Add 1/2" for seam allowance. For the length, as an example, we needed 72". We did not want the rod cover to have tight gathers, therefore we used 1 1/4 times rather than 1 1/2 times. In other words, 72" divided by 4 = 18". We added the 18" to 72", giving us a 90" length. If you wish, add another 1" for the hem. If your circumference, as an example, is 4", cut 4 1/2" strips. Join them together on the short ends to arrive at 91". Turn under 1/4", then another 1/4" on short ends of the joined strips, and press. Top stitch the hem in place. With right sides facing, stitch a 1/4" seam along the long edges. Reinforce stitching at both ends. Turn right side out, and pull over the shower curtain rod.

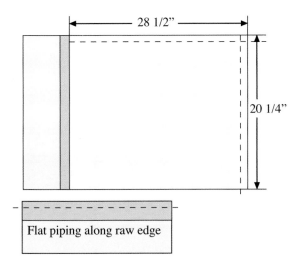

Flat piping along raw edge

PILLOWCASES

Cutting for two standard cases. Finished size: 20" x 32"

MATERIALS

FABRIC I (LT. YELLOW SOLID)   Need 1 3/4 yards
Cut: Two - 28 1/2" x 40 1/2" for pillowcase body.
FABRIC II (MED. YELLOW PRINT)   5/8 yard
Cut: Two - 8 1/2" x 40 1/2" for border.
FABRIC III (LT. GREEN PRINT)   Need 1/8 yard
Cut: Two - 1 1/4" x 40 1/2" for flat piping.

Assembly instructions for one pillowcase:
1. Place short ends of Fabric III strip right sides together, and using 1/4" seam, stitch the ends, forming a circle. Fold the 1 1/4" circle in half lengthwise, wrong sides together, matching raw edges, and press.
2. Place short ends of 8 1/2" x 40 1/2" strip of Fabric II right sides together and stitch the ends, forming another circle. Fold the 8 1/2" circle in half lengthwise, wrong sides together, again matching raw edges, and press.
3. Refer to diagram above, and place the 1 1/4" strip, raw edges together on the Fabric II circle as shown. Using a scant 1/4" seam, stitch around the edge.
4. Fold the 28 1/2" x 40 1/2" piece of Fabric I right sides together for a measurement of 20 1/4" x 28 1/2".
Stitch raw edges together as shown. Turn right side out.
Place 4 1/4" circular end with Fabric III flat piping around raw edge of pillowcase. Stitch around the circle using 1/4" seam. Fold out and press.

TRIANGLE-SQUARE PILLOW

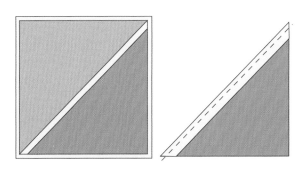

Pillow finishes to 20" square.

MATERIALS

FABRIC I (MED. GREEN SOLID) Need 1 1/8yds.
Cut: One 20 1/2" wide strip. From this cut:
      * One - 20 1/2" square
      * One - 13 1/2" x 20 1/2" (backing)
Cut: One 13 1/2" wide strip. From this, cut:
      * One - 13 1/2" x 20 1/2" (backing)
FABRIC II (MED. GREEN PRINT) Need 3/4 yard
Cut: One 20 7/8" square (for triangle). Cut in half diagonally. Discard one triangle.
FABRIC III (MED. YELLOW PRINT) Need 1/8 yard
Cut: Three 1" wide strips for flat piping.
      * Cut one strip 32" long for diagonal. Trim to fit triangle long edge.
      * Cut border accent piping into four 20 1/2"lengths.

1. Press piping for diagonal, wrong sides together and place on long edge of triangle, raw edges matching. Stitch piping in place, about 1/8" from seam allowance.
2. Place triangle right sides together on top of Fabric I, 20 1/2" square with raw edges matching. Use 1/4" seam, and stitch triangle in place along the diagonal edge. Fold out and press. Top stitch the triangle along outer edges to keep it in place.
3. Using the 1" x 20 1/2" strips of Fabric III, press them in half lengthwise. Place each along outer edges of pillow top, raw edges matching, and top stitch in place as in Step 1.
4. For hems on pillow back, turn under 1/4"; then another 1/4" on 20 1/2" edge of both backing pieces. Press, and top stitch.
5. Place backing pieces right sides together on pillow top. The hemmed edges will overlap approximately 3" in the center. Stitch around outer edge of pillow, using a 1/4" seam. Turn right side out, and stuff with 20" pillow form. See page 24 for diagram.

RUFFLED PILLOW

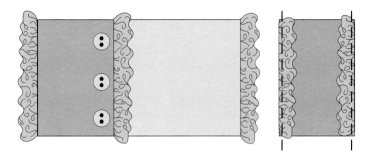

Pillow finishes to 14" x 20".

MATERIALS
FABRIC I (LT. PINK PRINT)   **Need 1/2 yard**
 * Cut One - 14 1/2" x 15 1/2" (pillow back)
 * Cut: One - 12 1/2" x 14 1/2" (pillow front)

FABRIC II (MED. PINK SOLID)   **Need 1/2 yard**
 * Cut: Three 4" x 30". (for ruffles)

FABRIC III (DK. PINK PRINT)   **Need 1/2 yard**
Cut: One - 8 1/8" x 14 1/2" (pillow front)
       One - 14 1/2" x 16 1/2" (pillow back)
Three 1 1/8" covered or flat light pink buttons.

1. To make the ruffles, fold the three 4" x 30" pieces from Fabric II in half lengthwise, right sides together. Stitch short ends 1/4" from edge. Turn the ruffle right side out and press. Run a gathering stitch 1/8" from ruffle edges, and gather each ruffle to 14" length. Baste the ruffles in place as shown on Fabric III pillow front. Ruffles should be 1/4" in from pillow edges.

2. Place Fabric I pillow front right sides facing on one 14 1/2" end of Fabric III pillow front, raw edges matching. Stitch, using 1/4" seam. Open out. Pull center ruffle towards Fabric I pillow front. Top stitch along the Fabric III edge, close to the ruffle so that it stays towards Fabric I front section. Place the remaining ruffle along raw edge of Fabric I pillow top. Baste in place with raw edges matching. Pin the ruffles away from outer edges so that they do not catch in the seams when the back is added.

3. Refer to diagram at right, and turn under 1/4"; then another 1/4" on 14 1/2" edges of both backing pieces. Press, and top stitch to form the hem. Refer to diagram at right for finishing.

FLOWER BLOCK PILLOW

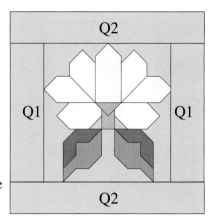

Follow instructions on page11 for Making One Block. Make one of Block B.

Pillow finishes to 20" circle, which includes flange.

FABRIC I (LT. GREEN PRINT)   **Need 1 1/2 yards**
Cut two 5 1/2" x 11" pieces, (Q1) and two 5" x 20 1/2" pieces (Q2). Cut two 13 1/2" x 20 1/2" pieces for backing.
Muslin and batting: Cut a 20 1/2" square.

1. Join Q1 pieces to opposite sides of flower block; then add Q2 strips to the top and bottom as shown.
Sandwich batting between top and muslin. We ditched the patchwork and quilted along seams.

2. For backing, make hem as for Diagonal Pillow. Place the backing pieces right sides facing on pillow top. Pin securely. Draw a 20 1/2" circle on a piece of tissue paper. Center on pillow top, and cut pillow top around outer edges of circle, cutting the backing also. Stitch around outer edges of pillow using 1/4" seam. Turn right side out.

3. Draw a 16" circle on tissue paper. For the flange, center this pattern on pillow top and pin in place. Top stitch around outer edge of tissue paper circle, through all layers, forming the flange. Stuff with 16" round pillow form.

BACKING A PILLOW

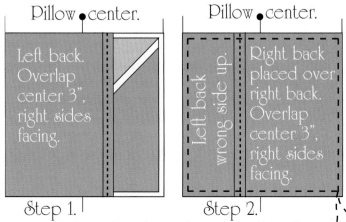

Turn right side out and insert pillow form.

Spring at Dusk
tablecloth

Fresh spring buds pop out of a navy background on this fabulous tablecloth. A quick new technique is used for the scallops, and the matching valance pulls this lovely dining area together. A real conversation piece for that special dinner party!

Tablecloth finished size with scallops: 68 1/2" x 98 1/2". 13 1/2" drop includes green frame.

Center section finishes to: 42" x 72"

Techniques Used: Diagonal corners, diagonal ends, and strip sets used as diagonal corners.

MATERIALS

Fabric I (navy textured print)
Need 219 5/8"   6 1/2 yds

Fabric II (pale yellow solid)
Need 19 1/8"   3/4 yard

Fabric III (med. yellow print)
Need 13 7/8"   1/2 yard

Fabric IV (dark yellow print)
Need 5 1/8"   1/4 yard

Fabric V (light lavender print)
Need 7 1/4"   3/8 yard

Fabric VI (dark lavender print)
Need 6 3/4"   3/8 yard

Fabric VII (light green solid)
Need 5"   1/4 yard

Fabric VIII (med. green print)
Need 24"   7/8 yard

Fabric IX (dark green print)
Need 29"   1 yard

Fabric X (bright pink print)
Need 3 1/2"   1/4 yard

Backing   **5 3/4 yards**

25

CUTTING

FROM FABRIC I, CUT: (NAVY TEX-TURED PRINT)
- **One 36" x 40" for 2 1/2" wide bias binding**.
- **One 9 7/8" wide strip. From this, cut:**
  * Two - 9 7/8" squares (Q22) Cut in half diagonally.
  * Four - 2 1/4" x 9 3/4" (Q4)
  * Four - 2 1/2" x 9 1/2" (Q17)
- **Five 8 1/2" wide strips. From these, cut:**
  * Four - 8 1/2" x 9 1/2" (Q18)
  * Eight - 8 1/2" squares (Q15)
  * Twenty-four - 2 1/2" x 8 1/2" (Q16)
  * Four - 2" x 8 1/2" (Q7)
  * Eight - 1 1/2" x 8 1/2" (Q19)
  Stack these cuts:
  * Eight - 1 1/4" x 4 1/4" (C3, D3)
  * Sixteen - 1 1/8" x 2" (B5b, B21b, C14, D14)
- **One 6 1/2" wide strip. From this, cut:**
  * Four - 6 1/2" x 10" (Q5)
- **One 6" wide strip. From this, cut:**
  * Two - 6" x 10 1/2" (Q9)
  Stack these cuts:
  * Eight - 2 7/8" x 3 5/8" (C29, D29)
- **One 5" wide strip. From this, cut:**
  * Four - 5" x 10" (Q8)
- **One 4 3/8" wide strip. From this, cut:**
  * Four - 4 3/8" squares (B20)
  Stack this cut:
  * Two - 1 1/4" x 22 1/2" (Q3)
- **Four 3 1/2" wide strips. From these, cut:**
  * Four - 3 1/2" x 16 1/2" (Q10)
  * Four - 3 1/2" x 16" (Q6)
  * Four - 1 1/2" x 3 1/2" (A4)
  * Four - 1 3/8" x 3 3/8" (B9)
  * Sixteen - 1 1/8" x 3 1/8" (C6, C23, D6, D23)
- **One 3 3/8" wide strip. From this, cut:**
  * Eight - 3 3/8" x 4 1/8" (C16, D16)
  * Four - 1" squares (B18a)
- **Two 3 1/8" wide strips. From these, cut:**
  * Eight - 3 1/8" x 4 5/8" (B2, B25)
  * Sixteen - 1" x 3 1/8" (C5, C26, D5, D26)
  * Eight - 2 7/8" squares (C2, D2)
- **Two 2 5/8" wide strips. From these, cut:**
  * Eight - 2 5/8" squares (C17, D17)
  * Eight - 1 7/8" x 2 5/8" (C28a, D28a)
  * Sixteen - 1 1/4" x 2 5/8" (B4, B23, C18, D18)
  Stack this cut:
  * Twenty-four - 1 1/4" squares (B3a, B6b, C13a, C21a, D13a, D21a)
  * Four - 1" x 2 1/2" (A13)
- **Eleven 2 1/2" wide strips. From these, cut:**
  * Four - 2 1/2" x 37 1/2" (Q21) Piece two together to = two 74 1/2" lengths.
  * Four - 2 1/2" x 22 1/2" (Q20) Piece two together to = two 44 1/2" lengths.
  * Four - 2 1/2" x 3" (A14)

  * Eight - 2 1/2" squares (C12, D12)
  * Fifty-two - 1 1/2" x 2 1/2" (A10, E4, F4)
  * Fifty-two - 1 3/8" x 2 1/2" (B8, E11, F11)
  * Eight - 1 3/8" x 2 3/8" (B1, B24)
- **Two 2" wide strips. From these, cut:**
  * Eight - 2" x 5 1/2" (C20, D20)
  * Four - 2" x 4 1/2" (A5)
  * Eight - 1 7/8" squares (C1a, D1a)
  * Four - 1 5/8" x 2 1/8" (B14)
- **Twenty-four 1 1/2" wide strips. From these, cut:**
  * One - 1 1/2" x 22 1/2" (Q1)
  * Two - 1 1/2" x 16 1/2" (Q11)
  * Two - 1 1/2" x 11" (Q2)
  * Twenty-six - 1 1/2" x 4 1/2" (A6, E6, F6)
  * 480 - 1 1/2" squares (A1a, A3b, A7a, A11b, A12a, A15a, B11a, E1b, E3a, E7a, E10a, F1b, F3a, F7a, F10a)
  * Sixteen - 1 3/8" squares (C10a, C11a, D10a, D11a)
- **One 1 3/4" wide strip. From this, cut:**
  * Sixteen - 1 3/4" x 2 1/4" (C9, C27, D9, D27)
- **Two 1 1/8" wide strips. From these, cut:**
  * Eight - 1 1/8" x 2 1/8" (B12)
  * Forty - 1 1/8" squares (B3b, B7a, B10b, B22a, C15a, C19a, D15a, D19a)
- **Nine 1" wide strips. From these, cut:**
  * Four - 1" x 25 1/2" (Q12)
  * Forty-eight - 1" x 4 1/2" (E2, F2)
  * Sixteen - 1" x 2 3/8" (C7, C25, D7, D25)

FROM FABRIC II, CUT: (PALE YELLOW SOLID)
- **One 3 3/8" wide strip. From this, cut:**
  * Eight - 3 3/8" squares (B5, B21)
  * Four - 2 5/8" x 3 3/8" (B10)
  Stack this cut:
  * Four - 1 1/4" squares (B6d)
- **One 3 1/8" wide strip. From this, cut:**
  * Eight - 3 1/8" squares (C4, C22)
- **One 2 5/8" wide strip. From this, cut:**
  * Four - 2 5/8" x 4 1/8" (B6)
  * Eight - 2 1/2" squares (A11a, A12)
- **Four 2 1/2" wide strips. From these, cut:**
  * Thirty-six - 2 1/2" x 4" (A7, E7)

FROM FABRIC III, CUT: (MEDIUM YELLOW PRINT)
- **Four 2 1/2" wide strips. From these, cut:**
  * Two - 2 1/2" x 5" (A15)
  * Four - 2 1/2" x 4 1/2" (A11)
  * Thrity-two - 2 1/2" x 3 5/8" (E10)
  * Four - 2 1/4" x 2 1/2" (C11)
- **One 2 1/4" wide strip. From this, cut:**
  * Four - 2 1/4" x 4 1/4" (C10)
  * Eight - 1" x 2 1/4" (C9, C27)
  * Four - 2" squares (D10b)
- **One 1 5/8" wide strip. From this, cut:**
  * Sixteen - 1 5/8" squares (F9)

FROM FABRIC IV, CUT: (DK. YELLOW PRINT)
- **One 2 5/8" wide strip. From this, cut:**
  - * Four - 2 5/8" x 4" (B6a)
  - * Eight - 2 5/8" squares (B3, B22)
- **One 2 1/2" wide strip. From this, cut**
  - * Four - 2 1/2" squares (B7)
  - * Eight - 2" squares (B5a, B21a)
  - * Four - 1 7/8" squares (B10a)

FROM FABRIC V, CUT: (LT. LAVENDER PRINT)
- **Two 2 1/2" wide strips. From these, cut:**
  - * Sixteen - 2 1/2" x 4" (F7)
  - * Four - 2 1/4" x 2 1/2" (D11)
- **One 2 1/4" wide strip. From this, cut:**
  - * Four - 2 1/4" x 4 1/4" (D10)
  - * Eight - 1" x 2 1/4" (D9, D27)

FROM FABRIC VI, CUT: (DK. LAVENDER PRINT)
- **One 3 5/8" wide strip. From this, cut:**
  - * Sixteen - 2 1/2" x 3 5/8" (F10)
- **One 3 1/8" wide strip. From this, cut:**
  - * Eight - 3 1/8" squares (D4, D22)

FROM FABRIC VII, CUT: (LIGHT GREEN SOLID)
- **Two 2 1/2" wide strips. From these, cut:**
  - * Fifty-two - 1" x 2 1/2" (A8, E8, F8)
  - * Twenty-four - 1 1/4" squares (C8, C17b, C24, D8, D17b, D24)
- **One 1 7/8" wide strip. From this, cut:**
  - * Four - 1 7/8" squares (B17)

FROM FABRIC VIII, CUT: (MED. GREEN PRINT)
- **Five 2 1/2" wide strips. From these, cut:**
  - * Fifty-two - 2 1/2" squares (A1, E3, F3)
  - * Forty-eight - 1 1/2" x 2 1/2" (E1a, F1a)
  - * Twelve - 1 1/8" squares (B12a, B14b)
- **One 2" wide strip. From this, cut:**
  - * Eight - 2" x 2 1/8" (B13)
  - * Sixteen - 1 1/4" x 2" (C13, C21, D13, D21)
- **Two 1 7/8" wide strips. From these, cut:**
  - * Sixteen - 1 7/8" x 2 5/8" (C15, C19, D15, D19)
  - * Sixteen - 1 7/8" squares (C17a, D17a)
  - * Four - 1 5/8" x 1 7/8" (B14a)
- **Three 1 1/2" wide strips. From these, cut:**
  - * Sixty - 1 1/2" squares (A2a, A3a, A4a, E5a, F5a)
  - * Four - 1 1/4" x 1 5/8" (B18)
  - * Eight - 1" x 2 1/8" (B11)
- **One 1 1/4" wide strip. From this, cut:**
  - * Thirty-two - 1 1/4" squares (C1b, C7a, C25a, C28b, D1b, D7a, D25a, D28b)

FROM FABRIC IX, CUT: (DK. GREEN PRINT)
- **Three 1 7/8" wide strips. From these, cut:**
  - * Sixteen - 1 7/8" x 2 7/8" (C1, C28, D1, D28)
  - * Sixteen - 1 7/8" x 2 3/8" (C7, C25, D7, D25)
  - * Four - 1" x 2 7/8" (B16)
  - * Four - 1" x 1 5/8" (B15)
  - * Four - 1" x 1 1/4" (B19)
- **Fourteen 1 1/2" wide strips. From these, cut:**
  - * Four - 1 1/2" x 36 1/2" (Q13) Piece two together to = two 72 1/2" lengths.
  - * Four - 1 1/2" x 22 1/2" (Q14) Piece two together to = two 44 1/2" lengths.
  - * Fifty-two - 1 1/2" x 3 1/2" (A3, E1, F1)
  - * Fifty-two - 1 1/2" x 2 1/2" (A2, E5, F5)
- **One 1 3/8" wide strip. From this, cut:**
  - * Eight - 1 3/8" x 2 1/8" (B1a, B24a)
  - * Eight - 1 3/8" x 2" (B5b, B21b)
- **One 1" wide strip. From this, cut:**
  - * Sixteen - 1" squares (B13a)
  - * Eight - 1" x 2 1/8" (B11)

FROM FABRIC X, CUT: (BRIGHT PINK PRINT)
- **One 1 7/8" wide strip. From this, cut:**
  - * Eight - 1 7/8" squares (B6c, C10b)
  - * Fifteen - 1 5/8" squares (E9)
- **One 1 5/8" wide strip. From this, cut:**
  - * Seventeen - 1 5/8" squares (add to E9 above)
  - * Four - 1 1/2" squares (A9)

BLOCK A ASSEMBLY

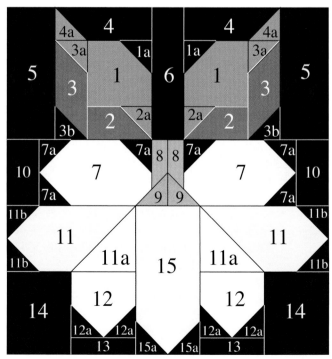

Block A. Make 2. When completed, block should measure 10 1/2" x 11".

28

1. Use diagonal corner technique to make two each of mirror image units 1, 2, 3, 4, 7, and 11. Make two of Unit 12, and one of Unit 15. To make combined units 7-8, refer to block diagram for correct placement of mirror image units. Join Unit 8 to Unit 7; then add diagonal corner, Unit 9.

2. To assemble the block, begin by joining mirror image units 1 and 2. Add Unit 3 to the sides as shown; then add Unit 4 to the top, matching leaf seams. Join Unit 5 to sides as shown. Join these two combined unit sections to opposite sides of Unit 6 to complete the leaf section of the block.

3. Join mirror image combined units 7-9 together as shown, matching Unit 9 seams. Add Unit 10 to opposite sides. Join units 12 and 13; then add Unit 14 to the sides of these combined units as shown. Refer to block diagram and join these combined units to the bottom of Unit 11, matching petal seams. Join these combined units to opposite sides of Unit 15 as shown. Join combined units 7-10 to the top to complete the flower section.

4. Join the leaf and flower sections together to complete the block. Make 2.

BLOCK B ASSEMBLY

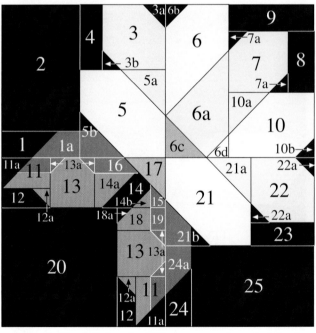

Block B. Make 4. When completed, block should measure 11" square.

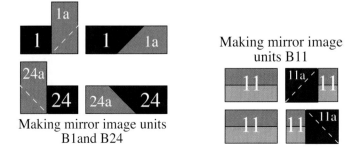

Making mirror image units B1 and B24

Making mirror image units B11

Making mirror image units B5, and B21.

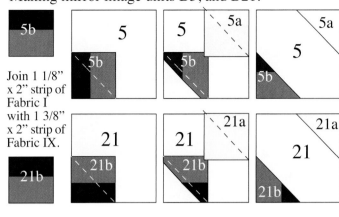

Join 1 1/8" x 2" strip of Fabric I with 1 3/8" x 2" strip of Fabric IX.

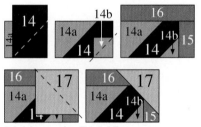

Making Unit B6.

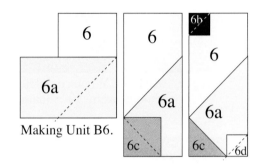

Making units B14-17

These instructions are for one block.

1. Use diagonal corner technique to make two each of mirror image units 11 and 12. Make two of Unit 13. Make one each of units 3, 5, 7, 10, 21, and 22.

2. Use diagonal end technique to make one each of units 1, 6, 14, and 24 as shown on this page. Refer to diagrams to make these units. Note that diagonal end for Unit 6 is made first; then diagonal corners are added

3. Unit 11 is made by joining 1" x 2 1/8" strips of fabrics VIII and IX, making a small strip set. Diagonal corner 11a is then added.

4. Units 5 and 21 are shown above. Note that the main difference is in the strip set diagonal corners. Here we have used a small strip set as a diagonal corner. Follow the instructions given for the strip set. Refer to the diagram for correct placement for both units 5 and 21. Stitch diagonal, trim seam and press; then add diagonal corners 5a and 21a.

5. To make combined units 14-17, refer to diagram above. Join diagonal end, Unit 14 first; then add diagonal corner 14b. Trim seam and press. Join Unit 15 to right side; then add Unit 16 across the top. Join diagonal corner, Unit 17. Trim seam and press. Make 4.

BLOCKS C AND D ASSEMBLY

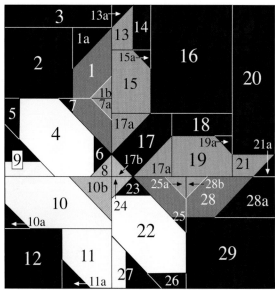

Block C. Make 4. When completed, block should measure 10" square.

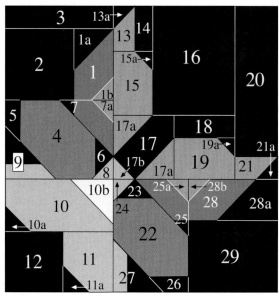

Block D. Make 4. When completed, block should measure 10" square.

1. Blocks C and D are constructed exactly the same. There is a color difference, so refer to Block D diagram frequently for the color change.

2. Use diagonal corner technique to make one of units 1, 10, 11, 13, 15, 17, 19, and 21. Use diagonal end technique to make one of Unit 28.

3. Refer to the step-by-step diagram on page 31 for making combined units 4-9 and 22-27. Here we have used small strip sets as diagonal corners. Make these combined units, again referring to Block D diagram for color changes.

4. To assemble the blocks, begin by joining units 1 and 2; then add Unit 3 to top of the combined 1-2 units. Join combined units 4-9 to bottom of combined 1-3 units, matching leaf seam.

5. Join units 11 and 12; then add Unit 10 to the top of the 11-12 combined units. Join these units to the bottom of the 1-9 combined units to complete the left side of the block.

6. For the right side of the block, join units 13 and 14; then add Unit 15 to bottom of these combined units. Join Unit 16 to the right side of combined 13-15 units. Join units 18 and 19; then add Unit 17 to left side of these combined units. Join the two combined unit sections together, matching leaf seams. Join units 20 and 21; then add these units to the right side of combined 13-19 units, again matching leaf seam.

7. For both blocks, join units 28 and 29; then add combined units 22-27 to left side of these combined units, matching seams. For both blocks, join the bottom combined units to the top combined units, matching seams where necessary.

8. Join the left side of the flower to the right side of the flower, carefully matching seams to complete the blocks. Make 4 of Block C, and 4 of Block D.

BLOCKS E AND F ASSEMBLY

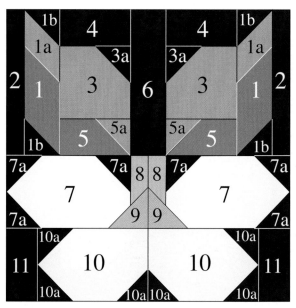

Block E. Make 16. When completed, block should measure 8 1/2" square.

1. Blocks E and F are assembled exactly the same. The only difference is a change of color in the flower. Refer frequently to the block diagrams above and on page 31 for correct placement of color.

2. Use diagonal corner technique to make two each of mirror image units 3, 5, 7, and 10. Use diagonal end technique to make two of mirror image Unit 1, shown on following page. For Unit 1, make diagonal end first; then add diagonal corners 1b.

3. To assemble the block, begin by joining units 1 and 2, referring to block diagram for correct position of mirror image units. Join units 4, 3, and 5 in a vertical row, and add this row to the sides of 1-2 combined units, matching leaf seams. Join these mirror image combined units to opposite sides of Unit 6 to complete the leaf section of the block.

4. Join Unit 8 to side of Unit 7 as shown; then add diagonal corner, Unit 9. Join these two combined unit sections together. Join units 11, 10, 10, and 11 in a horizontal row. Join this row to bottom of combined 7-9 units.

5. Join the flower section to the leaf section, matching stem and leaf seams to complete the block. Make 8.

Making units C4-C9, C22-C27. For D4-D9, and D22-D27, refer to Block D diagram for color changes.

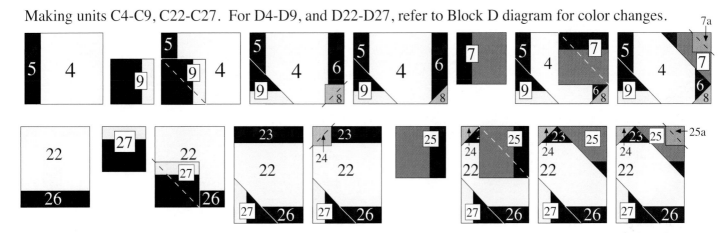

The diagram above shows how to assemble the units given in the title. The major difference is the way the strip set diagonal corners are placed, and color changes for Block D. Refer to Block D diagram for those changes. The following description is for the top diagram (units C4-C9). For the bottom diagram, refer to the placement of the strip set units, as they are placed differently, although the cut sizes and fabrics are identical. To begin, join units 4 and 5. Join 1" x 2 1/4" strip of Fabric III with 1 3/4" x 2 1/4" strip of Fabric I for Unit 9. This will now be used as a diagonal corner. For all strip set diagonal corners, if you want your strip set to end up horizontally, it must be placed vertically. If you want it to end up vertically, it must be placed horizontally.

Place diagonal corner, Unit 9 as shown, with raw edges matching. Stitch diagonal seam, trim and press. Add Unit 6 to the right side. Join diagonal corner Unit 8. Join 1" x 2 3/8" strip of Fabric I with1 7/8" x 2 3/8" strip of Fabric IX for Unit 7. Use this strip set as a diagonal corner. Place as shown on top right corner of combined units with raw edges matching. Stitch diagonal, trim seam and press. Join diagonal corners 7a. Refer to the bottom illustration to make units 22-27.

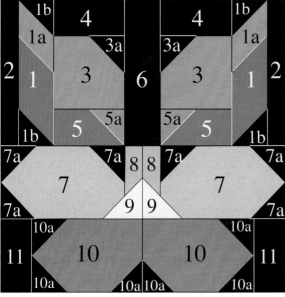

Block F. Make 8. When completed, block
should measure 8 1/2" square.

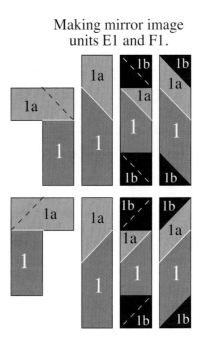

Making mirror image
units E1 and F1.

TABLECLOTH ASSEMBLY. BLOCKS B AND D CENTER.

Refer to the tablecloth diagram frequently throughout these instructions for correct placement of blocks and sashing.

1. To assemble the center section, begin by joining two of Block B to opposite sides of Q2 sashing. Make 2. Join Q1 sashing between the two Block B sets; then join Unit Q3 to opposite sides as shown.

2. Join two Block D's, referring to diagram for correct position. Make 2. Join Unit Q4 to opposite ends of the combined Block D's. Join the Block D sets to opposite sides of the center as shown.

CENTER SECTION TOP AND BOTTOM ASSEMBLY

1. Referring to the tablecloth diagram, begin at the top part of the center section. Join two of Block F as shown. Join Unit Q9 to leaf side of Block A as shown. Join Unit Q10 to opposite sides of the Q9-Block A section; then add the combined Block F's. Join Unit Q11 to the bottom of this combination. Join Unit Q12 to opposite sides as shown Make 2..

2. The sides are mirrored, so correct placement of the blocks is important. Refer to diagram on page 32 for correct placement of the following: join Unit Q5 to top of Block C; then add Unit Q6 to the side of the Q5-Block C combination. Join Q7 to top of Block F; then add Unit Q8 to the side as shown. Join this combination to the bottom of the Block C combination. Make a total of 4. Join the sides to opposite sides of the Block A-Block F section. Make 2.

3. Join the top and bottom of the center section to the center as shown. Join previously pieced Q13 borders to opposite sides of the center; then add Q14 borders to the top and bottom.

SCALLOPED BORDER ASSEMBLY

1. For side borders, begin by folding the ends of the scallops wrong sides together, on a 45° angle. Press them in place. Join scallops to top of each Block E and each Unit Q15 as shown. Press seams towards the scallops. Make a row of five Block E's with Unit Q15 between them as shown. Join Unit Q19 to opposite short ends. Seam allowance for the scallops will overlap. Make two of these rows.

2. Join previously pieced Unit Q21 to bottom of the Block E flower row. Make two. Join these rows to the sides of the center section, pressing seams towards Unit Q21.

3. For top and bottom borders, join scallops Q16 to the top of each remaining Block E. Join scallop Q17 to the top of Unit Q18. Referring to quilt diagram, make a row of three Block E flowers with Unit Q18 between them. Scallops will overlap. Join Unit Q19 to opposite ends of this row; then add Unit Q20 to the bottom as shown. Join triangle Q22 to opposite sides. Make 2. Join these scallop rows to top and bottom of tablecloth to complete it.

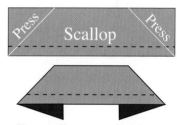

For scallops, turn under corners on a 45° angle and press. Join into seam with corners pressed under.

QUILTING AND FINISHING

Mary quilted a beautiful heart shaped feather motif with swirls at the ends in all of the open spaces. Her special little finishing touch of colored swirls coming out of each flower enhanced each bloom.

Cut 2 1/4" wide bias binding from Fabric I, and bind your tablecloth.

VALANCE

Refer to page 22 for making a valance. Here we had a 46" wide window and used E and F blocks. We put 1" wide navy sashing at the top and bottom of each flower block to give it a more open look.

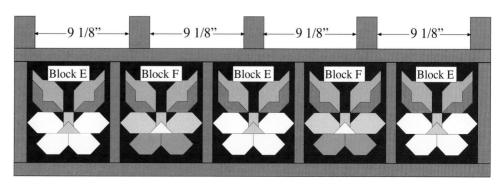

Although the strips between the various squares are small, this design is good practice for any beginner who wants to achieve accurate, "scant" 1/4" seams.

Because we live in this environment, I am crazy about this wall quilt.

Whether you live in the pines, or in the city, the charm and elegance of this design will be certain to get anyone's attention!

In The Pines

Wall Quilt Finishes To: 62 3/8" square.
Techniques used: Diagonal Corners

MATERIALS

Fabric I (light blue marble print)
Need 11 3/4"   3/8 yard

Fabric II (medium blue print)
Need 83 1/4""   2 1/2 yards

Fabric III (dark blue print)
Need 25 3/4"   7/8 yard

Fabric IV (light green batik)
Need 5 3/4"   1/4 yard

Fabric V (medium green batik)
Need 5 3/4"   1/4 yard

Fabric VI (dark green batik)
Need 5 3/4"   1/4 yard

Fabric VII (light brown batik)
Need 5"   1/4 yard

Fabric VIII (medium brown batik)
Need 37"   1 1/8 yard

Fabric IX (dark brown batik)
Need 5"   1/4 yard
Backing   4 yards

CUTTING

FROM FABRIC I, CUT: (LIGHT BLUE MARBLE PRINT)
- One 11 3/4" wide strip. From this, cut:
  * Two - 9" x 11 3/4" (Q3, Q4)
  Stack these cuts:
  * One - 4 7/8" x 20 1/4" (Q2)
  * One - 4 7/8" x 15 7/8" (Q1)

FROM FABRIC II, CUT: (MEDIUM BLUE PRINT)
- Eight 6 3/4" wide strips. From these, cut:
  * Four - 6 3/4" x 30 3/4" (Q9) Piece two together to = two 61" lengths. Trim length if necessary.
  * Four - 6 3/4" x 24 1/2" (Q8) Piece two together to = two 48 1/2" lengths. Trim length if necessary.
  * One - 1 3/4" x 5 1/8" (A8b)
  * One - 2 3/8" x 4 1/2" (A3b)
  * Seven - 1 1/2" x 4" (B8b, C8b)
  * Seven - 2" x 3 1/2" (B3b, C3b)
  * Fourteen - 1" x 3 1/2" (B1d, B8d, C1d, C8d)
  From scrap, cut:
  * One - 2 3/8" x 3 1/4" (A8a)
  * Three - 1 3/4" x 3 1/4" (A1c, A3a, A7b)
  * Eighteen - 1 1/8" x 3 1/4" (A1a, A2a, A4a, A7a, A8c, A9a, A11)
  * Forty-two - 1" x 3" (B1b, B2b, B9b, C1b, C2b, C9b)
  * Seven - 2" x 2 1/2" (B8a, C8a)
  * Two - 2" squares (A10a)
- Four 2 1/2" wide strips. From these and scrap, cut:
  * Twenty-one - 1 1/2" x 2 1/2" (B1c, B3a, B7b, C1c, C3a, C7b)
  * 126 - 1" x 2 1/2" (B1a, B2a, B4a, B7a, B8c, B9a, B11, C1a, C2a, C4a, C7a, C8c, C9a, C11)
- Four 1 7/8" wide strips. From these, cut:
  * Two - 1 7/8" x 34 1/4" (Q6)
  * Two - 1 7/8" x 31 1/2" (Q5)
  * Eight - 1 3/4" squares (A16a, B10a)
- One 1 3/4" wide strip. From this, cut:
  * One - 1 3/4" x 14 5/8" (A14)
  * One - 1 3/4" x 13 3/8" (A15)
- Eight 1 1/4" wide strips. From these, cut:
  * Eight - 1 1/4" x 12 1/2" (C15)
  * Eleven - 1 1/4" x 11" (B14, C14)
  * Three - 1 1/4" x 10 1/4" (B15)
  * Six - 1 1/4" squares (B16a)
  From scrap, cut:
  * Two - 1 1/8" x 4 1/2" (A1d, A8d)
  * Six - 1 1/8" x 3 7/8" (A1b, A2b, A9b)
  * One - 1 1/8" x 1 3/4" (A6)
  * One - 1 1/8" square (A13)
  * Seven - 1" x 1 1/2" (B6, C6)
  * Seven - 1" squares (B13, C13)

FROM FABRIC III, CUT: (DK. BLUE PRINT)
- Two - 12 7/8" wide strips. From these, cut:
  * Four - 12 7/8" squares (Q7) Cut in half diagonally.

FROM FABRIC IV, CUT: (LT. GREEN BATIK)
- One 3 1/4" wide strip. From this, cut:
  * Four - 3 1/4" squares (A1)
  * One - 2 5/8" x 3 1/4" (A7)
  * One - 1 1/8" x 3 1/4" (A5)
  * Three - 2" x 2 1/2" (B7)
  * Three - 1" x 2 1/2" (B5)
- One 2 1/2" wide strip. From this, cut:
  * Twelve - 2 1/2" squares (B1)

FROM FABRIC V, CUT: (MED. GREEN BATIK)
- One 3 1/4" wide strip. From this, cut:
  * Five - 3 1/4" squares (A2, A9)
- One 2 1/2" wide strip. From this, cut:
  * Fifteen - 2 1/2" squares (B2, B9)

FROM FABRIC VI, CUT: DARK GREEN BATIK)
- One 3 1/4" wide strip. From this, cut:
  * Four - 3 1/4" squares (A3, A8)
  * One - 2 5/8" x 3 1/4" (A4)
  * One - 1 1/8" x 3 1/4" (A12)
  * Three - 2" x 2 1/2" (B4)
  * Three - 1" x 2 1/2" (B12)
- One 2 1/2" wide strip. From this, cut:
  * Twelve - 2 1/2" squares (B3, B8)

FROM FABRIC VII, CUT: (LT. BROWN BATIK)
- Two 2 1/2" wide strips. From these, cut:
  * Sixteen - 2 1/2" squares (C1)
  * Four - 2" x 2 1/2" (C7)
  * Four - 1" x 2 1/2" (C5)

FROM FABRIC VIII, CUT (MEDIUM BROWN BATIK)
- One 3 1/4" wide strip. From this, cut:
  * One - 3 1/4" square (A10)
  * One - 1 3/4" x 3" (A16)
  * Fourteen - 2 1/2" squares (B10, C2, C9)
- Eight 2 1/2" wide strips. Seven for straight-grain binding. From remaining strip, cut:
  * Nine - 2 1/2" squares (add to 2 1/2" sq. above)
- One 1 3/4" wide strip. From this, cut:
  * One - 1 3/4" square (A14a)
  * Three - 1 1/4" x 2" (B16)
  * Three - 1 1/4" squares (B14a)
- Eight 1 1/2" wide strips. From these, cut:
  * Four - 1 1/2" x 31 3/4" (Q11) Piece together to = two 63" lengths. Trim to fit if necessary.
  * Four - 1 1/2" x 30 3/4" (Q10) Piece together to = two 61" lengths. Trim to fit if necessary.

FROM FABRIC IX, CUT: (DK. BROWN BATIK)
- Two 2 1/2" wide strips. From these, cut:
  * Twenty - 2 1/2" squares (C3, C8, C10)
  * Four - 2" x 2 1/2" (C4)
  * Four - 1" x 2 1/2" (C12)

BLOCKS A AND B ASSEMBLY

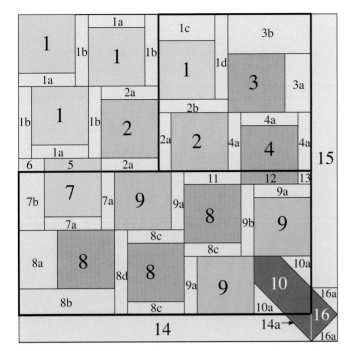

Block A. Make 1. When completed, block should measure 15 7/8" square.

Block B. Make 3. When completed, block should measure 11 3/4" square.

TREE TOP LEFT SECTION ASSEMBLY

1. Blocks A and B are assembled exactly the same way. The only difference between the blocks is the size. Block B is smaller. To begin, use diagonal corner technique to make one of units 10, 14, and 16.

2. We have divided the blocks off into sections, beginning with the top left section. To assemble this section, begin by joining Unit 1a to three Unit 1's. Referring to the top left corner, join Unit 1b to right side of right side of two Unit 1's as shown. Join these Unit 1's together.

3. For remaining Unit 1, turn so that Unit 1a is on the bottom. Join Unit 1b to opposite sides of Unit 1. Join units 5 and 6. Add these combined units to the bottom of the 1-1a-1b unit. Join Unit 2a to top and bottom of Unit 2; then add this combination to the right side of the 1-5-6 combined units. Join this section to the previously joined Unit 1's.

TREE TOP RIGHT SECTION ASSEMBLY

1. Begin by joining Unit 1c to top of Unit 1. Join Unit 1d to the right side; then add Unit 2b to the bottom. Join Unit 2a to left side of Unit 2; then join this to bottom of combined units 1-1c-1d-2b.

2. Join Unit 3a to right side of Unit 3; then add Unit 3b to the top. Join one Unit 4a to the top long edge of Unit 4; then join remaining units 4a to opposite sides. Join the combined Unit 4 section to the bottom of the combined Unit 3 section. Join 3-4 section to right side of 1-2 section. Join the combined 1-2-3-4 section to the right side of the combined 1-2-5-6 section to complete the top of the tree.

TREE BOTTOM SECTION ASSEMBLY

1. Join one Unit 7a to bottom of Unit 7; then add remaining Unit 7a to right side of combined 7-7a section. Join Unit 7b to left side of these combined units. For Unit 8, join Unit 8a to left side; then add Unit 8b across the bottom. Join the 7 and 8 combined units together as shown.

2. Join Unit 9a to right side of Unit 9. Join Unit 8c to top and bottom of one Unit 8; then add Unit 8d to left side of the 8-8c combined units. Join these combined units to the bottom of combined Unit 9. Join this section to the right side of combined units 7-8 as shown.

3. Join Unit 8c to bottom of remaining Unit 8; then add Unit 9b to the right side. Join Unit 9a to the left side of one Unit 9; then add the 9-9a combined units to the bottom of combined units 8-8c-9b. Join Unit 9a to top of remaining Unit 9; then add Unit 10 to the bottom of these combined units. Join this combination to the right side of other combined units. Join units 11, 12, and 13 in a horizontal row, and add to the top of the 8-9-10 combined units, matching seams. Join these units to right side of other combined units.

4. Join the top and bottom sections together, carefully matching seams.

COMPLETING THE TREE BLOCKS

1. To complete the trees, join Unit 14 to the bottom of the tree, matching tree trunk seams. Join units 15 and 16; then add them to the right side of the tree, again matching tree trunk seams.

PINE CONE BLOCK C ASSEMBLY

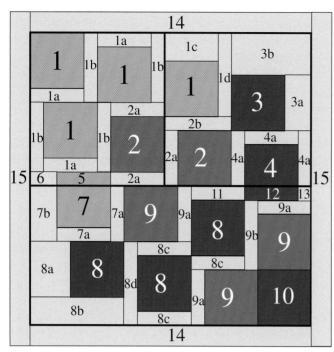

Block C. Make 4. When completed, block should measure 12 1/2" square.

PINE CONE TOP LEFT SECTION ASSEMBLY

1. To assemble the top left section, begin by joining Unit 1a to three Unit 1's. Referring to the top left corner, join Unit 1b to right side of two Unit 1's as shown. Join these Unit 1's together.
2. For remaining Unit 1, turn so that Unit 1a is on the bottom. Join Unit 1b to opposite sides of Unit 1. Join units 5 and 6. Add these combined units to the bottom of the 1-1a-1b unit. Join Unit 2a to top and bottom of Unit 2; then add this combination to the right side of the 1-5-6 combined units. Join this section to the previously combined Unit 1's.

PINE CONE TOP RIGHT SECTION ASSEMBLY

1. Join Unit 1c to the top of remaining Unit 1; then add Unit 1d to the right side. Join Unit 2b to the bottom. Join Unit 2a to the left side of Unit 2; then add these combined units to the bottom of the Unit 1 combination.
2. Join Unit 3a to the right side of Unit 3; then add Unit 3b to the top as shown. Join one Unit 4a to the top long edge of Unit 4; then add remaining 4a units to opposite sides. Join these Unit 4 combined units to the bottom of Unit 3 combination.
3. Join the 3-4 combined units to the right side of the 1-2 combined units to complete the top right section. Join this section to the side of the top left section, matching seams.

PINE CONE BOTTOM SECTION ASSEMBLY

1. The bottom of the pine cone is assembled the same as for "Tree Bottom Section Assembly" - Steps 1-4. Follow these instructions for the bottom of the pine cone.
2. Join Unit 14 to top and bottom of pine cone; then add Unit 15 to opposite sides. Make 4.

QUILT CORNER ASSEMBLY

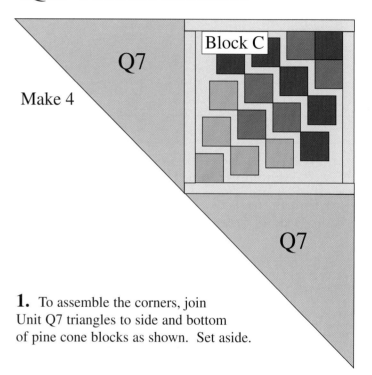

1. To assemble the corners, join Unit Q7 triangles to side and bottom of pine cone blocks as shown. Set aside.

QUILT CENTER ASSEMBLY

1. To assemble the center section, join Block B, Unit Q4, and Block B in a row. Join Unit Q3 to top of remaining Block B. Join Unit Q1 to side of Block A as shown; then add Unit Q2 to bottom of Q1-Block A combination. Join the top Block B-Q4-Block B row to the top of Block A section, matching seams where necessary.
2. Join Unit Q5 to opposite sides of center trees; then add Unit Q6 to top and bottom.

Quilt top center asssembly. Assemble on the straight.

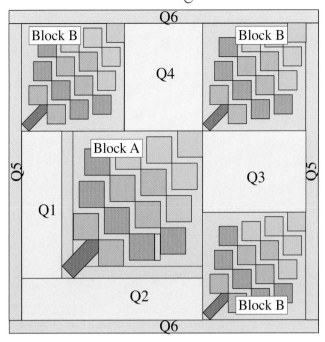

QUILT BORDERS & FINISHING

1. Turn center section around so that trees are "on point." Join the previously pieced triangular corners, pressing seams towards center.

2. Join border Q8 to opposite sides of center section; then add Unit Q9 to top and bottom. Join outer border Q10 to opposite sides of quilt top; then add border Q11 to top and bottom.

3. Mary Nordeng's quilting on this design is exquisite. Mary rarely marks her quilts, and the pine cones and pine boughs are all worked on a long arm machine freehand.

4. Use seven 2 1/2" wide strips of Fabric VIII for straight-grain binding and bind your quilt.

Forget Me Not

The title of this ensemble is very appropriate, especially for me. Through all of the years that we have designed quilts and accessories, this stands out among them all as my favorite. After the quilt design was completed, I wanted to set the scene for the most elegant bedroom I could think of.

You can make this happen in your home. Window treatments are surprisingly easy to do! This is the stuff dreams are made of.................Enjoy!

Quilt Finishes To: 97" x 106".

Techniques used: Diagonal Corners, Diagonal Ends, Triangle-Squares, Triangle-Squares with Diagonal Corners, Strip Sets, and Strip Sets with Diagonal Corners.

MATERIALS

Fabric I (ivory with blue print)
Need 208 1/2"   6 yards

Fabric II (light blue print)
Need 88 1/4"   2 5/8 yards

Fabric III (medium blue print)
Need 85 3/8"   2 1/2 yards

Fabric IV (dark blue print)
Need 13 1/2"   1/2 yard

Fabric V (navy textured print)
Need 161"   4 3/4 yards

Fabric VI (light green print)
Need 18"   5/8 yard

Fabric VII (medium green print)
Need 13"   1/2 yard

Fabric VIII (dark green print)
Need 21"   3/4 yard

Fabric IX (yellow print)
Need 3"   1/4 yard

Backing   **8 5/8yards**

Medium blue batiste 6"   1/4 yard

Light blue batiste   6"   1/4 yard

CUTTING

FROM FABRIC I, CUT: (IVORY WITH BLUE PRINT)
- **Five 11 1/2" wide strips. From these, cut:**
  * Two - 11 1/2" x 12 1/2" (G5)
  * Eight - 11 1/2" squares (B37)
  * Six - 7 3/4" x 11 1/2" (F14)
  Stack this cut:
  * Ten - 4 1/2" squares (C19, D21, E21, F16a, G7a)
  From scrap, cut:
  * Twenty-nine - 1 1/2" squares (A4a, A6a, A7a, A9a, A18b, A21b, A35b, A40a, A42, A50b, A53b, A55b)
- **Eight 7 1/2" wide strips. From these, cut:**
  * Eight - 7 1/2" x 29 1/2" (Q2, Q8)
  * Eight - 4 1/4" x 7" (F17, G6)
  * Eight - 3 3/4" x 7" (F15, G8)
  From scrap, cut:
  * Forty-eight - 1 1/2" sq. (add to 1 1/2" sq. above)
- **Four 6 3/4" wide strips. From these, cut:**
  * Six - 6 3/4" x 9" (F13a)
  * Eight - 6 3/4" squares (F13b, G2)
  * Two - 4 3/4" x 6 3/4" (G1)
  * Three - 6 3/8" x 8 1/2" (F11)
  Stack these cuts:
  * Six - 2" x 3" (F7)
  * Six - 1 7/8" squares (F10b)
- **Four 5 1/2" wide strips. From these, cut:**
  * Four - 5 1/2" x 18 1/2" (Q7)
  * Four - 5 1/2" x 13 1/2" (Q6)
  * Six - 2 1/2" x 5 1/2" (F4)
  * Eight - 1 1/2" x 5 1/2" (A54)
- **Two 5 1/4" wide strips. From these, cut:**
  * Ten - 5 1/4" squares (F14b, G5c)
  Stack this cut:
  * Eight - 2 1/2" x 3 1/2" (A52)
  * Eighteen - 1 1/2" x 2 1/2" (A49, A51a, A56)
- **Two 4 1/2" wide strips. From these, cut:**
  * Sixteen - 4 1/2" sq. (add to 4 1/2" sq. above)
  Stack this cut:
  * Six - 1 1/2" x 2 1/2" (add to above)
- **One 4 1/4" wide strip. From this, cut:**
  * One - 4 1/4" x 21 1/2" (G3)
  * Two - 4 1/4" squares (G2c)
  Stack this cut:
  * Six - 1 5/8" squares (F9b)
- **One 3 1/2" wide strip. From this, cut:**
  * Six - 3 1/2" squares (F5a)
  * Three - 2 1/2" x 6 1/2" (F1)
- **Two 2 1/2" wide strips. From these, cut:**
  * Twenty - 2 1/2" squares (A8, F5b, F6a)
  * Two - 2 1/4" squares (G1c)
  * Twelve - 2 1/8" squares (F9a, F10a)
- **One 2" wide strip. From this, cut:**
  * Twelve - 2" squares (F6c, F11d)
  * Ten - 1 1/2" squares (add to 1 1/2" sq. above)
- **Two 1 5/8" wide strips. From these, cut:**
  * Three - 1 5/8" x 18 1/2" (F12)
  * One - 1 1/2" x 21 1/2" (G4)
- **Three 1 1/2" wide strips. From these, cut:**
  * Fifty-seven - 1 1/2" sq. (add to 1 1/2" sq.)

FROM FABRIC II, CUT: (LIGHT BLUE PRINT)
- **Two 7 3/4" wide strips. From these, cut:**
  * Eight - 7 3/4" squares (F14a, G5a)
  Stack these cuts:
  * Six - 3 1/8" x 3 3/8" (F10)
  * Six - 1 3/4" squares (F9c)
- **One 6 3/4" strip. From this, cut:**
  * Two - 6 3/4" squares (G2b)
  * Two - 4 3/4" squares (G1b)
  * Thirty-nine - 1 1/2" squares (A12b, A39a, A46a, A47, A49a, B17b, B19, F6d)
- **One 5" wide strip. From this, cut:**
  * Six - 5" squares (F11a, F11b)
  * Eighteen - 1 1/2" squares (add to 1 1/2" sq.)
- **Eleven 3 1/2" wide strips. From these, cut:**
  * Four - 3 1/2" x 29 1/2" (Q2)
  * Four - 3 1/2" x 16 1/2" (Q5)
  * Six - 3 1/2" x 4 1/2" (F5)
  * Four - 3 1/2" squares (Q4a)
  * Seventy-four - 2 1/2" x 3 1/2" (A4, A33, A50, B7, B11, B33, C5, D5, E5, F2)
  * Sixteen - 1 1/2" x 3 1/2" (A5, A21)
- **One 3" wide strip. From this, and scrap cut:**
  * Ten - 3" squares (F16b, G1a, G7b)
  Stack this cut:
  * Thirteen - 1 1/2" squares (add to 1 1/2" sq.)
- **Three 2 1/2" wide strips. From these, cut:**
  * Twenty- 2 1/2" squares (B24, F1a, F4b)
  * Forty - 1 1/2" x 2 1/2" (A19, A23, A28, A41)
- **Eight 1 1/2" wide strips for Strip Set 2.**

FROM FABRIC III, CUT: (MED. BLUE PRINT)
- **Two 13 1/2" wide strips. From these, cut:**
  * Four - 13 1/2" squares (Q1)
  Stack this cut:
  * 153 - 1 1/2" squares (A3, A19a, A21a, A38, A41a, A43, A45, A50a, B9, B11a, B28, C3, D3, E3)
- **One 9 1/4" wide strip. From this, cut:**
  * Six - 6 3/4" x 9 1/4" (F13)
- **One 7 3/4" wide strip. From this, cut:**
  * Two - 7 3/4" squares (G5b)
  Stack this cut:
  * Fourteen - 3 1/2" squares (B23, F11c)
- **One 7" wide strip. From this, cut:**
  * Eight - 4 1/2" x 7" (F16, G7)
  * Twelve - 1 1/2" squares (add to 1 1/2" sq.)
- **Six 3 1/2" wide strips. From these, cut:**
  * Six - 3" x 3 1/2" (F6)
  * Eighty-four - 2 1/2" x 3 1/2" (A7, A12, A15, A39, A40, B5, B17, B31, C4, D4, E4)
  * Six - 1 1/4" squares (F6b)
- **One 3" wide strip. From this, cut:**
  * Eight - 3" squares (F14c, G2a)
  * Six - 2" x 3" (F8)
  * Six - 1 1/2" squares (add to 1 1/2" sq. above)
- **One 2 7/8" wide strip. From this, cut:**
  * Six - 2 7/8" x 3 3/8" (F9)
  * Three - 2 1/2" squares (F3)
  * Six - 2" squares (F4a)

- **Five 1 1/2" wide strips. From these, cut:**
  - * Eight - 1 1/2" x 3 1/2" (B30)
  - * Twenty-four - 1 1/2" x 2 1/2" (A46, A51, B13)
  - * Fifty-three - 1 1/2" squares (add to 1 1/2" sq)

FROM FABRIC IV, CUT: (DK. BLUE PRINT)
- **Nine 1 1/2" wide strips. Eight for strip sets 1 and 2. From remainder, cut:**
  - * Sixteen - 1 1/2" squares (A20, A44)

FROM FABRIC V, CUT: (NAVY PRINT)
- **Four 10 1/2" wide strips. From these, cut:**
  - * Eight - 10 1/2" squares (Q1a, Q2a)
  - * 140 - 1 1/2" squares (A11, A12a, A15a, A22,A27, A28a, A33a, B1a, B3a, B4a, B5a,B7a, B14a, B16, B17a, B18, B24a, B25a,B26a,B31a, B33a, B36b,C4a, C5a, C6b, C7a, C10b, C11a, C12a, C13b, C14b,C15b, D4a, D5a, D6b, D7a, D10b, D11a, D12a, D13b, D14b, D15b, D17a, E4a, E5a, E6b, E7a, E10b, E11a, E12a, E13b, E14b, E15b, E17a)
- **Two 8 1/2" wide strips. From these, cut:**
  - * Eight - 4 1/2" x 8 1/2" (B32)
  - * Eight - 3 3/8" x 8 1/2" (C18, D20, E20)
  - * Two - 2 1/2" x 8 1/2" (D18, E18)
  - * Thirty-five - 1 1/2" squares (add to 1 1/2" sq.)
- **One 7 1/2" wide strip. From this, cut:**
  - * Four - 7 1/2" squares (Q8a)
- **Three 4 1/2" wide strips. From these, cut:**
  - * Eight - 4 1/2" squares (B6)
  - * Thirteen - 2 1/2" x 4 1/2" (B2, C8, D8, E8)
  - * Eight - 1 1/2" x 4 1/2" (A14)
  - * Seventy-five - 1 1/2" squares (add to 1 1/2" sq.)
- **Five 3 1/2" wide strips. From these, cut:**
  - * Four - 3 1/2" x 7 1/2" (Q4)
  - * Eight - 3 1/2" squares (B21)
  - * Eight - 2 1/2" x 3 1/2" (B34)
  - * Fifty-six - 1 1/2" x 3 1/2" (A13, A17, A30, A31, A32, A34, B35a)
  - * Forty-six - 1 1/2" squares (add to 1 1/2" sq.)
- **Fourteen 2 1/2" wide strips. Eleven for straight-grain binding. From remaining strips, cut:**
  - * Ten - 2 1/2" x 6 1/2" (C16, D16, E16)
  - * Eighteen - 2 1/2" squares (B12, C9, D9, E9)
- **Twelve 2" wide strips. From these, cut:**
  - * Four - 2" x 40" (Q9, Q10)
  - * Four - 2" x 29 1/4" (Q10) Piece two to opposite sides of 40" strip to = two 97 1/2" lengths.
  - * Four - 2" x 27 3/4" (Q9) Piece two to opposite sides of 40" strip to = two 94 1/2" lengths.
- **Three 1 1/2" wide strips. From these, cut:**
  - * Eight - 1 1/2" x 2 1/2" (A16)
  - * Eight - 1 1/2" x 2 3/8" (C17, D19a, E19a)
  - * Fifty-two - 1 1/2" squares (add to 1 1/2" sq.)

FROM FABRIC VI, CUT: (LT. GREEN PRINT)
- **Twelve 1 1/2" wide strips. From these, cut:**
  - * Thirty-two - 1 1/2" x 3 1/2" (A18, A35, A55, B36)
  - * Fifty-five - 1 1/2" x 2 1/2" (A6, A53, B3, B14, B26, C7, C12, D7, D12, E7, E12)

- * 150 - 1 1/2" squares (A17b, A26, A29, A34b, A48, A49b, A54b, B1b, B4b, B15, B20a, B22a, B25b, B35b, C6a, C13a, C15a, C17b, D6a, D13a, D15a, D17b, D19b, E6a, E13a, E15a, E17b, E19b)

FROM FABRIC VII, CUT: (MEDIUM GREEN PRINT)
- **One 6 1/2" wide strip. From this, cut:**
  - * Four - 6 1/2" squares (Q2b)
  - * Two - 3 1/2" x 6 1/2" (Q3)
  - Stack this cut:
  - * Sixteen - 1 1/2" squares (A10, A13b, C10a,C14a, D10a, D14a, E10a, E14a)
- **One 3 1/2" wide strip. From this, cut:**
  - * Eight - 3 1/2" squares (Q4b, Q8b)
- **Two 1 1/2" wide strips. From these, cut:**
  - * Thirteen - 1 1/2" x 2 1/2" (A9, C11, D11, E11)
  - * Ten - 1 1/2" squares (add to 1 1/2" sq. above)

FROM FABRIC VIII, CUT: (DK. GREEN PRINT)
- **Fourteen 1 1/2" wide strips. From these, cut:**
  - * Eight - 1 1/2" x 4 1/2" (B22)
  - * Eight - 1 1/2" x 3 1/2" (B20)
  - * 144 - 1 1/2" x 2 1/2" (A13a, A17a, A18a, A34a, A35a, A53a, A54a, A55a, B1, B4, B25, B35,B36a, C6, C10, C13, C14, C15, C17a, D6, D10, D13, D14, D15, D17, D19, E6, E10, E13, E14, E15, E17,E19)
  - * Eighty - 1 1/2" squares (A6b, A9b, A11, A27, A29, A31a, A48, A51b, B14b, B16)

FROM FABRIC IX, CUT: (LT. YELLOW PRINT)
- **Two 1 1/2" wide strips for Strip Set 1**

FROM MEDIUM BLUE BATISTE, CUT:
- **Two 2 1/2" x 35 1/2" (bow) Piece two together to = 70" length.**

FROM LIGHT BLUE BATISTE, CUT:
- **Two 2 1/2" x 35 1/2" (bow) Piece two together to = 70" length.**

STRIP SETS FOR THE BLOCKS

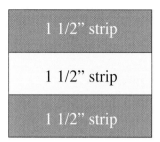
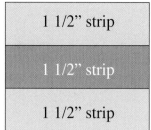

Strip Set 1. Make 2. Cut into fifty - 1 1/2" segments for units A1/A2, A24/A25, A36/A37, B8/B10, B27/B29, C1/C2, D1/D2, E1/E2.

Strip Set 2. Make 4. Cut into eighty-four 1 1/2" segments for units A2/A3, A37/A38,B9/B10, B28/B29 C2/C3, D2/D3, and E2/E3.

1. Refer to page 6 for instructions on how to make strip sets. Follow the instructions above and make the required number of strips for each strip set.

2. The diagrams show the number of strip sets to make, the size of the strips, and the units that the strip set segments will be used for. Cut the strip sets into the number of 1 1/2" segments that are required. You may wish to count the number of units and place the segments into their own zip top bag with the unit numbers marked on the bag. This organizes the units for block assembly when needed later.

3. Refer to the diagrams below. After cutting Strip Set 2 into the required number of segments, diagonal corner Unit 3 will be added. This saves an amazing amount of time, and if they are chain pieced using The Angler 2, this step will go quickly. The seams from diagonal corner Unit 3 will overlap Unit 2, 1/4" for your seam allowance.

Step 1

Strip Set 2 cut into 1 1/2" segment.

Step 2

Join diagonal corner Unit 3, right sides together with raw edges matching. Trim seam and press.

Step 3

Join second diagonal corner 3.

Trim seam and press.

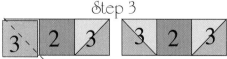

Save what is left of your strip sets. They can be used later for pillowcase blocks and panel screen blocks.

BLOCK A ASSEMBLY

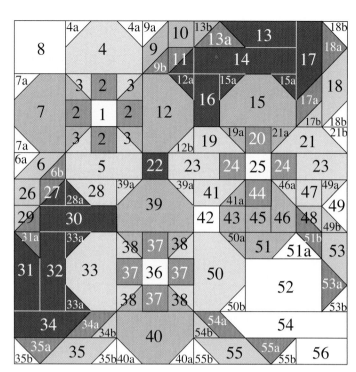

Block A. Make 8. When completed, block should measure 13 1/2" square.

1. Use diagonal corner technique to make one of units 4, 6, 7, 9, 12, 15, 19, 21, 28, 31, 33, 39, 40, 41, 46, 49, and 50. Use diagonal end technique to make one of units 13, 17, 18, 34, 35, 51, 53, 54, and 55. Refer to diagrams on this page and page 45 for correct placement of diagonal end units.

2. Use triangle-square technique to make one of units 11, 27, 29, and 48. Follow instructions and diagrams below, and on following page.

Place 1 1/2" squares of fabrics VI and VIII right sides facing and raw edges matching. Stitch diagonal and press for units A29 and A48.

Place 1 1/2" squares of fabrics V and VIII right sides facing and raw edges matching. Stitch diagonal and press for units A11 and A27, and B16.

Making Unit A54

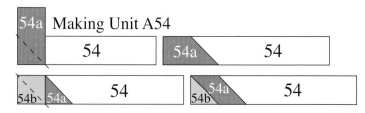

3. To assemble the block, begin by joining Strip Set 2 to top and bottom of Strip Set 1 (units 1, 2, and 3). Refer to block diagram for correct placement of color in the triangle-squares. Match all seams. Join Unit 4 to the top of the combined strip sets. Join units 7 and 8; then add them to left side of strip set center. Join units 10 and 11; then add Unit 9 to left side of combined units 10-11; then add Unit 12 to the bottom as shown. Join these combined units to right side of flower.

4. Join units 13 and 14. Join units 15 and 16; then add these combined units to the bottom of combined 13-14 units. Join units 17 and 18; then add them to the right side of combined units 13-16. Join units 19, 20, and 21 in a horizontal row. Add this row to the bottom of the 13-18 combined units. Join the left combined unit section to the right combined unit section, matching seams. Join units 6, 5, 22, 23, Strip Set 1, and Unit 23 in a horizontal row. Add this row to the bottom of other combined units to complete the top section of Block A.

5. To assemble the bottom section of Block A, join units 26, 27, and 28 in a horizontal row. Join units 29 and 30. Add these combined units to bottom of the 26-28 horizontal row. Join units 31, 32, and 33 in a row. Add to the bottom of other combined units as shown, matching 31a leaf seam. Join units 34 and 35, matching leaf seams. Add these combined units to the bottom of combined units 26-33.

6. Join Strip Set 2, Strip Set 1, and Strip Set 2 together (units 37-38, and 36-37). See block diagram for correct placement of color in the triangle-squares. Match all seams. Join Unit 39 to the top of the strip set combination, and Unit 40 to the bottom. Add this section to right side of other combined units, matching seams where necessary.

7. Join units 42 And 43; then add Unit 41 to top of these combined units, matching 41a seam. Join units 44 and 45; then add Unit 46 to right side of these combined units. Join the combined 41-43 units to left side of the combined 44-46 units. Join units 47 and 48; then add Unit 49 to right side. Join these combined units to the right side of 41-46 combined units. Join units 51 and 52; then add Unit 50 to left side of these combined units and Unit 53 to the right side. Add to bottom of other combined units, matching seams. Join units 55 and 56; then add Unit 54 to top of the 55-56 combined units, matching leaf seam. Join this section to bottom of 41-53 combined units.

8. Join this right flower section to the left combined units, again matching seams. Join the top of Block A to the bottom, matching all seams where necessary to complete Block A. Make 8.

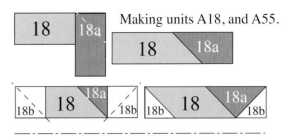

Making units A18, and A55.

Making mirror image units A35, and A53. For Unit A53, refer to block diagram and omit one diagonal corner as shown.

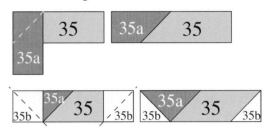

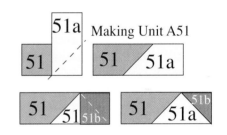

Making Unit A51

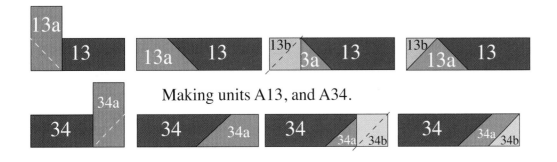

Making units A13, and A34.

45

BLOCK B ASSEMBLY

Step 1. Make block as shown below.

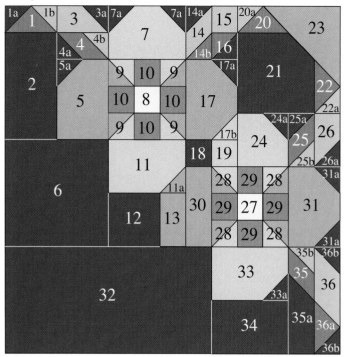

Block B. Make 8. When completed, block should measure 13 1/2" square.

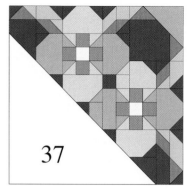

Step 2. Join diagonal corner B37. DO NOT trim center seam on diagonal corner as it is a light fabric on top of a dark fabric, and the dark will show through.

TIP

Join all multiple diagonal corners in alphabetical order.

1. Use diagonal corner technique to make one of units 1, 3, 4, 5, 7, 11, 14, 17, 20, 22, 24, 25, 26, and 33. Use diagonal end technique to make one of units 35 and 36, shown below right. Refer to diagrams on page 44 for making triangle-square Unit 16.

2. To assemble the block, begin by joining units 1 and 2. Join units 3, 4, and 5 in a vertical row; then join them to right side of the 1-2 combined units. Join Unit 6 to the bottom of the combined units. Join Strip Set 2, Strip Set 1, and Strip Set 2 (units 9-10 and 8-10) as shown; then add Unit 7 to the top of the strip sets, and Unit 11 to the bottom. Join units 12 and 13. Add these combined units to the flower center row. Join this row to right side of the 1-6 combined units.

3. Join units 15 and 16; then add Unit 14 to left side of these combined units. Add Unit 17 to the bottom. Join units 18 and 19; then add them to the bottom of Unit 17. Join units 20 and 21; then add Unit 22 to right side of these combined units as shown. Join diagonal corner, Unit 23 to top right corner of the 20-22 combined units. Join units 24, 25, and 26. Join these combined units to the bottom of combined units 20-23, matching leaf seam.

4. Join combined units 20-26 to right side of combined units 14-19, matching seams. For remaining flower center, join Strip Set 2, Strip Set 1, and Strip Set 2 in a row (units 28-29 and 27-29) as shown. Join Unit 30 to left side of the flower center, and Unit 31 to the right side. Join this section to the bottom of combined units 14-26, matching seams. Join the right side of the block (just completed) to the left side of the block, matching seams.

5. For the bottom of the block, join units 33 and 34; then add Unit 32 to the left side of the 33-34 combination. Join units 35 and 36, matching leaf seams; then add these combined units to combined units 32-34. Join the bottom of the block to the top of the block, again matching seams.

6. To complete the block, join diagonal corner Unit 37 to bottom left corner as shown in block diagram above. Make 8 of Block B.

Making Unit B35

Making Unit B36

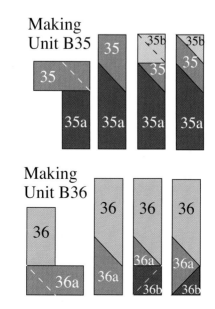

BLOCKS C, D, AND E ASSEMBLY

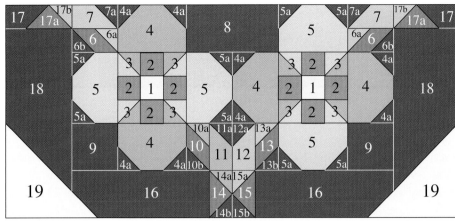

Block C. Make 3. When completed, block should measure 9 1/2" x 20 1/4".

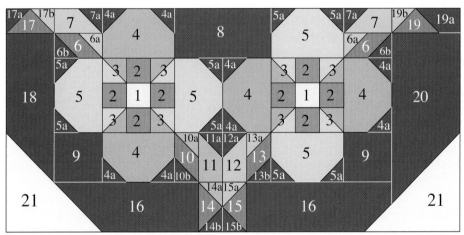

Block D. Make 1. When completed, block should measure 9 1/2" x 19 3/8".

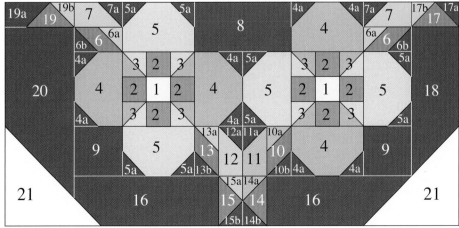

Block E. Make 1. When completed, block should measure 9 1/2" x 19 3/8".

Blocks C, D, and E are basically the same. D and E are mirror images because of their positions on the quilt. Some instructions apply to all three blocks. Exceptions will be designated. Instructions are for one block of each.

1. Use diagonal corner technique to make four each of units 4 and 5. Make two each of mirror image Units 6, 7, and 17. Make one of units 10, 11, 12, 13, 14, and 15. Use diagonal end technique to make two each of mirror image units 17 and 19.

2. To assemble the blocks, begin by making the center of each flower. Join Strip Set 2, Strip Set 1, and Strip Set 2 (units 2-3 and 1-2) as shown. For blocks C and D, refer to block diagrams, and join Unit 4 to top and bottom of one flower center, and Unit 5 to top and bottom of remaining flower center. Placement of these units are in reverse for Block E.

3. Refer to block diagrams for correct placement of these mirror image units. For left side of C and D blocks, join units 7, 6, 5, and 9 in a vertical row. Add this row to left side of flower center section. For right side of C and D blocks, join mirror image units 7, 6, 4, and 9 in a vertical row. Join this row to right side of remaining flower center. For E block, refer to block diagram. Units 7, 6, 4 and 9 are joined to the left side of left flower center, and mirror images 7, 6, 5, and 9 are joined to the right side of the remaining flower.

4. For blocks C and D center section, join units 4 and 5; then add Unit 8 to top of these combined units. Join units 10, 11, 12, and 13 in a row as shown. Join to the bottom of combined units 4-5-8. Join the two flowers together as shown. Join units 16, 14, 15, and 16 in a horizontal row. Add this row to the bottom of the flowers.

5. Being a mirror image of Block D, Block E is made in reverse. The 4-5 units are reversed, as are the 13, 12, 11, and 10 units. Refer to block diagram and join these units. For the bottom, join units 16, 15, 14, and 16; then add this row to the bottom of the flowers.

6. For Block C sides, join mirror image diagonal end, Unit 17 and Unit 18. Join to opposite sides of the flowers, matching seams. Join diagonal corner, Unit 19 to bottom corners of the block. Do not trim center seam of the diagonal corner, as the darker fabric will show through.

7. For left side of Block D, join diagonal corner Unit 17 to Unit 18. Add these combined units to the left side of the block. For the right side, join diagonal end Unit 19 to Unit 20. Join to right side of the block. Join diagonal corner Unit 21 to bottom corners of the block. Do not trim center seam of diagonal corner.

8. For left side of Block E, join diagonal end Unit 19 and

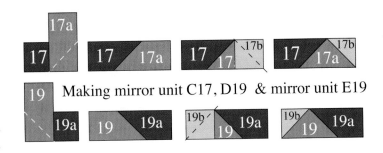

Making mirror unit C17, D19 & mirror unit E19

Unit 20; then add to left side of the block. For the right side, join diagonal corner Unit 17 to Unit 18; then add to right side of the block. Join diagonal corner Unit 21 to bottom corners of the block. Do not trim center seam of diagonal corner. Make 3 of Block C, and one each of blocks D and E.

BLOCK F ASSEMBLY

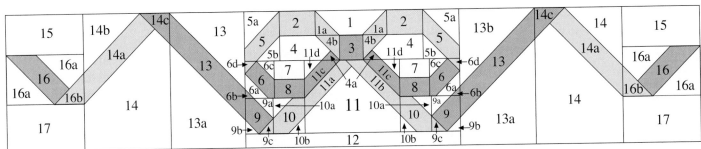

Block F. Make 3. When completed, block should measure 11 1/2" x 58 1/2".

For blocks F and G, DO NOT trim the center seam of light colored background fabric, as darker fabric will show through. Join all diagonal corners in alphabetical order.

1. Use diagonal corner technique to make two each of mirror image units 4, 5, 6, 9, 10, 14, and 16. Use this technique to make one of units 1, and 11. Use diagonal end technique to make two of mirror image Unit 13.

2. To assemble the bow, begin in the center and join Unit 2 to opposite sides of Unit 1. Join mirror image Unit 4 to opposite sides of Unit 3, referring to block diagram for correct placement of Unit 4.. Join these two combined unit sections together, matching seams; then add mirror image Unit 5 to opposite sides of combined units.

3. Join units 7 and 8; then join mirror image Unit 6 to sides of these combined units. Join mirror image units 9 and 10. Add these combined units to bottom of units 6-8.

4. Join these mirror image combined units to opposite sides of Unit 11, matching bow seams; then add Unit 12 to the bottom. Join combined units 1-5 to top of the 6-12 combined units to complete the center of the bow.

5. Refer to the diagram at right for making diagonal end, mirror image Unit 13. Make diagonal end first; then add

diagonal corner 13b as shown. Join mirror image Unit 14 to side of Unit 13 as shown in block diagram. Match the ribbon seam. Join units 15, 16, and 17 in a row, referring to block diagram for correct position of mirror image Unit 16. Make 2. Join these rows to side of Unit 14, again matching ribbon seam.

6. Join mirror image combined units 13-17 to opposite sides of bow center to complete the block. Make 3.

Making mirror image Unit F13

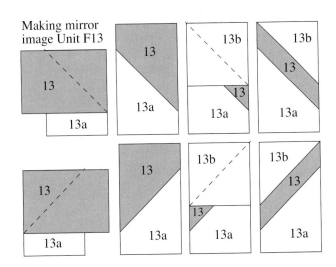

BLOCK G ASSEMBLY

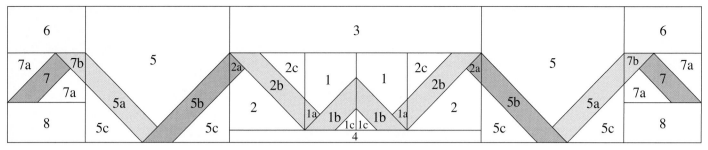

Block G. Make 1. When completed, block should measure 11 1/2" x 58 1/2".

1. Use diagonal corner technique to make two each of mirror image units 1, 2, 5, and 7. Join all diagonal corners in alphabetical order. For light background diagonal corners that are on top of darker fabrics, do not trim the center seam as the dark fabric will show through. Both the diagonal corner and triangle-square techniques are used for Unit 2. Refer to the diagram and instructions below to make mirror image, Unit 2.

2. To assemble the block, begin in the center and join the two Unit 1's as shown. Join mirror image Unit 2 to opposite sides of combined Unit 1's, matching seams; then add Unit 3 to the top, and Unit 4 to the bottom. Join units 6, mirror image Unit 7, and Unit 8 in a vertical row. Make 2. Join these rows to opposite sides of mirror image units 5; Join these combined units to opposite sides of center section, matching ribbon seams, to complete the block. Make 1.

Making mirror Unit G2

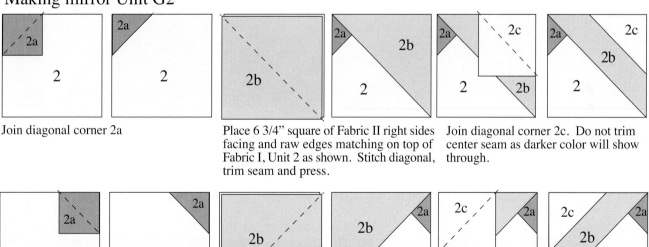

Join diagonal corner 2a

Place 6 3/4" square of Fabric II right sides facing and raw edges matching on top of Fabric I, Unit 2 as shown. Stitch diagonal, trim seam and press.

Join diagonal corner 2c. Do not trim center seam as darker color will show through.

QUILT CENTER SECTION ASSEMBLY

1. Use diagonal corner technique to make four of units Q1, and four of mirror image Unit Q4 and Q8.

2. To assemble the quilt, begin in the center, and referring to the quilt diagram above, join four of Block A together as shown, matching seams. Join Block B's together in pairs as shown, again matching seams. Join one pair to the top of the combined A blocks, and one to the bottom.

3. Join Unit Q1 to the top and bottom of remaining two pairs of Block B as shown. Join these rows to opposite sides of the center section, matching seams where necessary.

4. Join units Q5, mirror image Unit Q4, Q3, mirror image Unit Q4, and Q5 in a vertical row. Make two rows and join to opposite sides of center section.

5. Join a 3 1/2" x 29 1/2" strip of Fabric II to a 7 1/2" x 29 1/2" strip of Fabric I. Make four. These joined strips now become Unit Q2. Referring to quilt diagram, join mirror image units Q2a, and Q2b diagonal corners to short ends of Q2 units, adding the diagonal corners in alphabetical order. Join two of the Q2 strips together as shown in quilt diagram, with diagonal corner seams matching. Add one pair to top of center section, and one pair to the bottom, again matching seams.

6. Join Block G to the top of the center section as shown; then add one Block F to the bottom.

QUILT SIDE SECTION ASSEMBLY

1. To assemble the side sections of the quilt, refer to the quilt diagram, and begin with Block A in the top left corner. Notice its position. Join Unit Q6 to right side of Block A; then add Unit Q7 to the bottom. Make four. When you are assembling the sides of the quilt, the Block A combination can simply be turned for correct positioning.

2. Join two of Unit Q8 together, matching seams on the diagonal corners. Make two. Join Block F to sides of the combined Q8's, checking the quilt diagram for correct positioning of Block F bows. Join the Block A combination to top and bottom of the bow section as shown. Make 2. Join these rows to opposite sides of the quilt as shown.

3. Join previously pieced Q9 borders to opposite sides of the quilt; then join pieced Q10 borders to the top and bottom.

QUILT SCALLOP SECTION

1. For the bottom scallops, join the three Block C's in a horizontal row, matching Fabric I seams. Join Block D to left side of the row; then add Block E to the right side, again matching seams. Join this row to the bottom of the quilt as shown to complete the quilt top.

BATISTE BOW

1. For the bow at quilt top center, cut short ends of pieced 70" lengths of batiste on a 45° angle. Place right sides together and stitch around, leaving about a 4" opening. Trim corners. Turn right side out and press. Slip stitch opening closed. Tie in a large bow, approximately the same size as the pieced bows on the quilt. The bow may either be pinned to the quilt, or hand stitched in place.

MATERIALS FOR TWO PILLOWCASES

☐ **Fabric I (ivory with blue print)**
Need 89"   2 5/8 yards

☐ **Fabric II (light blue print)**
Need 3 1/2"   1/4 yard

☐ **Fabric III (medium blue print)**
Need 3 1/2"   1/4yard

☐ **Fabric IV (dark blue textured print)**
Need 1 1/2"   1/8 yard

☐ **Fabric V (navy textured print)**
Need 33 3/4"   1 yard

☐ **Fabric VI (light green print)**
Need 3"   1/8 yard

☐ **Fabric VII (dark green print)**
Need 3"   1/8 yard

☐ **Fabric VIII (yellow print)**
Need 3 1/2" sq.   Scrap

CUTTING FOR TWO PILLOWCASES

☐ **FROM FABRIC I, CUT: (IVORY WITH BLUE PRINT)**
• **Two 44 1/2" wide strips. From these, cut:**
    * Two - 25" x 44 1/2" (pillowcases)
    * Two - 4 1/2" x 5 1/2 (A10)
    * Sixteen - 1 1/2" squares (A4b, A6c)

☐ **FROM FABRIC II, CUT: (LT. BLUE PRINT)**
• **One 3 1/2" wide strip. From this, cut:**
    * Eight - 2 1/2" x 3 1/2" (A5)
    * Sixteen - 1 1/2" squares (A3)

☐ **FROM FABRIC III, CUT: (MED. BLUE PRINT)**
• **One 3 1/2" wide strip. From this, cut:**
    * Eight - 2 1/2" x 3 1/2" (A4)
    * Sixteen - 1 1/2" squares (A3)

☐ **FROM FABRIC IV, CUT: (DK. BLUE PRINT)**
• **One 1 1/2" wide strip. From this, cut:**
    * Sixteen - 1 1/2" squares (A2)

☐ **FROM FABRIC V, CUT: (NAVY PRINT)**
• **One 22 1/2" wide strip. From this, cut:**
    * Two - 15" x 22 1/2" (pillowcases)
    * One - 8 1/4" x 22 1/2" (pillowcases)
• **One 8 1/4" wide strip. From this, cut:**
    * One - 8 1/4" x 22 1/2" (add to above)
    * Four - 2 1/2" x 5 1/2" (A9)
    * Twenty-nine- 1 1/2" squares (A4a, A5a, A6a, A7a, A8a)
• **Two 1 1/2" wide strips. From these, cut:**
    * Thirty-five - 1 1/2" sq. (add to 1 1/2" sq. above)

FROM FABRIC VI, CUT: (LT. GREEN PRINT)
- **Two 1 1/2" wide strips. From these, cut:**
  - * Sixteen - 1 1/2" x 2 1/2" (A7)
  - * Thirty-two - 1 1/2" squares (A6b, A8b)

FROM FABRIC VII, CUT: (DK. GREEN PRINT)
- **Two 1 1/2" wide strips. From these, cut:**
  - * Thirty-two - 1 1/2" x 2 1/2" (A6, A8)

FROM FABRIC VIII, CUT: (LT. YELLOW PRINT)
- **Four - 1 1/2" squares (A1)**

FOR BATISTE BOWS, CUT:
- **Two 3" x 40"**

PILLOWCASE ASSEMBLY

Assembly instructions for one pillow case. Cutting for two standard cases. Finished size: 22" x 31 3/4"

1. Place one 8 1/4" x 22 1/2" piece of Fabric V right sides facing, on Block A. Stitch together along one long side. Press open. Place one 15" x 22 1/2" piece of Fabric V on top of Block A section, right sides facing. Stitch each short side together, forming a circle.

2. Fold the 15" circle in half lengthwise, wrong sides together, matching raw edge, and press.

3. Fold one 25" x 44 1/2" piece of Fabric I right sides together for a measurement of 22 1/4" x 25". Stitch one side and bottom together as shown. Turn right side out. Place 7 1/2" circular end along raw edge of pillowcase. Stitch around the circle using 1/4" seam. Fold out and press. Serge seams if desired.

PILLOWCASE BLOCK A ASSEMBLY

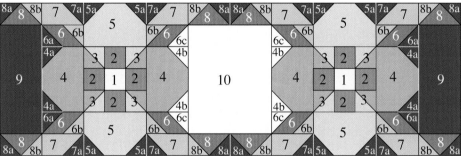

Pillowcase Block A. Make 2. When completed block should measure 7 1/2" x 22 1/2".

1. Use diagonal corner technique to make eight each of mirror image units 6, 7, and 8. Use this technique to make four each of units 4 and 5.

2. To assemble the block, use four 1 1/2" segments of Strip Set 2, (left over from the quilt strip sets), and two of Strip Set One. Refer to page 44 for making the strip set diagonal corners.

3. Join the strip sets for the center of each flower as shown. Join Unit 5 to top and bottom of each flower center. Refer to block diagram above frequently for correct position of all mirror image units For inner flower petals, join mirror image units 7, 6, 4, 6, and 7 in a vertical row. Make two. Join these mirror image rows to the inner side of the flowers, matching seams.

4. Join two mirror image Unit's 8 together with leaf tips matching as shown. Make two. Join to top and bottom of Unit 10. Join the flowers to opposite sides of Unit 10.

5. For outer flower petals and leaves, once again join mirror image units 7, 6, 4, 6, and 7 in a vertical row. Make two. Join these mirror image rows to opposite sides of the block, matching seams. Join mirror image Unit 8 to top and bottom of Unit 9. Make two. Join these combined units to outer ends of the block, matching seams to complete Block A. Make two.

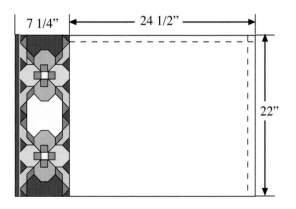

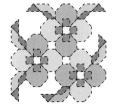

MATERIALS FOR PANEL SCREEN

☐ **Fabric I (ivory with blue print)**
Need 9"   3/8 yard

☐ **Fabric II (light blue print)**
Need 10"   1/2 yard

☐ **Fabric III (medium blue print)**
Need 10"   1/2 yard

☐ **Fabric IV (dark blue print)**
Need 4 1/2"   1/4 yard

☐ **Fabric V (navy textured print)**
Need 59 1/2"   1 7/8 yards

☐ **Fabric VI (light green print)**
Need 4 1/2"   1/4 yard

☐ **Fabric VII (medium green print)**
Need 1 1/2"   1/8 yard

☐ **Fabric VIII (dark green print)**
Need 6"   1/4 yard

☐ **Fabric IX (yellow print)**
Need 1 1/2"   1/8 yard

☐ **Fabric X (med. blue batiste)**
Need 147"   4 1/4 yards
Muslin   1 1/8 yards
Batting cut from 44" width 1 1/8 yards

CUTTING

☐ **FROM FABRIC I, CUT: (IVORY WITH BLUE PRINT)**
- **Two 4 1/2" wide strips. From these, cut:**
  * Twelve - 4 1/2" squares (A20)

☐ **FROM FABRIC II, CUT: (LT. BLUE PRINT)**
- **Two 3 1/2" wide strips. From these, cut:**
  * Twenty-four - 2 1/2" x 3 1/2" (A5)
- **Two 1 1/2" wide strips for Strip Set 2.**

☐ **FROM FABRIC III, CUT: (MED. BLUE PRINT)**
- **Two 3 1/2" wide strips. From these, cut:**
  * Twenty-four - 2 1/2" x 3 1/2" (A4)
- **Two 1 1/2" wide strips. From these, cut:**
  * Forty-eight - 1 1/2" squares (A3)

☐ **FROM FABRIC IV, CUT; (DK. BLUE PRINT)**
- **Three 1 1/2" wide strips. Two for Strip Set 1, and one for Strip Set 2.**

☐ **FROM FABRIC V, CUT; (NAVY PRINT)**
- **Two 16 1/2" wide strips. From these, cut:**
  * Six - 11" x 16 1/2" (backing for blocks)
  * Six - 2" x 15" (for casing)
- **Four 2 1/2" wide strips. From these, cut:**

  * Twelve - 2 1/2" x 7 1/2" (A17)
  * Six - 2 1/2" x 4 1/2" (A15)
  * Twelve - 2 1/2" squares (A6)
- **Eleven 1 1/2" wide strips. From these, cut:**
  * Six - 1 1/2" x 16 1/2" (A16)
  * Twelve - 1 1/2" x 5 1/2" (A11)
  * Twelve - 1 1/2" x 2 1/2" (A12)
  * 144 - 1 1/2" squares (A4a, A5a, A7a, A8a, A9a, A10a, A14b, A18a, A19a)

☐ **FROM FABRIC VI, CUT: (LT. GREEN PRINT)**
- **Three 1 1/2" wide strips. From these, cut:**
  * Thirty - 1 1/2" x 2 1/2" (A9, A13, A14)
  * Twelve - 1 1/2" squares (A10b, A19b)

☐ **FROM FABRIC VII, CUT: (MED. GREEN PRINT)**
- **One 1 1/2" wide strip. From this, cut:**
  * Six - 1 1/2" x 2 1/2" (A8)
  * Twelve - 1 1/2" squares (A7b, A18b)

☐ **FROM FABRIC VIII, CUT: (DARK GREEN PRINT)**
- **Four 1 1/2" wide strips. From these, cut:**
  * Twenty-four - 1 1/2" x 2 1/2" (A7, A10, A18, A19)
  * Forty-eight - 1 1/2" squares (A12a, A13a, A14a)

☐ **FROM FABRIC IX, CUT: (YELLOW PRINT)**
- **One 1 1/2" wide strip for Strip Set 1.. cut:**

☐ **FROM FABRIC X, CUT: (MED. BLUE BATISTE)**
- **Three - 40" x 49" (gathered panels between blocks)**

   CUT: Six 12 1/2" x 18 1/2" pieces of muslin and batting for quilting the blocks.

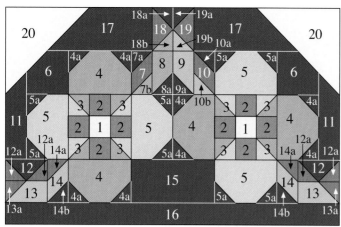

Block A. Make 6. When completed Block
should measure 10 1/2" x 16 1/2"

PANEL SCREEN BLOCK A ASSEMBLY

1. Use diagonal corner technique to make four each of
units 4 and 5. Make two each of mirror image units 13 and
14. Make two of Unit 12. Make one of units 7, 8, 9, 10, 18,
and 19. Make one of each strip set as shown on page 44.

2. To assemble the blocks, use twenty-four 1 1/2" segments
of Strip Set 2, and twelve of Strip Set One. Refer to page 44
for making the strip set diagonal corners.

3. Join the strip sets for the center of each flower as shown.
Join Unit 5 to opposite sides of left flower; then join Unit 4
to opposite sides of right flower. Join the two flowers together to complete the center row. For the top row, join Unit 6,
Unit 4, Unit 7, Unit 8, Unit 9, Unit 10, Unit 5, and Unit 6 in
a horizontal row. Join this row to the top of the center row,
matching all seams. Join Unit 11 to opposite sides of the two
combined rows.

4. For the bottom row, begin by joining Unit 12, and mirror
image Unit 13 as shown. Join mirror image Unit 14 to sides
of combined units 12-13. Refer to diagram for correct placement of the mirror image units. Join units 4, 15, and 5 in a
row; then add combined units 12-14 to opposite sides. Join
Unit 16 across the bottom of the row as shown. Join this row
to bottom of flowers, again matching seams.

5. Join units 17, 18, 19, and 17 in a horizontal row. Join this
row to top of block. Join diagonal corner, Unit 20 to opposite sides of the block as shown. Do not trim the center seam
of the diagonal corner as the darker color beneath it will show
through. Make 6.

QUILTING BLOCK A

1. For each block, cut a piece of batting and a piece of
muslin 12 1/2" x 18 1/2". Place the batting on top of the
muslin; then center the block top, right sides up on the batting. Pin all 3 layers together, pinning from the center to the
outer edges.

2. Quilt "in the ditch" around all patchwork and add other
decorative quilting if desired.

PREPARING THE BATISTE FOR SCREEN PANEL

1. On the 49" sides of the batiste, turn under 1/4"; then
another 1/4" and press. This forms your side hems. Top
stitch in place.

2. Run a gathering stitch along both 40" ends of the
batiste. Gather to 16". Place the bottom of the block (Unit
16), and the gathered end of the batiste right sides together. Using 1/4" seam, stitch the batiste to the block, beginning and ending 1/4" from edges.

3. Repeat Step 2 with the opposite gathered edge of the
batiste, making certain that all right sides are the same.
Press seams towards block. Make one for each panel.

PANEL SCREEN FINISHING

1. For casing, turn under 1/4" on all sides and press.
Center casing at the top of one long side of the backing and
approximately 1/2" below the top raw edge. Pin in place.

Block top

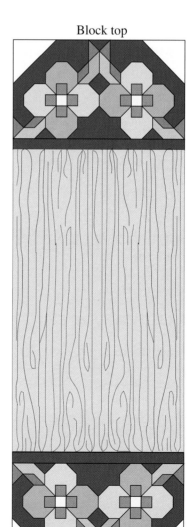

Top stitch two long
ends to form the cas-
ing.

On remaining long
raw edge of backing,
turn under 1/2" for
bottom of backing
and press.

2. Place the backing
and the block right
sides together, with
the casing at the top.
Using 1/4" seam,
stitch around three
sides of the block
through all thickness-
es, leaving the bot-
tom of the block
open. Clip corners
and turn right side
out. Press.

3. Pin backing, block
and gathered batiste
together, so that
pressed edge of back-
ing is over the stitched
line a bit. Top stitch in
place through all
thicknesses.

Block top

GATHERED BATISTE PILLOW

Pillow finishes to 20" square.

MATERIALS

Fabric I (navy print)   1/2 yard
Fabric II (med. blue print)   5/8 yard
Fabric III (med. blue batiste)   3/4 yard
Fabric IV (light blue batiste)   1/8 yard

CUTTING

Fabric I (navy print)
Cut one 14 1/2" square
Fabric II (med. blue print)
Cut one 20 1/2" wide strip. From this, cut:
     * Two - 13 1/2" x 20 1/2" (backing)
     * Two - 3 1/2" x 20 1/2" (Unit 2 borders)
     * Two - 3 1/2" x 14 1/2" (Unit 3 borders)
Fabric III (med. blue batiste)
Cut one 22" x 30"
Fabric IV (light blue batiste)
Cut one 2 1/2" x 24" for bow.

PILLOW ASSEMBLY

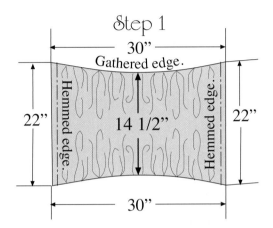

1. On the 30" side of the batiste, find the center and draw a gentle curve from the center to the outer edge. There should be 14 1/2" at the center point as shown. Cut the curves. Turn under 1/4"; then another 1/4" on the 22" sides of the batiste. Top stitch in place for the hemmed sides. Run a gathering stitch along the curved 30" sides. Gather to 14" wide. This curved side will allow enough give so that you can pull the batiste towards the center and tie with a bow.

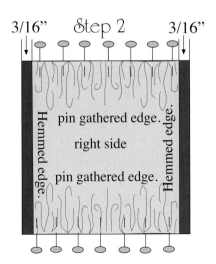

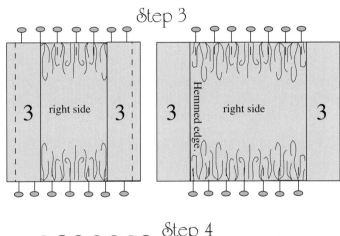

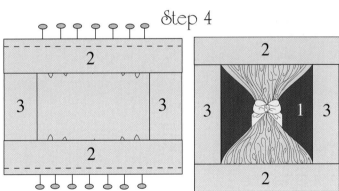

2. Using 1/4" seams, join Unit 3 to opposite sides of the navy square, being careful not to catch batiste in stitching. Open Unit 3 out, and press seams towards Unit 3.
3. Join Unit 2 to top and bottom of pillow top, catching gathered batiste into seams at top and bottom. Open out and press seams towards Unit 2.

Pin gathered edges to top and bottom of 14 1/2" square of navy, 1/4" from side edges as shown. Place batiste right side up on top of the navy square which is also right side up. Baste gathered ends 3/16" from each raw edge.

MAKING THE BOW

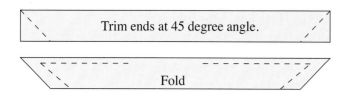

Fold the 2 1/2" x 24" piece of Fabric IV, in half length-wise, right sides together. Trim ends on a 45° angle as shown. Stitch around raw edges, leaving a 3"opening to turn. Trim corners. Turn right side out and press. Pull gathered batiste together in the center of the pillow top, and tie with the bow.

BACKING THE PILLOW

Turn under 1/4"; then another 1/4" on one 13 1/2" side of each backing piece, forming a hem. Refer to page 24 for backing a pillow. Stuff with 20" pillow form.

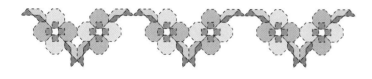

RUFFLED CENTER PILLOW

Pillow finishes to 18" square.

MATERIALS
Fabric I (navy print)	**3/4 yard**
Fabric II (med. blue batiste)	**1/2 yard**

CUTTING
Fabric I (navy print)
Cut one 13" wide strip. From this, cut:
 * Two - 13" x 18 1/2" (backing)
Cut two 4 1/2" wide strips. From these, cut:
 * Two - 4 1/2" x 18 1/2" (2)
 * Two - 4 1/2" x 10 1/2" (1)
Fabric II (med. blue batiste)
Cut two 5 1/2" wide strips. From these, cut:
 * Two - 5 1/2" x 40" (ruffle)
Muslin And Batting:
Cut one 20 1/2" square of each.

MAKING THE RUFFLE

Join the two 5 1/2" x 40" strips of Fabric II together on the short ends, forming a circle. Fold in half lengthwise wrong sides together. Run a basting stitch approximately 3/16" around raw edge and gather. Pin right sides together to 10 1/2" center square as shown. Adjust gathers to fit where necessary. Tuck the corners in and pin in place. Using 1/4" seam, stitch around the 10 1/2" square, securing the ruffle.

COMPLETING THE PILLOW TOP

1. Using 1/4" seams, join Uniit 1 to top and bottom of the 10 1/2" square, securing the ruffle at top and bottom.
Open out and press. Join Unit 2 to opposite sides of the pillow, again catching the ruffle in the seam. Open out and press.
2. Place the 20 1/2" square of batting on top of the 20 1/2" square of muslin; then center the pillow top on the batting. Mary quilted a swirl design with leaves in the center, and a matching leaf and vine design on the outer edges. Trim batting and backing to match the top.
3. Turn under 1/4"; then another 1/4" on one 13" side of the backing, forming a hem. Refer to page 24 for backing a pillow. Stuff with 18" pillow form.

MAKING THE WINDOW TREATMENT

1. Measure the width and length of your window. To establish the amount of batiste needed, you will first need to decide how long you want your swag on the sides. Add this measurement for both side lengths to the width. We decided to make the length of the sides come well below the window. Use the entire width of the fabric (for instance, 40" x 230").

2. Turn under 1/4"; then another 1/4" on all four sides. Top stitch this hem in place.

3. Find the center of your swag, which should be placed behind the center sconce. Drape as desired, forming a swag between the sconces.

4. We had a bay window, and purchased a curtain rod for a bay window. Measure your window and purchase a rod for the correct size.

5. For the batiste, measure the width and the desired length for your curtain. Add 1" to each width for side hem, and 4" to the length for hem and casing.

6. For sides, turn under 1/2"; then another 1/2" and top stitch in place for the hem. Repeat for hem on the bottom edge. For the top edge casing, turn under 1/4"; then 2" and pin in place. Top stitch along hemmed edge, forming a casing. Place the curtain on the rod.

7. Measure the length of your window and double it. This will establish the length of your ribbons for the bow. Refer to page 51 for making a bow from the light blue batiste.

Find the center of the ribbon and pin it at the top of the rod letting one ribbon fall in front, and one in back of the curtain. The bow may be tied in front of the curtain, or at the bottom if you desire. We suggest pinning the ribbons in place on the back so that they do not slip.

Forget Me Not Tablecloth

Forget Me Not Tablecloth

Tablecloth Finishes To: 72 1/2" square.
Techniques used are the same as for the quilt.

MATERIALS FOR TABLECLOTH

☐ **Fabric I (ivory with blue print)**
Need 73 1/2"   2 1/4 yards

☐ **Fabric II (light blue print)**
Need 38 1/2"   1 1/4 yards

☐ **Fabric III (medium blue print)**
Need 37 1/2"   1 1/8 yards

☐ **Fabric IV (dark blue print)**
Need 13 1/2"   1/2 yard

☐ **Fabric V (navy textured print)**
Need 125 3/8"   3 3/4 yards

☐ **Fabric VI (light green print)**
Need 18"   5/8 yard

☐ **Fabric VII (medium green print)**
Need 9 1/4"   3/8 yard

☐ **Fabric VIII (dark green print)**
Need 21"   3/4 yard

☐ **Fabric IX (yellow print)**
Need 3"   1/8 yard
Backing   **2 1/2 yards**

CUTTING

☐ **FROM FABRIC I, CUT; (IVORY WITH BLUE PRINT)**
- **Three 11 1/2" wide strips. From these cut:**
  * Eight - 11 1/2" squares (B37)
  Stack these cuts:
  * Four - 2 1/2" x 3 1/2" (A52)
  * Four - 2 1/2" squares (A8)
  * Four - 1 1/2" x 5 1/2" (A54)
  * Twelve - 1 1/2" x 2 1/2" (A49, A51a, A56)
  * Sixty-six - 1 1/2" squares (A4a, A6a, A7a, A9a, A18b, A21b, A35b, A40a, A42, A50b, A53b, A55a)
- **One 9 1/2" wide strip. From this, cut:**
  * Four - 9 1/2" squares (Q7)
- **Three 4 1/2" wide strips. From these, cut:**
  * Twenty-four - 4 1/2" squares (C19)
- **Eight 2" wide strips. From these, cut:**
  * Four - 2" x 27 1/2" (Q6) Piece two together to = two 54 1/2" lengths.
  * Four - 2" x 26" (Q5) Piece two together to = two 51 1/2" lengths.
  * Six - 1 1/2" squares (add to 1 1/2" sq. above)

☐ **FROM FABRIC II, CUT: (LT. BLUE PRINT)**
- **Six 3 1/2" wide strips. From these, cut:**
  * Eighty-four - 2 1/2" x 3 1/2" (A4, A33, A50, B7, B11, B33, C5)
  * Eight - 1 1/2" x 3 1/2" (A5, A21)
  * Seven - 2 1/2" squares (B23)
- **One 2 1/2" wide strip. From this, cut:**
  * One - 2 1/2" square (add to B23 above)
  * Twenty - 1 1/2" x 2 1/2" (A19, A23, A28, A41)
- **Ten 1 1/2" wide strips. Eight for Strip Set 2. From remainder, cut:**
  * 40 - 1 1/2" squares (A12b, A39a, A46a, A47, A49a, B17b, B19)

☐ **FROM FABRIC III, CUT; (MED. BLUE PRINT)**
- **Six 3 1/2" wide strips. From these, cut:**
  * Ninety-two - 2 1/2" x 3 1/2" (A7, A12, A15, A39, A40, B5, B17, B31, C4)
- **Eleven 1 1/2" wide strips. From these, cut:**
  * Eight - 1 1/2" x 3 1/2" (B30)
  * Sixteen - 1 1/2" x 2 1/2" (A46, A51, B13)
  * 224 - 1 1/2" squares (A3, A19a, A21a, A38, A41a, A43, A45, A50a, B9, B11a, B28, C3)

☐ **FROM FABRIC IV, CUT: (DK. BLUE PRINT)**
- **Nine 1 1/2" wide strips. Eight for strip sets 1 and 2. From remainder, cut:**
  * Eight - 1 1/2" squares (A20, A44)

☐ **FROM FABRIC V, CUT: (NAVY PRINT)**
- **One 10 7/8" wide strip. From this, cut:**
  * Two - 10 7/8" squares (Q1) Cut in half diagonally.
  Stack these cuts:
  * Eight - 3 1/2" squares (B21)
  * Four - 1 1/2" x 4 1/2" (A14)
  * Four - 1 1/2" x 2 1/2" (A16)
- **Three 8 1/2" wide strips. From these, cut:**
  * Eight - 4 1/2" x 8 1/2" (B32)
  * Twenty-four - 2 1/2" x 8 1/2" (C16)
  Stack this cut:
  * Seventy-five - 1 1/2" squares (A11, A12a, A15a, A22, A27, A28a, A33a, B1a, B3a, B4a, B5a, B7a, B14a, B16, B17a, B18, B24a, B25a, B26a, B31a, B33a, B36b, C4a, C5a, C6b, C7a, C10b, C11a, C12a, C13b, C17a)
- **One 4 1/2" wide strip. From this, cut:**
  * Eight - 4 1/2" squares (B6)
- **Three 3 1/2" wide strips. From these, cut:**
  * Thirty-two - 1 1/2" x 3 1/2" (A13, A17, A30, A31, A32, A34, B35a)
  Stack this cut:
  * Forty - 1 1/2" squares (add to 1 1/2" sq. above)
- **Four 3 3/8" wide strips. From these, cut:**
  * Four - 3 3/8" x 15" (Q4)
  * Four - 3 3/8" x 12 1/8" (Q3)
  Stack this cut:
  * Sixty-four - 1 1/2" sq. (add to 1 1/2" sq. above)
- **Seventeen 2 1/2" wide strips. Eight for straight-grain binding. From remainder, cut:**

* Twenty-four - 2 1/2" x 6 1/2" (C18)
* Twenty - 2 1/2" x 4 1/2" (B2, C8)
* Eight - 2 1/2" x 3 1/2" (B34)
* Thirty-two - 2 1/2" squares (B12, C9)
- **Twelve 1 1/2" wide strips. From these, cut:**
    * 313- 1 1/2" squares (add to 1 1/2" sq. above)

FROM FABRIC VI, CUT: (LT. GREEN PRINT)
- **Twelve 1 1/2" wide strips. From these, cut:**
    * Twenty - 1 1/2" x 3 1/2" (A18, A35, A55, B36)
    * Sixty-eight - 1 1/2" x 2 1/2" (A6, A53, B3, B14, B26, C7, C12)
    * 156 - 1 1/2" squares (A17b, A26, A29, A34b, A48, A49b, A54b, B1b, B4b, B15, B20a, B22a, B25b, B35b, C6a, C13a, C15a, C17b)

FROM FABRIC VII, CUT: (MED. GREEN PRINT)
- **One 9 1/4" wide strip. From this, cut:**
    * Two - 9 1/4" squares (Q2) Cut in half diagonally. Stack these cuts:
    * Sixteen - 1 1/2" x 2 1/2" (A9, C11)
    * Thirty-two - 1 1/2" sq. (A10, A13b, C10a, C14a)

FROM FABRIC VIII, CUT: (DK. GREEN PRINT)
- **Fourteen 1 1/2" wide strips. From these, cut:**
    * Eight - 1 1/2" x 4 1/2" (B20)
    * Eight - 1 1/2" x 3 1/2" (B22)
    * 168 - 1 1/2" x 2 1/2" (A13a, A17a, A18a, A34a, A35a, A53a, A54a, A55b, B1, B4, B25, B35, B36a, C6, C10, C13, C14, C15, C17)
    * Forty-eight - 1 1/2" sq. (A6b, A9b, A11, A27, A29, A31a, A48, A51b, B14b, B16)

FROM FABRIC IX, CUT: (YELLOW PRINT)
- **Two 1 1/2" wide strips for Strip Set 1.**

BLOCK ASSEMBLY

1. Blocks A, B, and C are made the same as for the quilt. There are small differences which we will be specific about below. Follow the diagrams, instructions and graphic "how to" drawings for these blocks on pages 44-48. You will make 4 of Block A, eight of Block B, and 12 of Block C.

2. Refer to the diagram below for Block B. The block diagram shows that the top right corner is to be cut, after the block is assembled. It also shows that Unit 23 will not be used in the B block for the tablecloth. Note the dot/dash line. This is designated as a seam line. The dashed line is a cut line, and all top right corners for Block B are to be cut off as shown, 3" from the corner.

3. Assembly of Block C is the same as for the quilt, except that Unit C17 for the tablecloth has diagonal corners. Unit C17 for the quilt is a diagonal end.

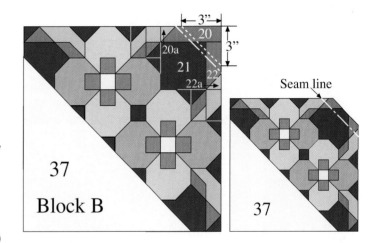

STRIP SETS FOR TABLECLOTH

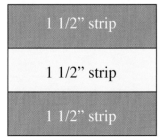

Strip Set 1. Make 2. Cut into Fifty-two - 1 1/2" segments for units A1/A2, A24/A25, A36/A37, B8/B10, B27/B29, C1/C2.

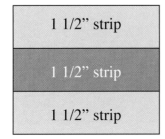

Strip Set 2. Make 4. Cut into ninety-six 1 1/2" segments for units A2/A3, A37/A38, B9/B10, B28/B29, C2/C3.

CORNER ASSEMBLY

1. For the corner of the center section, line Unit 3 up with bottom of triangle, Unit 2 as shown. Place the units right sides together, and using 1/4" seams, stitch Unit 3 to the triangle. Press seams towards Unit 3. Place Unit 4 across the bottom of joined units 2-3, right sides together. Stitch Unit 4 to triangle. Press open.

2. Line your ruler up along the long edge of the triangle and trim units 3 and 4 even with triangle as shown. Triangle includes seam allowance. Make 4.

TABLECLOTH ASSEMBLY

1. Refer to the diagram below, and begin by joining the four A blocks as shown. Join the B blocks in pairs with the Fabric I triangles matching. Join the triangular corners to the long edge of the Block B pairs as shown. Refer to the tablecloth diagram, and join two of the Block B and triangle corner pairs to opposite sides of combined Block A's, forming a long row.

2. Join Unit 1 triangles to opposite short sides of the remaining Block B pairs as shown, forming a large triangle. Join these triangles to opposite long sides of the center section, now forming a square.

3. Join previously pieced Unit 5 to opposite sides of the center section; then add Unit 6 to top and bottom. Join three of Block C's together, matching seams, forming a row. Make 4 rows. Join one to the top and one to the bottom of the tablecloth as shown. Join Unit 7 to opposite ends of the remaining joined C blocks. Join these rows to opposite sides of the tablecloth.

4. Quilt as desired. Make 320" of straight-grain binding from Fabric V, and bind your tablecloth.

60

This quilt, full of lace, buttons and bows will delight your favorite young one. It was fun to make, and a beginner who has learned our "Quick Piecing" techniques can achieve success with this design. One block makes chain piecing perfect for the project. We have included a diagram if you choose to make it into a queen size just by adding three more rows, and extending the border strips.

Quilt finishes to: 69 1/2" x 93".
Queen Size: 81" x 101
Technique Used: Diagonal corners.

MATERIALS

Fabric I (pink toile print)
Need 25"   7/8 yard

Fabric II (muslin)
Need 94 1/4"   2 3/4 yards

Fabric III (light peach print)
Need 17"   5/8 yard

Fabric IV (dark peach print)
Need 63 1/2"   1 7/8 yards

Fabric V (mint print)
Need 26 5/8"   7/8 yard

Fabric VI (medium teal print)
Need 45"   1 1/2 yards

Fabric VII (dark teal print)
Need 49 3/8"   1 1/2 yards

Quilt backing   5 1/4 yards
2 1/2" wide flat ivory lace
Need 396"   11 yards
7/8" wide ivory grosgrain ribbon
Need 354"   10 yards
Thirty-three - 3/4" flat peach buttons

CUTTING

FROM FABRIC I, CUT: (PEACH TOILE)
- **Two 12 1/2" wide strips. From these, cut:**
  - * Six - 12 1/2" squares (Q1).

FROM FABRIC II, CUT: (MUSLIN)
- **Three 5" wide strips. From these, cut:**
  - * Forty-four - 1 7/8" x 5" (A13)
  - Stack this cut:
  - * Thirty-four - 2 1/8" squares (A12a)
- **Eight 3 1/2" wide strips. From these, cut:**
  - * Twenty-two - 3 1/2" squares (A1)
  - * 110 - 2" x 3 1/2" (A2, A4, A6, A15)
  - * Twenty-eight - 1 3/8" x 1 1/2" (A10)
- **Three 2 7/8" wide strips. From these, cut:**
  - * Forty-four - 2 5/8" x 2 7/8" (A9)
- **Four 2 1/8" wide strips. From these, cut:**
  - * Ten - 2 1/8" squares (add to A12a)
  - * Nine - 2" squares (A3a, A5a, A8a, A16a)
- **Fifteen 2" wide strips. From these, cut:**
  - * Twenty-two - 2" x 9 1/2" (A7)
  - * Forty-four - 2" x 3" (A14)
  - * 123 - 2" squares (Add to 2" sq. above)
- **Three 1 3/8" wide strips. From these, and scrap, cut:**
  - * Sixteen - 1 3/8" x 1 1/2" (add to A10)
  - * Forty-four - 1 3/8" squares (A12b)

FROM FABRIC III, CUT: (LT. PEACH PRINT)
- **Two 3 1/2" wide strips. From these, cut:**
  - * Twenty-two - 3 1/2" squares (A3)
- **Five 2" wide strips. From these, cut:**
  - * Eighty-eight - 2" squares (A1a, A4a)

FROM FABRIC IV, CUT: (DK. PEACH PRINT)
- **Two 3 1/2 wide strips. From these, cut:**
  - * Twenty-two - 3 1/2" squares (A5)
- **Eight 3" wide strips. From these, cut:**
  - * Two - 3" x 40" (Q5)
  - * Two - 3" x 35" (Q6) Piece two together to = one 69 1/2" length.
  - * Four - 3" x 25 3/4" (Q5) Piece to opposite sides of 40" wide strips to = two 90 1/2" lengths.
- **Nine 2 1/2" wide strips for straight-grain binding.**
- **Five 2" wide strips. From these, cut:**
  - * Eighty-eight - 2" squares (A1b, A6a)

FROM FABRIC V, CUT: (MINT PRINT)
- **Four 3 1/2" wide strips. From these, cut:**
  - * Forty-four - 3 1/2" squares (A16)
- **Three 2 7/8" wide strips. From these, cut:**
  - * Forty-four - 2" x 2 7/8" (A8)
  - * Sixteen - 2" squares (A3a, A5a)
- **Two 2" wide strips. From these, cut:**
  - * Twenty-eight - 2" squares (add to A3a, A5a)

FROM FABRIC VI, CUT: (MED. TEAL PRINT)
- **Ten 4 1/2" wide strips. From these, cut:**
  - * Twelve - 4 1/2" x 20 1/2" (Q3)
  - * Twelve - 4 1/2" x 12 1/2" (Q2)

FROM FABRIC VII, CUT: (DARK TEAL PRINT)
- **Four 6 1/2" wide strips. From these, cut:**
  - * Twenty - 6 1/2" squares (Q4)
  - * Twelve - 2 1/4" x 5" (A12)
- **Four 2 1/4" wide strips. From these, cut:**
  - * Thirty-two - 2 1/4" x 5" (add to A12)
- **Three 2" wide strips. From these, cut:**
  - * Forty-four - 2" squares (A14a)
  - * Seventeen - 1 7/8" squares (A9a)
- **Three 1 7/8" wide strips. From these, cut:**
  - * Twenty-seven - 1 7/8" sq. (add to A9a)
  - * Forty-four - 1 3/8" x 1 7/8" (A11)
- **Two 1 3/8" wide strips. From these and scrap, cut:**
  - * Forty-four - 1 3/8" squares (A8b)

From 7/8" wide grosgrain ribbon, cut:
- Twenty - 10" long pieces to top stitch onto Q4.
- Eleven - 14" long pieces for bows.

From 3" wide flat lace, cut:
- Twelve -20 1/2" lengths (Q3)
- Twelve -12 1/2" lengths (Q2)

BLOCK A ASSEMBLY

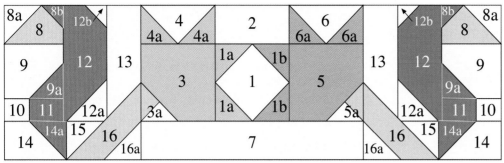

Block A. Make 22. When completed, block should measure 6 1/2" x 20 1/2".

These instructions are for one block. Use these instructions to make all 22 blocks.

1. Use diagonal corner technique to make two each of mirror image units 8, 9, 12, and 14. Make one each of units 1, 4, and 6. Refer to diagram directly below showing how to use triangle-squares as diagonal corners. Follow instructions and diagrams for units A3 and A5.

2. Refer frequently to block diagram at left for correct placement of all units.

3. To assemble the block, begin by joining units 1 and 2. Join units 3 and 4. Join units 5 and 6 as shown. Join the 3-4 combined units to the left side of combined units 1-2; then join combined units 5-6 to the right side. Join Unit 7 to the bottom of the combined units.

4. For the sides, refer to the block diagram, and diagram below for correct placement of mirror image units Join units 8 and 9. Join units 10 and 11. Join these two combined unit sections together as shown. Join units 12 and 13; then add them to the side of combined 8-11 units. Join units 14 and 15; then add these combined units to the bottom of the leaf units. Refer to the diagram below for joining diagonal corners 16 and 16a.

5. Refer to block diagram, and join the leaf sections just completed to opposite sides of the flowers, matching stem seams. Make 22.

6. For the lace block at top left of the following page, after lace is topstitched, join Unit Q2 to top and bottom of Unit Q1; then add Unit Q3 to opposite sides. Make 6.

Making units A3 and A5

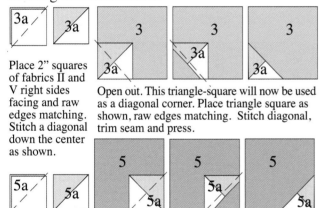

Place 2" squares of fabrics II and V right sides facing and raw edges matching. Stitch a diagonal down the center as shown.

Open out. This triangle-square will now be used as a diagonal corner. Place triangle square as shown, raw edges matching. Stitch diagonal, trim seam and press.

Joining mirror image diagonal corner 16 and 16a.

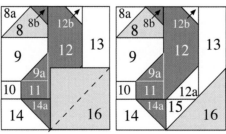 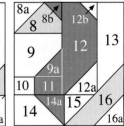

Join diagonal corner, Unit 16 as shown. Trim seam and press.

Join diagonal corner, Unit 16a as shown. Trim seam and press.

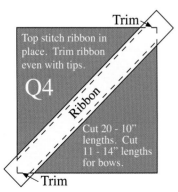

Top stitch ribbon in place. Trim ribbon even with tips.

Q4

Ribbon

Cut 20 - 10" lengths. Cut 11 - 14" lengths for bows.

Follow instructions and make 20 of Unit Q4.

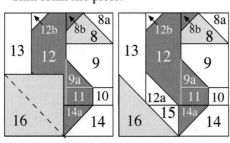

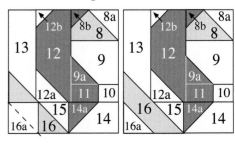

Cut twelve 20 1/2" lengths of lace for Unit Q3. Cut twelve 12 1/2" lengths of lace for Unit Q2. Top stitch lace in place along edge.

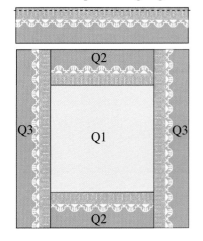

QUILT ASSEMBLY

1. To piece the quilt top, beginning at the top, join Row 1, Row 2, Row 1, Row 2, Row 1, and Row 3.

2. For the borders, join previously pieced Border Q5 to opposite sides of the quilt top. Join previously pieced border, Q6 to bottom of quilt as shown.

3. Tie eleven bows from 14" lengths of grosgrain ribbon. Cut the ends of the ribbon on a 45° angle. With grosgrain ribbon, this helps to keep it from raveling.

4. Place the bows as shown on the diagram at right, and place a peach button in the center of the bow. Sew the button on, through the bow, securing them both. Sew the buttons on each Block A.

QUILTING AND FINISHING

1. Mary quilted a beautiful wreath in the center of the lace block, and stippled behind the flowers on Block A. She quilted leaves inside the leaves, and used a half wreath on the Q4 units.

2. Make 350" of straight-grain binding from Fabric IV, and bind your quilt.

JOINING THE ROWS FOR QUILT ASSEMBLY

1. The quilt is assembled in rows. To piece Row 1, refer to the top row of the diagram below and begin piecing from left to right. Join Block A, lace block, two of Block A (refer to diagram), lace block and Block A. Make three of these rows.

2. For Row 2, refer to diagram below and join two Block A's, matching seams. Make two pairs. Join two of Unit Q4, checking diagram for correct placement of the diagonal ribbon. Make four pair. Refer to center of the row and join two of the pairs together, again checking correct position of the ribbon. Be sure to match the ribbon seams when joining the Q4 units. Make two of these rows.

3. For the bottom row, join one Q4 unit, BLock A, a pair of Q4 units, Block A, and one Q4 unit. Again check diagram for correct placement of the Q4 units.

ENVELOPE PILLOW

Pillow finishes to: 18" square.

MATERIALS

Medium teal   **5/8 yard**
One - 18 1/2" x 19"
Dark Teal   **5/8 yard**
Two - 10 1/2" x 18 1/2"
One - 18 1/2" square
7/8 yard of 2 1/2 " wide flat ivory lace.

1. Fold one 10 1/2" x 18 1/2" piece of dark. teal as illustrated. Cut from 1 1/4" to point as shown. Fold and cut two of these.

2. Turn under 1/4" on short end of lace and press. Baste lace to one triangular piece, right sides together and raw edges matching, gathering at point as shown.

3. Join the two triangular pieces right sides together, leaving the entire long end open. Lace will be sandwiched between the two triangular pieces. Trim corners, turn right side out and gently pull lace out at point and press. Refer to diagram at right and follow diagram and instructions.

4. On the 19" side of medium teal piece, turn under 1/4"; then another 1/4" and top stitch in place for hem. The hem will be under the flap when completed. Place this and the flap piece (with flap still remaining facing down), right sides facing and raw edges matching. Stitch the three remaining raw edges, being careful not

to catch lace in stitching. Pin out of the way if necessary. This will form the envelope.

5. Turn right side out. Press flap seam toward the envelope, and side seams inside. We used a snap and sewed a decorative button on the outside of the flap. Insert pillow form and close.

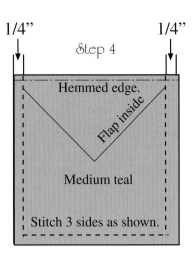

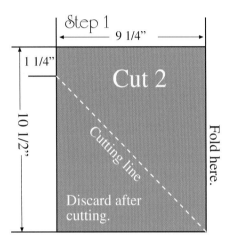

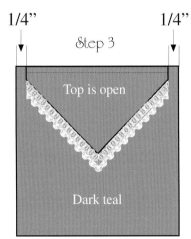

Join raw edges, right sides together leaving 1/4" for seam allowance on sides. Serge if desired.

MAKING THE QUILT QUEEN SIZE

The diagram below shows the addition of one row on all sides of the quilt to enlarge it to 81" x 101". Referring to page 65, you will make one of Row 3, and add it to the top of the quilt. The diagram shows the side rows which combine Unit 4 and Block A. The additions will require 8 of Block A, and 16 of Unit Q4.

Refer to page 11 for "Making One Block." This will show you how to multiply correctly to make one or more blocks.

Staffordshire Dog and Cat Beds

Pamper your pet with these adorable dog and cat beds designed by Mindy Kettner. We made canvas beds first, which can be stuffed with the filling of your choice. The beds have an overlap back, allowing for easy removal of the quilted cover for washing. For larger dogs, just add more borders! I can assure you that any breed will snuggle up and make the bed their own. In our case it had to be a baby bulldog! Believe it or not, my fellow animal lovers and quilters, I actually put an ad in the paper to find a litter of baby bulls!

Dog Bed finishes to: 26 1/2" x 32 1/2".

Cat Bed finishes to: 23" x 29"

Technique Used For Both Beds: Diagonal corners. diagonal ends, triangle-squares and triangle-squares used as diagonal corners.

MATERIALS FOR DOG BED

Fabric I (light blue print)
Need 12"   1/2 yard

Fabric II (white on white print)
Need 8 1/2"   3/8 yard

Fabric III (dark rust print)
Need 6 3/4"   1/4 yard

Fabric IV (medium brown print)
Need 6" square   Scrap

Fabric V (medium olive print)
Need 38 1/2"   1 1/4 yards

Fabric VI (dark gold print)
Need 1 3/4"   1/8 yard

Fabric VII (gold metallic print)
Need 2 1/2"   1/8 yard

Fabric VIII (solid black)
Need 6" square   Scrap

Fabric IX (red print)
Need 3" square   Scrap

Fabric X (dark olive print)
Need 10"   3/8 yard

Batting & Muslin   32" x 35" pieces for quilting.

CUTTING FOR DOG BED

FROM FABRIC I, CUT: (LT. BLUE PRINT)
- **One 6 1/2" wide strip. From this, cut:**
  - * Two - 4 1/4" x 6 1/2" (A8, B8)
  - * Two - 1 1/4" x 6 1/2" (A9, B9)
  - * Two - 2" x 5" (A18, B18)
  - * Two - 2" x 4 1/4" (A28, B28)
  - Stack this cut:
  - * Four - 1 1/4" x 2" (A31, B31)
- **One 3 1/2" wide strip. From this, cut:**
  - * Two - 3 1/2" squares (A19b, B19b)
  - * Two - 1 1/4" x 3 1/2" (A27, B27)
  - * Four - 1 1/4" squares (A30a, B30a)
- **One 2" wide strip. From this, cut:**
  - * One 2" x 18 1/2" (Q1)
  - * Eight - 2" squares (A7a, A10d, A29a, B7a, B10d, B29a)

FROM FABRIC II, CUT: (WHITE ON WHITE PRINT)
- **One 4 1/4" wide strip. From this, cut:**
  - * Two - 4 1/4" squares (A29, B29)
  - * Two - 3 1/2" x 4 1/4" (A26, B26)
  - * Two - 2" x 4 1/4" (A20, B20)
  - * Two - 4" x 5" (A17, B17)
  - * Two - 2" x 3 1/2" (A10a, B10a)
  - * Four - 1" x 2 1/2" (A12, A14, B12, B14)
  - * Four - 1 1/4" x 2" (A2, A27a, B2, B27a)
- **One 2 3/4" wide strip. From this, cut:**
  - * Two - 2 3/4" x 5" (A5, B5)
  - * Four - 1 1/4" x 2 3/4" (A24, A25, B24, B25)
  - * Four - 2 1/2" squares (A13, A19a, B13, B19a)
  - * Two - 2" squares (A10c, B10c)
- **One 1 1/2" wide strip. From this, cut:**
  - * Ten - 1 1/2" squares (A11a, A11b, A16, B11a, B11b, B16)
  - * Twenty - 1 1/4" squares (A1c, A4, A22, A23a, A24c, B1c, B4, B22, B23a, B24c)

FROM FABRIC III, CUT; (DK. RUST PRINT)
- **One 3 1/2" wide strip. From this, cut:**
  - * Two - 3 1/2" x 5" (A19, B19)
  - * Two - 2" x 3 1/2" (A23, B23)
  - * Four - 2" x 6 1/2" (A7, B7)
- **One 2" wide strip. From this, cut:**
  - * Two - 2" x 5" (A10, B10)
  - * Four - 2" squares (A5a, B5a)
  - * Two - 1 1/4" x 2" (A24b, B24b)
- **One 1 1/4" wide strip. From this, cut:**
  - * Sixteen - 1 1/4" squares (A9a, A10b, A13a, A18a, A18b, A20a, A21, A24a, B9a, B10b, B13a, B18a, B18b, B20a, B21, B24a)

FROM FABRIC IV, CUT: (MED. BROWN PRINT)
- **Four - 2 3/4" squares (A1, B1)**

FROM FABRIC V, CUT: (MED. OLIVE PRINT)
- **One 26 1/2" wide strip. From this cut:**
  - * Two - 20" x 26 1/2" (backing)
- **Four 2 1/2" wide strips. From these, cut:**
  - * Two - 2 1/2" x 28 1/2" (Q4)
  - * Two - 2 1/2" x 26 1/2" (Q5)
- **One 2" wide strip. From this, cut:**
  - * Two - 2" x 10 1/4" (A30, B30)
  - * Two - 1 1/4" x 5" (A6, B6)

FROM FABRIC VI, CUT: (DK. GOLD PRINT)
- **One 1 3/4" wide strip. From these, cut:**
  - * Two - 1 3/4" squares (A13b, B13b)
  - * Two - 1 1/2" squares (A11b, B11b)
  - * Two - 1 1/4" squares (A18b, B18b)
  - * Two - 1" x 3" (A15, B15)
  - * Two - 1" squares (A14a, B14a)

FROM FABRIC VII, CUT: (GOLD METALLIC PRINT)
- **One 2 1/2" wide strip. From this, cut:**
  - * Two - 2 1/2" squares (A11, B11)
  - * Two - 1 1/4" x 11 3/4" (A32, B32)

FROM FABRIC VIII, CUT: (SOLID BLACK)
- **Eight - 1 1/4" squares (A1a, A3, B1a, B3)**

FROM FABRIC IX, CUT: (RED PRINT)
- **Four - 1 1/4" squares (A1b, B1b)**

FROM FABRIC X, CUT: (DK. OLIVE PRINT)
- **Four 2 1/2" wide strips. From these, cut:**
  - * Two - 2 1/2" x 24 1/2" (Q2)
  - * Two - 2 1/2" x 22 1/2" (Q3)

DOG BED ASSEMBLY, BLOCKS A AND B

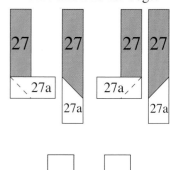

Making mirror image units
A27 and B27 for dogs.

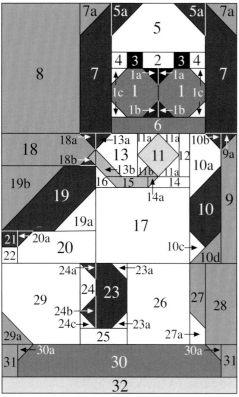

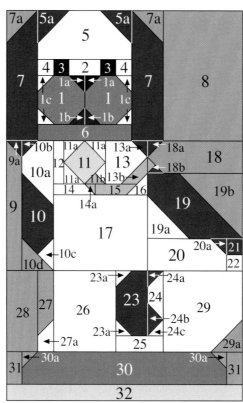

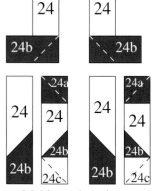

Block A. Make 1. When completed, block should measure 11 3/4" x 18 1/2".

Block B. Make 1. When completed, block should measure 11 3/4" x 18 1/2".

Making mirror image units A24 and B24 for dogs.

The blocks above are the same, except that they are mirror images. Refer to them frequently for correct placement of mirror image units. These instructions are for one block.

1. Use diagonal corner technique to make two each of mirror image units 1 and 7. Make one each of units 5, 9, 11, 13, 14, 18, 19, 20, 23, 29, and 30. Use diagonal end technique to make one of units 10, 24, and 27. Use triangle-square technique for units 11 and 18. Refer to diagrams of these, on this page, and on the following page.

2. To assemble the blocks, refer to the block diagram, and join the two mirror image Unit 1's as shown. Join units 4, 3, 2, 3, and 4 in a horizontal row; then add Unit 5 to the top of the row. Join these combined units to the top of com-

bined Unit 1's. Join Unit 6 to the bottom; then add mirror image Unit 7 to opposite sides of the head. Refer to block diagram for correct placement, and join Unit 8 to the side of Unit 7 as shown.

3. Join units 18 and 19. Join units 21 and 22; then add these combined units to the side of Unit 20 as shown, matching seams. Join combined units 20-22 to bottom of combined units 18-19.

4. For the collar and tag, refer to the diagram below for making Unit 11. Make this unit by using one triangle-square as a diagonal corner as shown. Join units 13, 11, and 12. Join units 14 and 15; then add these combined units to the bottom of the combined 13-11-12 units. Join diagonal corner, Unit 16 as shown in block diagram; then

Making mirror image units A11 and B11 for dog, and units A10 and B10 for cat.

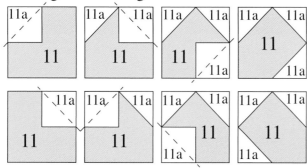

Place 1 1/4" squares of dark gold print and white on white print right sides facing and raw edges matching. Stitch diagonal, trim seam and press.

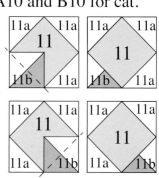

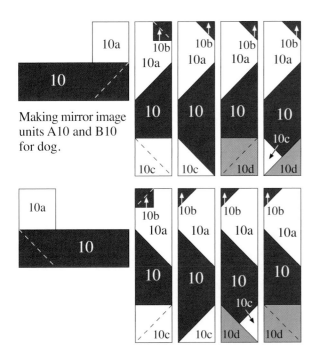

Making mirror image
units A10 and B10
for dog.

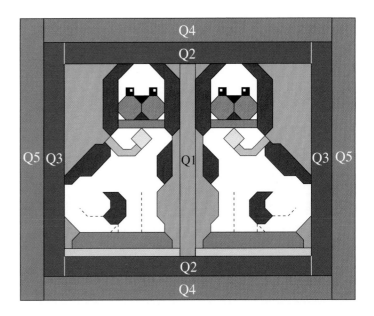

COMPLETING THE DOG BED

Making mirror image Unit 18 for dogs,
and Unit 24 for cats.

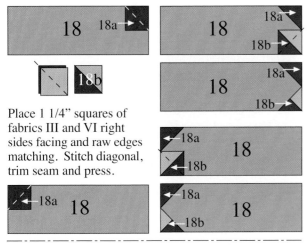

Place 1 1/4" squares of
fabrics III and VI right
sides facing and raw edges
matching. Stitch diagonal,
trim seam and press.

For cat, use 1 3/4" squares of fabrics II and IV.

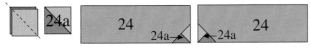

add Unit 17 to the bottom of the combined units. Join combined units 18-22 to side of combined units 11-17. Join units 9 and 10, matching seams, then join these combined units to side of dog center section as shown.

5. For the bottom section of the dog, join units 23 and 24; then add Unit 25 to the bottom of these combined units. Join units 26, 27, and 28; then add them to side of combined units 23-25. Join Unit 29 to opposite side. Join Unit 31 to opposite sides of Unit 30; then add Unit 32 to the bottom as shown. Join these combined units to the bottom of the dog body section.

6. Join the completed head section to the top of the dog center section, matching ear seams. Join the bottom section to the bottom of the center section, again matching seams. Make 1 of Block A, and 1 of Block B.

1. To complete the bed, join blocks A and B to opposite sides of Unit Q1. Join Unit Q2 to top and bottom of the bed; then add border Q3 to opposite sides. Join border Unit Q4 to top and bottom of bed/ then add border Unit Q5 to opposite sides to complete the bed top.

2. Refer to the dashed lines in the diagram above. Using a water erasable pen, draw these lines on each dog. Machine satin stitch the lines in dark rust, or chain stitch them with 6 strands of embroidery floss. Since a "little one" will be using the bed, we suggest the machine satin stitch.

3. Mary kept the quilting simple. She stippled the background and the dogs, and ditched the patchwork.

4. Turn under 1/4"; then another 1/4" on one 20" side of the backing, forming a hem. Hem two. Place backing pieces right sides together on bed top. The hemmed edges will overlap approximately 3" in the center. Stitch around outer edge of bed, using a 1/4" seam. Turn right side out.

5. We suggest making a simple canvas inside bed that is stuffed with the filling of your choice.

Cat Bed finishes to: 23" x 29"
Technique Used: Diagonal corners. diagonal ends, triangle-squares and triangle-squares used as diagonal corners.

MATERIALS FOR CAT BED

Fabric I (light blue print)
Need 11"   1/2 yard

Fabric II (medium gold print)
Need 1 3/4"   1/8 yard

Fabric III (metallic gold print)
Need 2 1/2"   1/8 yard

Fabric IV (dark gold print)
Need 7 1/2"   1/4 yard

Fabric V (white on white print)
Need 4 3/4"   1/4 yard

Fabric VI (navy print)
Need 37 1/2"   1 1/4 yards

Fabric VII (pink print)
Need 2"   1/8 yard

Fabric VIII (solid black)
Need 1 3/4" x 6" Scrap
Batting & Muslin 25" x 31" pieces
for quilting.

CUTTING FOR CAT BED

FROM FABRIC I, CUT: (LT. BLUE PRINT)
• **One 6 1/2" wide strip. From this, cut:**
  * Two - 2" x 6 1/2" (A7, B7)
  * Two - 5" x 6 1/4" (A9, B9)
  * Two - 2 1/2" x 5 3/4" (A24, B24)
  * Two - 2" x 4 1/4" (A18, B18)
  * Two - 3 3/8" squares (A25b, B25b)
  * Six - 1 1/4" x 2" (A17a, A23, A30, B17a, B23, B30)
• **One 2" wide strip. From this, cut:**
  * One - 2" x 18 1/2" (Q1)
  * Two - 2" squares (A28a, B28a)
• **Two 1 1/4" wide strips. From these, cut:**
  * Two - 1 1/4" x 17 3/4" (A31, B31)
  * Ten - 1 1/4" squares (A2a, A22a, A29a, B2a, B22a, B29a)

FROM FABRIC II, CUT: (MED. GOLD PRINT)
• **One 1 3/4" wide strip. From this, cut:**
  * Four - 1 3/4" squares (A24a, A25a, B24a, B25a)
  * Two - 1 1/2" squares (A10b, B10b)
  * Two - 1 1/4" squares (A12a, B12a)
  * Two - 1" x 2 1/4" (A13, B13)
  * Two - 1" squares (A15b, B15b)

FROM FABRIC III, CUT: (METALLIC GOLD PRINT)
• **One 2 1/2" wide strip. From this, cut:**
  * Two - 2 1/2" squares (A10, B10)
  * Two - 1 1/4" x 11 3/4" (A32, B32)

FROM FABRIC IV, CUT: (DK. GOLD PRINT)
• **One 5 3/4" wide strip. From this, cut:**
  * Two - 4 3/4" x 5 3/4" (A25, B25)
  * Two - 2" x 5 3/4" (A28, B28)
  * Two - 2 3/4" x 5" (A26, B26)
  * Two - 3 1/2" x 4 1/2" (A19, B19)
  * Two - 1 1/4" x 4 1/4" (A17, B17)
  Stack these cuts:
  * Four - 1 1/4" x 2 3/4" (A2, B2)
  * Six - 2" x 2 1/2" (A3, A6, B3, B6)
  * Two - 2" x 2 1/4" (A18a, B18a)
• **One 1 3/4" wide strip. From this, cut:**
  * Two - 1 3/4" squares (A24a, B24a)
  * Four - 1 1/4" x 1 3/4" (A5, B5)
  * Two - 1 1/4" x 2 1/4" (A20, B20)
  * Twenty - 1 1/4" squares (A1b, A14a, A15a, A21a, A22b, A27a, B1b, B14a, B15a, B21a, B22b, B27a)

FROM FABRIC V, CUT: (WHITE ON WHITE PRINT)
• **One 2 3/4" wide strip. From this, cut:**
  * Four - 2 3/4" squares (A1, B1)
  * Four - 1 1/4" x 2 3/4" (A21, A27, B21, B27)
  * Four - 1 3/4" x 2 1/2" (A11, A12, B11, B12)
  * Two - 2 1/4" x 3 1/4" (A15, B15)
  * Two - 1 3/4" x 2 1/4" (A14, B14)
  * Two - 1 1/4" squares (A26a, B26a)
• **One 2" wide strip. From this, cut:**
  * Two - 2" x 5" (A22, B22)
  * Eight - 1 1/2" squares (A10a, A10b, B10a, B10b)

FROM FABRIC VI, CUT: (NAVY PRINT)
• **One 23 1/2" wide strip. From this, cut:**
  * Two - 17 1/2" x 23 1/2" (backing)
• **Four 3" wide strips. From these, cut:**
  * Two - 3" x 24 1/2" (Q2)
  * Two - 3" x 23 1/2" (Q3)
• **One 2" wide strip. From this, cut:**
  * Two - 2" x 10 1/4" (A29, B29)
  * Two - 1 1/4" x 5" (A16, B16)

FROM FABRIC VII, CUT: (PINK PRINT)
• **One 2" wide strips. From these, cut:**
  * Eight - 2" squares (A6a, A7a, B6a, B7a)
  * Four - 1 1/4" squares (A1a, B1a)

FROM FABRIC VIII, CUT: (SOLID BLACK)
• **One 1 3/4" x 6" strip. From this, cut:**
  * Four - 1 1/4" squares (A4, B4)

CAT BED ASSEMBLY, BLOCKS A AND B

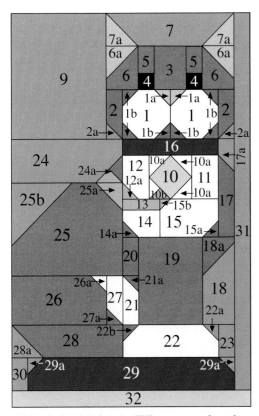

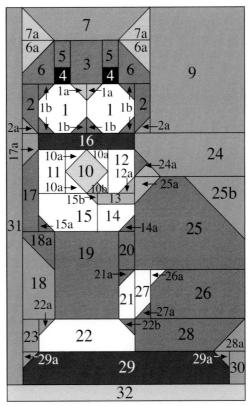

Block A. Make 1. When completed, block should measure 11 3/4" x 18 1/2".

Block B. Make 1. When completed, block should measure 11 3/4" x 18 1/2".

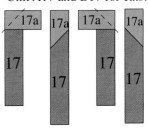

Making mirror image Unit A17 and B17 for cats.

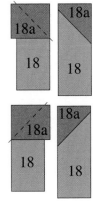

Making mirror image Unit A18 and B18 for cats.

The blocks above are the same, except that they are mirror images. These instructions are for one block.

1. Use diagonal corner technique to make two each of mirror image units 1, 2, and 6. Make one each of units 7, 10, 12, 14, 15, 21, 22, 24, 25, 26, 27, 28, and 29. Use diagonal end technique to make one of units 17 and 18, shown on this page. Use triangle-square technique for units 10 and 24. Refer to diagrams of these units on page 70 and page 71.

2. To assemble the blocks, refer to the block diagram, and join the two Unit 1's as shown. Join mirror image Unit 2 to opposite sides of combined Unit 1's. Join units 4 and 5; then join these combined units to opposite sides of Unit 3. Join mirror image Unit 6 to opposite sides of combined units 3-5. Add these combined units to top of combined units 1-2, matching seams; then join Unit 7 to the top, matching ear seams. Join Unit 9 to the side to complete the head section.

3. Join units 26 and 27. Join units 24, 25, combined units 26-27, and Unit 28 in a vertical row, matching seams. Set aside. Join units 12, 10, and 11, referring to block diagram for correct placement. Add Unit 16 to the top of these combined units. Join units 13 and 14; then add Unit 15 to the side of these combined units. Join units 13-15 to combined units 10-12. Join Unit 17 to the side as shown. Join units 18 and 19. Join units 20 and 21; then add these combined units to the side of combined units 18-19.

Join units 22 and 23. Join these combined units to the bottom of combined units 18-21, matching seams.

4. Join the chest/leg section to the cat's back section, matching seams. Join units 29 and 30; then add them to the bottom of the cat body. Join the head section to the body section, carefully matching seams. Join Unit 31 to the side of the cat as shown in block diagram; then join Unit 32 to the bottom. Make 1 of each block.

COMPLETING THE CAT BED

The dog and cat beds are finished the same way. The two differences are: borders for the cat bed end with Unit 3, and backing for the cat bed is hemmed on the 17 1/2" side. Follow steps 1-5 on page 71 for completing the dog bed.

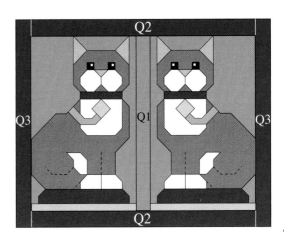

Shoe Boutique

About four years ago, my friend in Melbourne, Australia sent me beautiful miniature shoes for Christmas, which started my collection. When Mindy said "We have to do shoes", I was sold on the idea immediately. We had the best time embellishing the shoes on this lap quilt from everyone's old button and jewelry collections. This is really fun. Blocks are not difficult, lots of illustrations, and the results are well worth the time. It's a great conversation piece!

We used an ivory with a touch of blue for the background of each shoe block. All background in the cutting instructions are labeled "background."

This is a scrap quilt, and your stash should provide some great effects for the twelve shoe blocks in the quilt. The blocks make great gifts if made into smaller accessory items, such as pillows. We didn't have time to do it, but we envisioned the shoes on a table runner with matching place mats.

The materials list for the blocks are shown with each individual shoe. The materials list below is for the sashing and borders of the quilt.

Quilt finishes to 55 1/2" x 61 1/2"
Blocks A-C finish to: 12 1/2" x 15 1/2"
Blocks D-M finish to: 13 1/2" x 15 1/2"
Techniques Used: Diagonal corners, diagonal ends, and strip sets used as diagonal corners.

MATERIALS FOR QUILT SASHING AND BORDERS.

Fabric I (dark lavender print)
Need 47 1/2"   1 1/2 yards
Fabric II (light lavender print)
Need 10 1/2"   3/8 yard
Fabric III (white on white print)
Need 7 1/2"   3/8 yard
Fabric IV (gold print)
Need 7" x 9 1/2"   Scrap

MATERIALS AND CUTTING FOR BLOCK A

☐ **Fabric I (background)**
Need 8" 3/8 yard

■ **Fabric II (rusty floral print)**
Need 4 1/2" 1/4 yard

■ **Fabric III (black print)**
Need 1" 1/8 yard

☐ **FROM FABRIC I, CUT: (BACKGROUND)**
• **One 6 1/2" wide strip. From this, cut:**
  * Two - 6 1/2" squares (A10, A15)
  * One - 4" x 4 1/2" (A9)
  * One - 2" x 4 1/2" (A2)
  * One - 1" x 4 1/2" (A14a)
  * One - 4" x 15 1/2" (A16)
  Stack these cuts:
  * One - 2 1/2" square (A13)
  * One - 2" square (A1b)
  * One - 1 1/2" square (A1a)
• **One 1 1/2" wide strip. From this, cut:**
  * Two - 1 1/2" x 9" (A5)

■ **FROM FABRIC II, CUT: (RUSTY FLORAL PRINT)**
• **One 4 1/2" wide strip. From this, cut:**
  * One - 4 1/2" x 5 1/2" (A6)
  * One - 3 1/2" x 4" (A7)
  * One - 2" x 4" (A3)
  * One - 3 1/2" x 5" (A1)
  * One - 1" x 3" (A14)
  * One - 2" x 6 1/2" (A12)

■ **FROM FABRIC III, CUT: (BLACK PRINT)**
• **One 1" wide strip. From this, cut:**
  * One - 1" x 6 1/2" (A11)
  * One - 1" x 4" (A8)
  * One - 1" x 2" (A4)

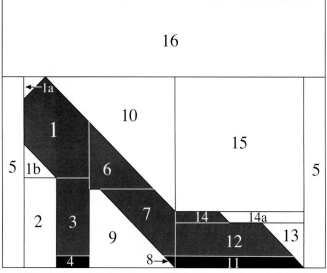

Block A. Make One. When completed, block
should measure 12 1/2" x 15 1/2".

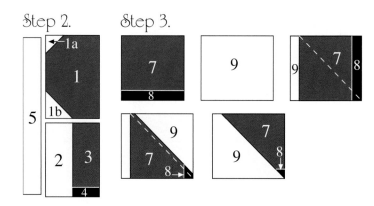

STEP 1. Use diagonal corner technique to make one of Unit 1. Use diagonal end technique to make one of Unit 14, shown on page 77.

STEP 2. Join units 3 and 4; then add Unit 2 to left side of the 3-4 combined units. Join Unit 1 to top; then add Unit 5 to left side.

STEP 3. For combined units 7 and 8, join 2" x 6 1/2" strip of Fabric II with 1" x 6 1/2" strip of Fabric III. This will now be used as a diagonal corner. Place on Unit 9 as shown. Stitch diagonal, trim seam and press.

Step 4

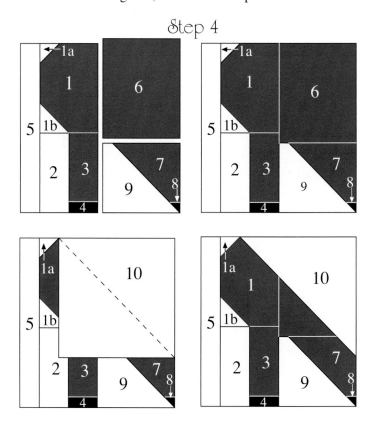

STEP 4. Join Unit 6 to top of combined units 7-9; then add these combined units to combined units 1-5. Place diagonal corner Unit 10, raw edges matching at top right corner. Stitch diagonal, trim seam and press. Do not trim center seam of diagonal corner as the background is lighter than the shoe, and the darker fabric will show through.

BLOCK A ASSEMBLY CONTINUED

Making Unit A14

STEP 5. Join units 11 and 12; then add diagonal corner Unit 13 as shown. Join units 15 and 14. Join these combined units to top of combined units 11-13. Join remaining Unit 5 to right side of the combined 11-15 units. Join the front of the shoe to the back, matching seams; then add Unit 16 across the top to complete the block.

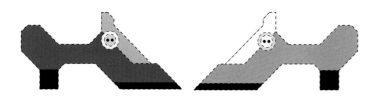

MATERIALS AND CUTTING FOR BLOCK B

	Fabric I (background)
	Need 7 1/2" 3/8 yard
	Fabric II (mint green print)
	Need 4 1/2" 1/4 yard
	Fabric III (black print)
	Need 3 1/2" 1/4 yard
	Fabric IV (dark teal print)
	Need 5" square Scrap
	Fabric V (gold print)
	Need 2" x 5" Scrap

FROM FABRIC I, CUT: (BACKGROUND)
- **One 7 1/2" wide strip. From this, cut:**
  * One - 7 1/2" square (B31)
  * One - 1" x 7 1/2" (B32)
  * One - 4 1/2" x 7" (B10)
  * One - 1 1/2" x 5" (B7)
  * One - 2" x 4" (B24)
  * Two - 1 1/2" x 4" (B8, B9)
  * One - 2 1/2" x 3" (B30)
  * One - 1 1/2" x 3" (B23)
  * One - 2" square (B27)
  * Stack these cuts:
  * One - 1 1/2" x 14 1/2" (B11)
  * One - 1 1/2" x 12 1/2" (B33)
  * Two - 1 1/2" squares (B12a)

FROM FABRIC III, CUT: (MINT GREEN PRINT)
- **One 4 1/2" wide strip. From this, cut:**

  * One - 4 1/2" x 5" (B22)
  * One - 4" x 5" (B12)
  * One - 1 1/2" x 4" (B13)
  * One - 3" x 3 1/2" (B6)
  * One - 1" x 3 1/2" (B21)
  * One - 2 1/2" x 6 1/2" (B25)
  * Stack these cuts:
  * Two - 1 1/2" x 2 1/2" (B19, B23b)
  * Two - 1 1/2" x 2" (B7a, B8a)
  * One - 1 1/2" square (B20b)
  * Three - 1" squares (B5a, B15a, B20a)

FROM FABRIC III, CUT: (BLACK PRINT)
- **One 3 1/2" wide strip. From this, cut:**
  * One - 3 1/2" x 4 1/2" (B20)
  * One - 2" x 3 1/2" (B4)
  * One - 1" x 3 1/2" (B5)
  * One - 1 1/2" x 3" (B15)
  * Two - 1 1/2" x 2 1/2" (B13a, B16)
  * One - 1" x 2 1/2" (B29)
  * Two - 1 1/2" x 2" (B7b, B9a)
  * Stack these, cuts:
  * Two - 1 1/2" squares (B1, B3)
  * One - 1" x 6 1/2" (B26)
  * One - 1" x 1 1/2" (B18)

FROM FABRIC IV, CUT: (DK. TEAL PRINT)
- **One 2 1/2" square (B28)**
- **Two 1 1/2" squares (B23a, B30a)**

FROM FABRIC V, CUT: (GOLD PRINT)
- **Three 1 1/2" squares (B2, B14, B17)**

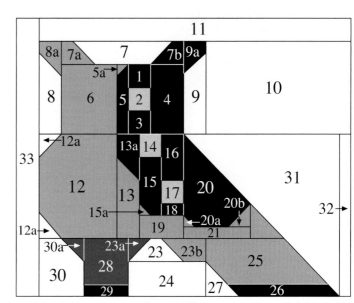

Block B. Make One. When completed, block should measure 12 1/2" x 15 1/2".

STEP 1. Use diagonal corner technique to make one of units 12, 15, 20, and 30. Use diagonal end technique to make one of units 7, 8, 9, 13, and 23, shown on page 78.

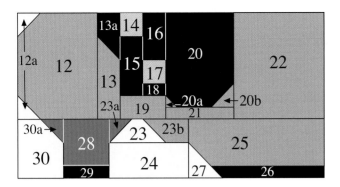

STEP 2. To assemble the shoe, refer to the block diagram on page 77, and begin by joining units 1, 2, and 3 in a vertical row; then add Unit 4 to the right side of the row, and Unit 5 to the left side. Join Unit 6 to

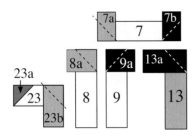

Unit 5. Join Unit 7 across the top of the 1-6 combined units; then add Unit 9 to the right side, and Unit 8 to the left side. Join Unit 10 to right side of Unit 9; then add Unit 11 across the top to complete the shoe top.

STEP 3. Refer to diagram above, and join units 12 and 13. Join units 14 and 15. Join units 16, 17, and 18 in a vertical row. Join combined units 14-15 and combined units 16-18; then add Unit 19 to the bottom of these units. Join com-

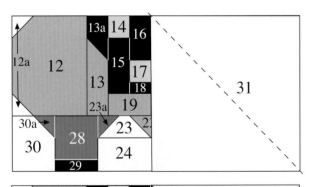

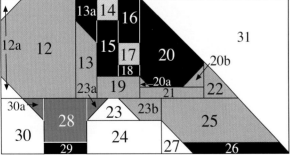

bined units 12-13 to left side of the shoe button section as shown. Join units 20 and 21; then add Unit 22 to the right side of these combined units. Join these units to the right side of button section.

STEP 4. For the bottom section of the shoe, join units 28

and 29; then add Unit 30 to the left side of these combined units. Join units 23 and 24. Join these combined units to right side of combined units 28-30. Join units 25 and 26; then add diagonal corner, Unit 27 to bottom left corner of the 25-26 combined units. Join the bottom section of the shoe to the center section, matching seams. Place diagonal corner, Unit 31 on the right side of the shoe as shown in the diagram. Be sure that raw edges are matching. Stitch diagonal and press. We do not suggest trimming the center seam of Unit 31 as the background fabric is a light color, and the dark colors will show through. Join Unit 32 to right side of Unit 31.

STEP 5. Join the shoe top to the shoe bottom, carefully matching seams. Join Unit 33 to left side to complete the block.

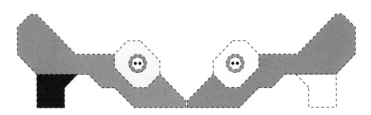

MATERIALS AND CUTTING FOR BLOCK C

☐ **Fabric I (background)**
Need 9"   3/8 yard

■ **Fabric II (bright salmon print)**
Need 4"   1/4 yard

■ **Fabric III (red batik)**
Need 1 1/2"   1/8 yard

☐ **Fabric IV (gold print)**
Need 2" x 3 1/2"   Scrap

☐   **FROM FABRIC I, CUT: (BACKGROUND)**
• **One 7 1/2" wide strip. From this, cut:**
    * One - 7 1/2" x 8" (C6)
    * One - 3 1/2" x 5 1/4" (C17)
    * One - 5" square (C13)
    * One - 3" x 5" (C11)
    * One - 4" square (C5)
    * One - 3" x 4" (C15)
    * One - 2 3/4" x 3 1/2" (C20)
    * One - 2 1/2" square (C4c)
    * One - 1 1/2" x 2 1/2" (C12a)
    Stack this cut:
    * Two - 2" squares (C4a, C14b)
    * One - 1 1/2" x 1 7/8" (C7)
    From scrap, cut:
    * One - 1 3/4" square (C14c)
    * Three - 1 1/2" squares (C3, C4b, C14a)
    * One - 1" square (C1a)
• **One 1 1/2" wide strip. From this, cut:**
    * One - 1 1/2" x 9 1/2" (C16)

FROM FABRIC II, CUT: (BRIGHT SALMON PRINT)
- **One 4" wide strip. From this, cut:**
  - * One - 4" square (C4)
  - * One - 1 1/2" x 4" (C12)
  - * One - 3" x 3 1/2" (C17a)
  - * One - 3" x 6" (C14)
  - * One - 2" square (C11a)
  - * One - 1 1/2" x 2" (C8)
  - * One - 1 1/8" x 1 1/2" (C10)
  - * One - 1" x 6 1/2" (C1)

 FROM FABRIC III, CUT: (RED BATIK)
- **One 1 1/2" wide strip. From this, cut;**
  - * One 1 1/2" x 3" (C18)
  - * One 1 1/4" square (C17b)
  - * One 1" x 6 1/2" (C2)
  - * One - 1" x 3 1/2" (C17a)

FROM FABRIC IV, CUT: (GOLD PRINT)
- **One - 1 1/2" square (C9)**
- **One - 1" x 1 1/2" (C19)**

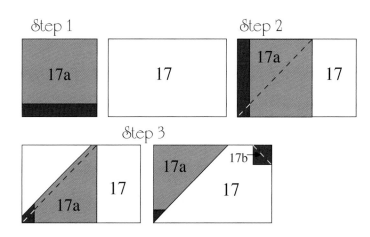

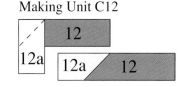
Making Unit C12

STEP 4. Use diagonal end technique to make one of Unit 12.

STEP 5. To assemble the shoe, join units 1 and 2; then add Unit 3 to left side of these combined units. Join units 4 and 5; then join Unit 6 to top of 4-5 units. Join these units to top of combined units 1-3.

STEP 6. Join units 7, 8, 9 and 10 in a horizontal row; then add Unit 13 to the top of this row, and Unit 11 to the bottom. Join Unit 12 to the bottom of Unit 11. Join units 14 and 15; then add Unit 16 to the right side of the 15-16 combined units. Add the combined 14-16 units to the right side of combined units 7-12.

STEP 7. Join units 18 and 19; then join Unit 17 to the left side of the 18-19 combined units, and Unit 20 to the right side. Join this heel section to the bottom of combined units 7-16. Join the shoe front to the shoe back, right sides facing. Match seams where necessary.

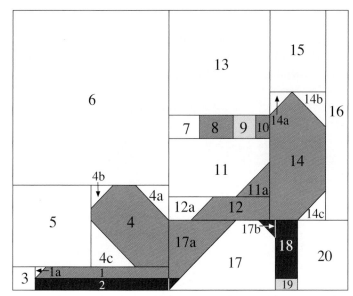

Block C. Make One. When completed, block should measure 12 1/2" x 15 1/2".

STEP 1. Refer to block diagram and use diagonal corner technique to make one each of units 1, 4, 11 and 14. Refer to diagram at top right, and join 3" x 3 1/2" strip of Fabric II with 1" x 3 1/2" strip of Fabric III. This now becomes a diagonal corner. .

STEPS 2 AND 3. Place right sides facing on Unit 17 as shown. Stitch diagonal, trim seam and press. Join diagonal corner 17b to complete the unit.

MATERIALS AND CUTTING FOR BLOCK D

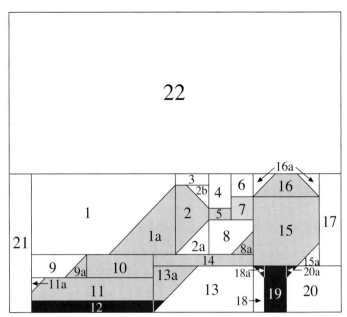

Block D. Make One. When completed, block should measure 13 1/2" x 15 1/2".

☐ Fabric I (background)
Need 7 1/2"   3/8 yard
▨ Fabric II (blue print)
Need 3 1/2"   1/4 yard
■ Fabric III (navy print)
Need 1 1/2"   1/8 yard
▨ Fabric IV (gold print)
Need 2" square   Scrap

☐   FROM FABRIC I, CUT: (BACKGROUND)
• **One 7 1/2" wide strip. From this, cut:**
    * One - 7 1/2" x 15 1/2" (D22)
    * One - 4" x 7" (D1)
    * One - 1 1/2" x 6 1/2" (D21)
    * One - 2 1/2" x 5" (D13)
    * One - 1 1/2" x 4 1/2" (D17)
    * One - 2 1/2" x 3" (D20)
    * One - 1 1/2" x 3" (D9)
    * One - 2" x 2 1/2" (D8)
    * One - 1" x 2 1/2" (D18)
    * One - 2" square (D2a)
    * One - 1 1/2" x 2" (D4)
    * One - 1" x 2" (D3)
From scrap, cut:
    * Five - 1 1/2" squares (D2b, D6, D15a, D16a)
    * One - 1 1/8" square (D11a)

▨   FROM FABRIC II, CUT: (BLUE PRINT)
• **One 3 1/2" wide strip. From this, cut:**
    * Two - 3 1/2" squares (D1a, D15)
    * One - 2" x 3 1/2" (D2)
    * Two - 1 1/2" x 3 1/2" (D10, D16)
    * One - 2" x 2 1/2" (D13a)
    * One - 1 1/2" x 6" (D11)
    * Two - 1 1/2" squares (D8a, D9a)
    * One - 1" x 1 1/2" (D5)
    * One - 1" x 5" (D14)

■   FROM FABRIC III, CUT: (NAVY PRINT)
• **One 1 1/2" wide strip. From this, cut;**
    * One - 1 1/2" x 2 1/2" (D19)
    * One - 1" x 6" (D12)
    * One - 1" x 2 1/2" (D13a)
    * Two - 1" squares (D18a, D20a)

▨   FROM FABRIC IV, CUT: (GOLD PRINT)
• **One - 1 1/2" square (D7)**

STEP 1. Refer to block diagram and use diagonal corner technique to make one each of units 1, 2, 8, 9, 11, 15, 16, 18, and 20. Refer to diagram below, and join 2" x 2 1/2" strip of Fabric II with 1" x 2 1/2" strip of Fabric III. This now becomes a diagonal corner.

STEP 2. Place right sides facing on Unit 13 as shown. Stitch diagonal, trim seam and press.

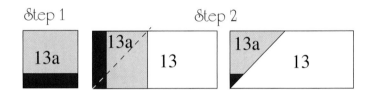

STEP 3. To piece the shoe, refer to block diagram, and begin by joining units 2 and 3; then add Unit 1 to left side of these combined units, matching seams. Join units 4 and 5. Join units 6 and 7. Join combined units 4-5 to left side of units 6-7 ; then add Unit 8 to the bottom of the combined units. Join these combined units to right side of combined units 1-3, again matching seams.

STEP 4. Join units 9 and 10. Join units 11 and 12. Add combined units 9-10 to top of units 11-12 as shown. Join units 13 and 14; then add these units to the right side of shoe toe combined units. Join this bottom shoe section to the bottom of combined units 1-8; then add Unit 21 to left side of the shoe.

STEP 5. For the shoe back, join units 15 and 16; then add Unit 17 to right side of combined units 15-16. Join units 18, 19, and 20. Join these combined units to the bottom of combined units 15-17, matching heel seam. Join the shoe back to the shoe front, matching seams; then add Unit 22 to the top of the shoe to complete the block.

MATERIALS AND CUTTING FOR BLOCK E

☐ **Fabric I (background)**
Need 8"   3/8 yard

▨ **Fabric II (teal print)**
Need 3 1/2"   1/8 yard

■ **Fabric III (black print)**
Need 2 1/2"   1/8 yard

☐ **FROM FABRIC I, CUT: (BACKGROUND)**
- **One 6" wide strip. From this, cut:**
  * One - 6" x 15 1/2" (E16)
  * One - 5 1/2" square (E12)
  * One - 3" x 5" (E4)
  * One - 2 1/2" x 5" (E15)
  * One - 1 1/2" x 4 1/2" (E7)
  * One - 4" x 8" (E8)
  * One - 3 1/2" square (E9a)
- **One 2" wide strip. From this, cut:**
  * One - 2" square (E5b)
  * One - 1 1/2" x 3 1/2" (E14)
  * One - 1 1/2" square (E1a)
  * Two - 1" squares (E5c, E13a)

▨ **FROM FABRIC II, CUT: (TEAL PRINT)**
- **One 3 1/2" wide strip. From this, cut:**
  * One - 3 1/2" x 8" (E9)
  * One - 1 1/2" x 3 1/2" (E13)
  * One - 3" x 7 1/2" (E10)
  * One - 2 1/2" x 3" (E6)
  * One - 2" x 3" (E1)
  * One - 2" x 2 1/2" (E5)
  * One - 1 1/2" x 2 1/2" (E3)
  * One - 1 1/2" square (E15a)
  * Two - 1" squares (E2a)

■ **FROM FABRIC III, CUT: (BLACK PRINT)**
- **One 2 1/2" wide strip. From this, cut:**
  * One - 2 1/2" square (E4a)
  * One - 1" x 2 1/2" (E2)
  * Two - 1 1/2" squares (E5a, E6a)
  * One - 1" x 3" (E11)

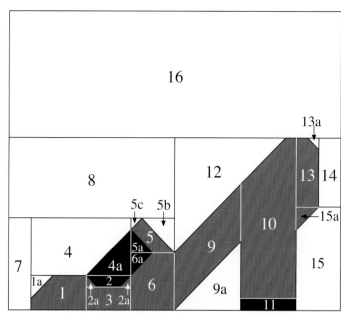

Block E. Make One. When completed, block should measure 13 1/2" x 15 1/2".

STEP 1. Refer to block diagram and use diagonal corner technique to make one each of units 1, 2, 4, 5, 6, 9, 13, and 15.

STEP 2. To piece the shoe, refer to block diagram, and begin by joining units 2 and 3; then add Unit 1 to left side of these combined units. Join unit 4 to the top of combined units 1-3; then add Unit 7 to left side. Join units 5 and 6. Join these units to the right side of toe combined units, matching seams; then add Unit 8 to the top.

STEP 3. Refer to diagram below and join units 10 and 11. Join Unit 9 to the left side of these combined units. Place diagonal corner, Unit 12, right sides facing and raw edges matching as shown. Stitch diagonal. Do not trim the center seam of the diagonal corner as it is a light fabric on top of a darker fabric, and the dark fabric may show through.

STEP 4. Join units 13 and 14; then add Unit 15 to bottom of these combined units, matching seams. Join the 13-15 combined units to 9-12 combined units as shown; then add the back of the shoe, just completed, to the front of the shoe, matching seams. Join Unit 16 across the top to complete the block

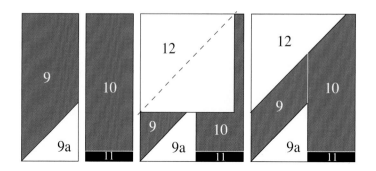

MATERIALS AND CUTTING FOR BLOCK F

Fabric I (background)
Need 7 1/2"   3/8 yard

Fabric II (dark green print)
Need 3 1/2"   1/4 yard

Fabric III (black print)
Need 3 1/2" x 6"   Scrap

Fabric IV (medium green batik)
Need 4" x 6 1/2"   Scrap

FROM FABRIC I, CUT: (BACKGROUND)
- **One 7 1/2" wide strip. From this, cut:**
  * One - 7 1/2" x 11 1/2" (F15)
  * One - 3 1/2" x 7" (F10)
  * One - 1 1/2" x 7" (F9)
  * One - 2 1/2" x 5 1/2" (F11)
  * One - 4 1/2" x 8 1/2" (F5)
  * One - 3" x 4" (F6)
  * One - 1 1/2" x 4" (F2)
  * One - 2 1/2" x 3 1/2" (F14)
  * One - 2" x 2 1/2" (F4)
  * One - 2" square (F1a)
  * One - 1 1/2" square (F1b)
  * Two - 1" squares (F1c, F8a)

FROM FABRIC II, CUT: (DK. GREEN PRINT)
- **One 3 1/2" wide strip. From this, cut:**
  * One - 3 1/2" x 4" (F1)
  * One - 3" square (F10b)
  * One - 2" x 2 1/2" (F11b)
  * One - 2" x 5 1/2" (F12)
  * One - 2" x 4" (F7)
  * One - 1 1/2" square (F6a)
  * One - 1" square (F11a)

FROM FABRIC III, CUT: (BLACK PRINT)
- **One - 2" x 2 1/2" (F3)**
- **One - 1" x 5 1/2" (F13)**
- **One - 1" x 2 1/2" (F11b)**

FROM FABRIC IV, CUT: (MED. GREEN BATIK)
- **One - 3 1/2" x 4 1/2" (F10a)**
- **One - 1 1/2" square (F8)**

Making Unit 10

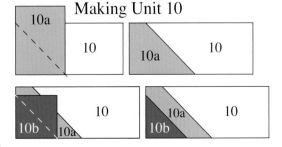

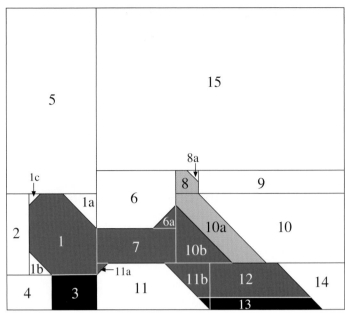

Block F. Make One. When completed, block should measure 13 1/2" x 15 1/2".

STEP 1. Refer to block diagram and use diagonal corner technique to make one each of units 1, 6, and 8. Use diagonal end technique to make one of units 10, and combined units 12-14, shown below. For Unit 10, make diagonal end first; then add diagonal corner 10b. For combined units 12-14, join 2" x 5 1/2" piece of Fabric II with 1" x 5 1/2" piece of Fabric III. Join diagonal end, Unit 14, to this small strip set.

Making units 12 thru 14

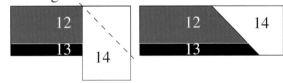

STEPS 2 AND 3. Refer to diagram of Unit 11 below, and join 2" x 2 1/2" strip of Fabric II with 1" x 2 1/2" strip of Fabric III. This now becomes a diagonal corner. Place on Unit 11, right sides together and raw edges matching. Stitch diagonal, trim seam and press. Join diagonal corner 11a.

Step 2   Step 3

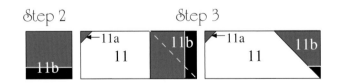

STEP 4. To piece the shoe, refer to block diagram, and begin by joining units 1 and 2. Join units 3 and 4; then add these combined units to bottom of 1-2 units, matching seams. Join Unit 5 to top of heel units. Join units 6 and 7. Join units 8 and 9; then add Unit 10 to bottom of 8-9 combined units, matching seams. Join combined units 6-7 to left side of combined units 8-10, again matching seams.

BLOCK F ASSEMBLY CONTINUED

STEP 5. Join unit 11 and combined units 12-14. Join this section to bottom of combined units 6-10; then add Unit 15 to the top. Join the shoe back to the shoe front, matching seams to complete the block.

MATERIALS AND CUTTING FOR BLOCK G

Fabric I (background)
Need 7 1/2"   3/8 yard
Fabric II (light lavender print)
Need 3 1/2"   1/4 yard
Fabric III (dark lavender print)
Need 3" x 5 1/2"   Scrap
Fabric IV (yellow print)
Need 3"   1/4 yard
Fabric V (dark purple print)
Need 1 1/2" x 3"   Scrap

FROM FABRIC I, CUT: (BACKGROUND)
• **One 7 1/2" wide strip. From this, cut:**
  * Two - 1 1/2" x 7 1/2" (G8, G19)
  * One - 6 1/2" x 15 1/2" (G20)
  * One - 3" x 5 1/2" (G18)
  * One - 3 1/2" x 5" (G1a)
  * One - 2 1/2" x 4" (G11)
  * One - 3" x 3 1/2" (G3)
  * One - 2" x 3 1/2" (G10)
  * One - 2 1/2" square (G9a)
  Stack these cuts:
  * Three - 2" squares (G15b, G16, G17a)
  * Two - 1 1/2" x 2" (G7, G14)
  * Three - 1 1/2" squares (G1b, G2a, G9b)
  * Two - 1" squares (G2b, G9c)

FROM FABRIC II, CUT; (LIGHT LAVEN-DER PRINT)
• **One 3 1/2" wide strip. From this, cut:**
  * One - 3 1/2" x 4 1/2" (G1)
  * One - 2" square (G4a)
  * One - 1 1/2" x 2" (G6)
  * One - 1 1/2" x 6" (G2)
  * One - 1 1/2" x 5 1/2" (G12)
  * Two - 1 1/2" squares (G13, G15a)

FROM FABRIC III, CUT: (DARK LAVEN-DER PRINT)
• **One - 2 1/2" x 3" (G4)**
• **One - 2" square (G3a)**

FROM FABRIC IV, CUT: (YELLOW PRINT)

• **One 3" wide strip. From this, cut:**
  * One - 3" x 4 1/2" (G15)
  * One - 2 1/2" x 3" (G17)
  * One - 2 1/2" x 3 1/2" (G9)

FROM FABRIC V, CUT; (DARK PURPLE PRINT)
• **One 1" x 2 1/2" (G5)**

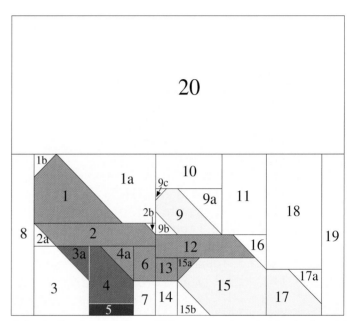

Block G. Make One. When completed, block should measure 13 1/2" x 15 1/2".

STEP 1. Refer to block diagram and use diagonal corner technique to make one each of units 2, 3, 4, 9, 15, and 17. Use diagonal end technique to make one of Unit 1, shown at right.

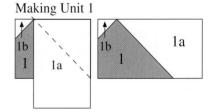

Making Unit 1

STEP 2. To piece the shoe, begin by joining units 1 and 2. Join units 4 and 5; then add Unit 3 to left side of these combined units. Join units 6 and 7. Join these combined units to right side of combined units 3-5, matching seams. Join combined units 1-2 to the top of the heel section, again matching seams; then add Unit 8 to left side of the combined shoe back units.

STEP 3. Join units 9 and 10; then add Unit 11 to right side of the 9-10 combined units. Join units 13 and 14; then join Unit 15 to right side of 13-14 combination. Add Unit 12 across the top; then join diagonal corner, Unit 16 to top right corner as shown. Join combined units 9-11 to top of combined units 12-16.

STEP 4. Join units 17 and 18; then add Unit 19 to right side of these combined units. Join these units to the right side of the shoe, matching seam. Join Unit 20 across the top to complete the block.

MATERIALS AND CUTTING FOR BLOCK H

☐ **Fabric I (background)**
Need 7 1/2"   3/8 yard

▨ **Fabric II (gold check)**
Need 5"   1/4 yard

◼ **Fabric III (dark rust check)**
Need 5" x 8"   Scrap

◼ **Fabric IV (black print)**
Need 2 1/2"   1/8 yard

☐ **FROM FABRIC I, CUT: (BACKGROUND)**
- **One 4 1/2" wide strip. From these, cut:**
  * One - 4 1/2" x 14" (H15)
  * One - 2" x 4 1/2" (H16)
  * One - 4" square (H8a)
  * One - 1" x 4" (H7)
  * One - 3 1/2" x 15 1/2" (H17)
  * One - 3 1/2" square (H15b)
- **One 3" wide strip. From this, cut:**
  * One - 3" x 5 1/2" (H12)
  * One - 3" square (H8b)
  * One - 1 1/2" x 3" (H14b)
  * One - 1 1/2" x 2 3/4" (H11)
  * One - 2 1/2" x 6" (H1)
  * One - 1 1/2" x 10" (H14)
  * One - 1 1/2" x 6 1/2" (H2)
  * One - 1 1/2" x 5 1/2" (H13)
  From scrap, cut:
  * One - 1 1/2" square (H9b)
  * One - 1 1/4" square (H10a)

▨ **FROM FABRIC II, CUT: (GOLD CHECK)**
- **One 5" wide strip. From this, cut:**
  * One - 5" x 5 1/2" (H8)
  * One - 3" x 3 1/4" (H9)
  * One - 1" x 2" (H6)

◼ **FROM FABRIC III, CUT: (DARK RUST PRINT)**
- **One 4 1/2" wide strip. From this, cut:**
  * One - 4 1/2" square (H15a)
  * One - 1 1/2" x 3 1/2" (H4)
  * One - 1 1/2" x 2 1/2" (H14a)

◼ **FROM FABRIC IV, CUT: (BLACK PRINT)**
- **One 2 1/2" wide strip. From this, cut:**
  * One - 2 1/2" x 3" (H1a)
  * One - 2" x 2 3/4" (H10)
  * One - 2" square (H9a)
  * One - 1 1/2" x 2" (H3)
  * One - 1 1/2" square (H14c)
  * One - 1" x 1 1/2" (H5)

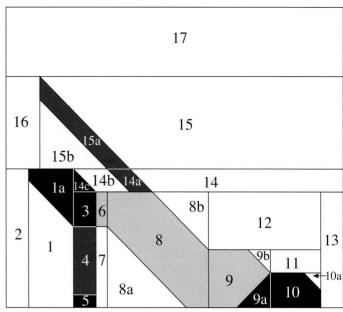

Block H.   Make One. When completed, block should measure 13 1/2" x 15 1/2".

STEP 1. Refer to block diagram and use diagonal corner technique to make one each of units 8, 9, 10 and 15. Use diagonal end technique to make one each of units 1 and 14, shown at right, and below. Unit 15 is a double diagonal corner. We do not suggest trimming the 15b center seam as the dark will show through the light fabric.

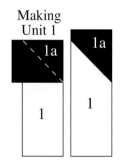

STEP 2. To piece the shoe, begin by joining units 1 and 2. Join units 3, 4 and 5 in a vertical row. Join units 6 and 7; then add them to the vertical row, matching Unit 6 seam. Join Unit 8, again matching seams. Join units 10 and 11; then add Unit 9 to left side of these combined units. Add Unit 12 across the top; then add Unit 13 to the right side. Join Unit 14 to the top of the combined units, matching strap seam. Join 1-2 combined units to left side of shoe to complete the shoe bottom.

STEP 3. Join units 15 and 16; then add Unit 17 across the top to complete the shoe top section. Join the two sections together, matching the strap seam to complete the block.

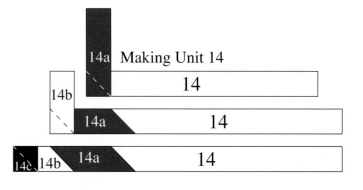

84

MATERIALS AND CUTTING FOR BLOCK J

☐ **Fabric I (background)**
Need 7 1/2"   3/8 yard
▨ **Fabric II (bright orange print)**
Need 3 1/2"   1/4 yard
■ **Fabric III (rust cane print)**
Need 2 1/2"   1/8 yard
▨ **Fabric IV (brown print)**
Need 1 1/2"   1/8 yard

☐ **FROM FABRIC I, CUT: (BACKGROUND)**
• **One 7 1/2" wide strip. From these, cut:**
  * One - 7 1/2" x 10 1/2" (J20)
  * One - 2" x 7 1/2" (J19)
  * Two - 1 1/2" x 6 1/2" (J16)
  * One - 4" x 5" (J18)
  * One - 2 1/2" x 3 1/2" (J3)
  * One - 1 1/2" x 3 1/2" (J2)
  * One - 3" square (J17a)
  Stack these cuts:
  * Five - 2 1/2" squares (J4a, J4b, J8, J13a, J14)
  * One - 2" x 3" (J10)
  * One - 2" x 2 1/2" (J5)
  * Four - 2" squares (J1a, J9a, J17b)
  * One - 1 1/2" square (J17c)
  * One - 1" square (J11a)

▨ **FROM FABRIC II, CUT: (BRIGHT ORANGE PRINT)**
• **One 3 1/2" wide strip. From this, cut:**
  * One - 3 1/2" x 5 1/2" (J4)
  * One - 2 1/2" x 3 1/2" (J1)
  * One - 3" x 4" (J17)
  * One - 2" x 3" (J9)
  * Three - 2" squares (J5a, J6, J12a)
  * One - 1 1/2" x 4" (J7)
  * One - 1" square (J5b)

■ **FROM FABRIC III, CUT: (RUST CANE PRINT)**
• **One 2 1/2" wide strip. From this, cut:**
  * One - 2 1/2" x 3 1/2" (J13)
  * One - 2" x 5 1/2" (J12)
  * One - 1 1/2" square (J10a)
  * One - 1" x 3" (J11)

▨ **FROM FABRIC IV, CUT: (BROWN PRINT)**
• **One 1 1/2" wide strip. From this, cut:**
  * One - 1 1/2" x 13 1/2" (J15)

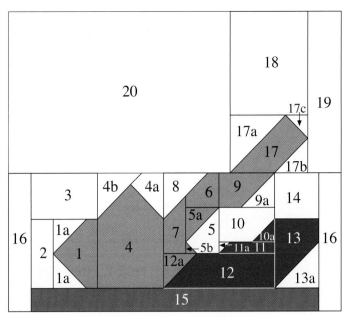

Block J. Make One. When completed, block should measure 13 1/2" x 15 1/2".

STEP 1. Refer to block diagram and use diagonal corner technique to make one each of units 1, 4, 5, 9, 10, 11, 12, 13 and 17. Unit 4 has overlapping diagonal corners. Join them in alphabetical order.

STEP 2. To piece the shoe, begin by joining units 1 and 2; then join Unit 3 to the top. Join Unit 4 to right side of 1-3 combined units. Join units 5 and 6; then add Unit 7 as shown. Join diagonal corner, Unit 8 to top left corner of the 5-7 combination. Join units 9, 10, and 11 in a vertical row. Join this row to combined 5-8 units; then add Unit 12 to the bottom, matching seams. Join units 13 and 14; then add them to the shoe back as shown.

STEP 3. Join the shoe back to the shoe front, matching seams. Join Unit 15 to the bottom; then add Unit 16 to opposite sides of the shoe. Join units 17 and 18; then join Unit 19 to the right side of these combined units, and Unit 20 to the left side. Join this top section to the shoe bottom section, matching the strap seam.

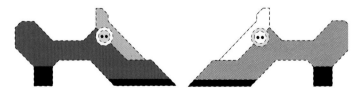

MATERIALS AND CUTTING FOR BLOCK K

☐ **Fabric I (background)**
Need 7 1/2"   3/8 yard
▨ **Fabric II (light pink print)**
Need 3 1/2"   1/4 yard
▨ **Fabric III (bright pink print)**
Need 4 1/2" x 9"   Scrap

FROM FABRIC I, CUT: (BACKGROUND)
- **One 7 1/2" wide strip. From this, cut:**
  - * Two - 1 1/2" x 7 1/2" (K13)
  - * One - 2 1/2" x 7" (K4)
  - * One - 6 1/2" x 15 1/2" (K14)
  - * One - 3 1/2" x 6 1/2" (K5)
  - * One - 2 1/2" x 4" (K3)
  - * One - 3" x 3 3/8" (K10)
  - * One - 2" x 3" (K12)
  - Stack these cuts:
  - * Three - 2" squares (K1b, K2a, K7b)
  - * One - 1 1/2" x 2" (K9)
  - * Two - 1 1/2" squares (K1a, K7a)

 FROM FABRIC II, CUT: (LT. PINK PRINT)
- **One 3 1/2" wide strip. From this, cut:**
  - * One - 3 1/2" square (K5a)
  - * One - 2 1/2" x 3" (K4a)
  - * One - 2" x 6 1/2" (K6)
  - * One - 2" x 5" (K7)
  - * One - 2" x 4" (K2)
  - * One - 2" square (K1d)
  - * Three - 1 1/2" squares (K1c, K8, K10a)

FROM FABRIC III, CUT: (BRIGHT PINK PRINT)
- **One - 4" square (K1)**
- **One - 2 5/8" x 3" (K11)**
- **One - 1 1/2" square (K10b)**

STEP 1. Refer to block diagram and use diagonal corner technique to make one each of units 1, 2, 5, 7, and 10. Use diagonal end technique to make one of Unit 4 as shown below.

STEP 2. To piece the shoe, begin by joining units 3, 1, and 2 in a row; then add Unit 4 to left side of these combined units. Join units 5 and 6; then add Unit 7 to right side of the 5-6 units. Join units 8 and 9; then add Unit 10 to right side of 8-9 combined units, matching seams. Join units 11 and 12; then add them to the right side of combined units 8-10. Join these units to the bottom of the 5-7 combined units, matching seam.

STEP 3. Join the front of the shoe to the back of the shoe, matching Unit 8 seam; then add Unit 13 to opposite sides of the shoe. Join Unit 14 across the top to complete the block.

Making Unit 4

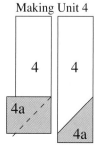

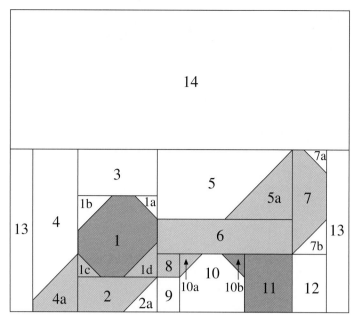

Block K. Make One. When completed, block should measure 13 1/2" x 15 1/2".

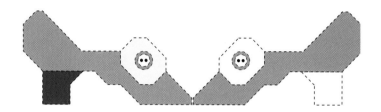

MATERIALS AND CUTTING FOR BLOCK L

Fabric I (background)
Need 7 1/2"   3/8 yard

Fabric II (grape batik)
Need 3"   1/8 yard

Fabric III (burgundy print)
Need 2 1/2" x 7 1/2"   Scrap

FROM FABRIC I, CUT: (BACKGROUND)
- **One 7 1/2" wide strip. From this, cut:**
  - * Two - 1 1/2" x 7 1/2" (L14)
  - * One - 6 1/2" x 15 1/2" (L15)
  - * One - 5" x 6" (L6)
  - * One - 3" x 5 1/2" (L7)
  - * One - 3" x 4 1/2" (L13)
  - * One - 1" x 3 1/2" (L3a)
  - * One - 2 1/2" x 3" (L2a)
  - * One - 2" x 3" (L4)
  - Stack this cut:
  - * Two - 2" x 2 1/2" (L5, L10)
  - * One - 2" square (L1a)
  - From scrap, cut:
  - * One - 1 1/2" square (L8a)

FROM FABRIC II, CUT: (GRAPE BATIK)
- **One 3" wide strip. From this, cut:**
  - One - 3" x 3 1/2" (L13a)
  - One - 3" square (L7b)
  - One - 2" x 3" (L9)
  - One - 1 1/2" x 3" (L8)
  - One - 2 1/2" x 4 1/2" (L11)
  - One - 2" x 7" (L1)
  - Two - 2" squares (L4b, L7a)
  - Two - 1 1/2" squares (L4a, L5a)
  - One - 1" x 5" (L3)
  - One - 1" square (L10a)

FROM FABRIC III, CUT: (BURGUNDY PRINT)
- **One - 1" x 7" (L2)**
- **One - 1" x 2 1/2" (L12)**

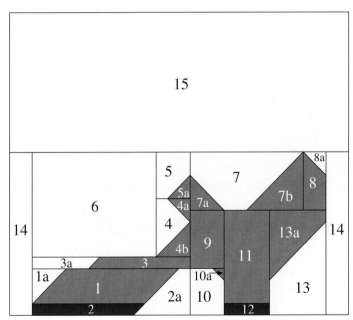

Block L. Make One. When completed, block should measure 13 1/2" x 15 1/2".

STEP 1. Refer to block diagram and use diagonal corner technique to make one each of units 1, 4, 5, 7, 8, and 10. Use diagonal end technique to make one each of combined units 1-2, 3, and 13, shown on this page.

Making Unit 13

Making combined units 1 and 2.

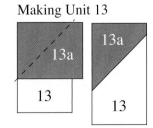

STEP 2. To piece the shoe, begin by joining units 1, and 2; then add diagonal end 2a. Join Unit 3 to the top of the 1-2 combined units. Join units 4 and 5, matching seams; then add Unit 6 to left side. Join these combined units to top of the 1-3 combined units to complete the shoe front.

STEP 3. For the shoe back, join units 7 and 8, matching seams. Join units 9 and 10. Join units 11 and 12; then add Unit 13 to right side of the 11-12 combined units. Join combined units 9-10 to the left side of the heel units; then add combined 7-8 units to the top, matching seams. Join the front of the shoe to the back of the shoe, again matching seams. Join Unit 14 to opposite sides of the shoe; then add Unit 15 across the top to complete the block.

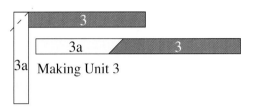

Making Unit 3

MATERIALS AND CUTTING FOR BLOCK M

Fabric I (background)
Need 8"   3/8 yard

Fabric II (light blue print)
Need 4 1/2"   1/4 yard

Fabric III (navy print)
Need 2 1/2" x 7 1/2"   Scrap

FROM FABRIC I, CUT: (BACKGROUND)
- **One 8" wide strip. From this, cut:**
  - One - 8" x 15 1/2" (M14)
  - Two - 1 1/2" x 6" (M12, M13)
  - One - 2 1/2" x 5 1/2" (M10)
  - One - 5" square (M11)
  - One - 4" square (M7a)
  - One - 2 1/2" x 4" (M4)
  - One - 1 1/2" x 4" (M6)
  - One - 3 1/2" square (M8b)
  - One - 2 1/2" square (M3)
  - From scrap, cut:
  - One - 2" square (M8a)
  - One - 1 1/2" square (M2a)

FROM FABRIC II, (LT. BLUE PRINT)
- **One 4 1/2" wide strip. From this, cut:**
  - One - 4 1/2" x 6" (M7)
  - One - 3 1/2" x 5 1/2" (M8)
  - One - 1 1/2" x 4 1/2" (M1)

FROM FABRIC III, CUT: (NAVY PRINT)
- **One 1 1/2" wide strip. From this, cut:**
    * One - 1 1/2" x 4 1/2" (M2)
    * One - 1 1/2" x 4" (M5)
    * One - 1" x 5 1/2" (M9)

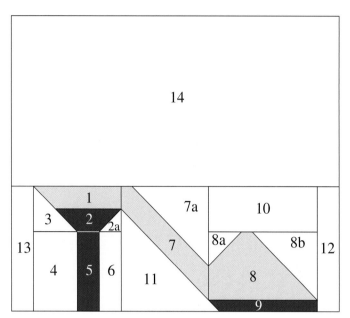

Block M.   Make One.   When completed, block should measure 13 1/2" x 15 1/2".

STEP 1. Refer to block diagram and use diagonal corner technique to make one each of units 2, 7, and 8. Refer to diagram below for making combined units 7-12. To make this unit, begin by joining units 10, 8, and 9 in a vertical row as shown. Join Unit 7 to left side and Unit 12 to right side. Place diagonal corner, Unit 11 right sides facing and raw edges matching on the bottom left corner. Stitch diagonal, trim seam and press.

Making combined units 7 thru 12

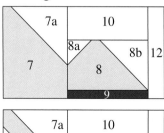
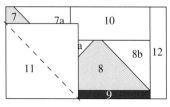
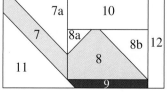

STEP 2. To piece the shoe, begin by joining units 1 and 2; then add diagonal corner, Unit 3, to left side as shown. Join units 4, 5, and 6 in a row; then add them to the bottom of combined units 1-2, matching heel seams. Join combined units 7-12 (previously made in Step 1) to right side of the heel section, again matching seams. Join Unit 13 to the left side; then add Unit 14 to the top as shown to complete the block.

CUTTING FOR QUILT DISPLAY WINDOW

FROM FABRIC I, CUT: (DK. LAVENDER PRINT)
- **Four 4 1/2" wide strips. From these, cut:**
    * Two - 4 1/2" x 28 1/2" (Q6)
    * Two - 4 1/2" x 21 5/8" (Q4)
    * Four - 4 1/2" squares (Q5a)
    * Two - 2 1/2" squares (Q7b)
- **Seven 2 1/2" wide strips for straight-grain binding.**
- **Eight 1 1/2" wide strips. From these, cut:**
    * Eight - 1 1/2" x 24" (Q3) Piece two together to equal four 47 1/2" lengths
    * Six - 1 1/2" x 13 1/2" (Q2)
    * Two - 1 1/2" x 12 1/2" (Q1)

FROM FABRIC II, CUT: (LT. LAVENDER PRINT)
- **Three 3 1/2" wide strips. From these, cut:**
    * Two - 3 1/2" x 7 1/2" (Q8)
    * Sixteen - 3 1/2" x 6 1/2" (Q7)

FROM FABRIC III, CUT: (WHITE ON WHITE PRINT)
- **Three 2 1/2" wide strips. From these, cut:**
    * Thirty-four - 2 1/2" squares (Q7a, Q8a)

FROM FABRIC IV, CUT: (GOLD PRINT)
- **Two - 4 1/2" x 6 3/8" (Q5)**

QUILT ASSEMBLY

STEP 1. Use diagonal corner technique to make sixteen of Unit Q7. Make two of Units Q8, and two of mirror image unit Q5.

STEP 2. Join Block A, Unit Q1, Block B, Unit Q1, and Block C in a row as shown. Join Unit Q3, previously pieced, to the bottom of the row. Join Block D, Unit Q2, Block E, Unit Q2, and Block F in a row. Again join Unit Q3 to the bottom of the row. Join Block G, Unit Q2, Block H, Unit Q2, and Block J in a row. Join remaining Unit Q3 to the bottom of the row. Join the four rows together, matching vertical placement of Q1 and Q2 units.

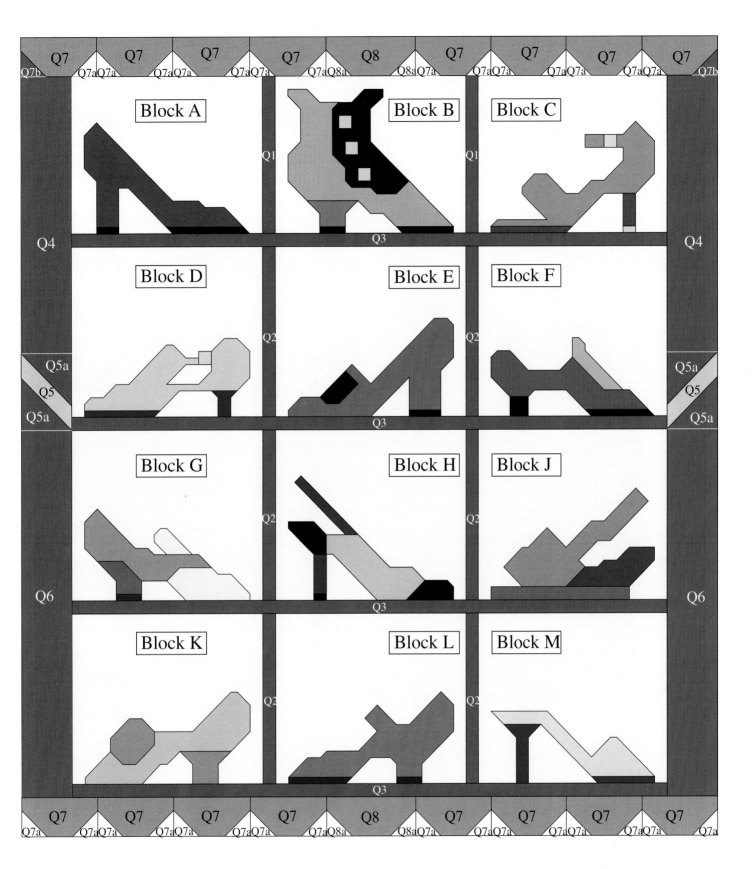

STEP 3. Refer to quilt diagram above for correct placement of mirror image Unit 5. Join units Q4, Q5, and Q6 in a vertical row. Make two. Join to opposite sides of the quilt top. Join the Q7 units together as shown, in horizontal rows of four. Refer to top row which shows a change in color for Q7b units. Make four rows. Join the rows to opposite sides of Unit Q8 as shown, matching seams. Join the row with the Q7b units to the top of the quilt, and the remaining row to the bottom of the quilt top.

STEP 4. Mary stippled the background behind the shoes, and quilted curved lines in the drapes and scallops with silver thread.

STEP 5. Refer to page 12, and piece seven 2 1/2" wide strips of Fabric I for straight-grain binding, and bind your quilt.

Log Cabin Duvet

What a great project this is for anyone who wants to dress up their comforter. The frayed seams are easy to do, and the blocks are perfect for any beginner. Fits a queen or king comforter.

Duvet Cover Finishes To: 92" x 106"
Technique Used: Strip Sets.
ALL SEAMS THROUGHOUT THIS PROJECT ARE 1/2".

MATERIALS FOR DUVET COVER

Fabric I (osnaburg)
Need 32 1/2"   1 yard

Fabric II (light gold homespun check)
Need 144 1/8"   4 1/4 yards

Fabric III (navy homespun check)
Need 162 7/8"   4 3/4 yards

Fabric IV (green homespun check)
Need 58 1/2"   1 7/8 yards

Fabric V (red homespun check)
Need 19 1/2"   3/4 yard

Fabric VI (dark gold homespun check)
Need 94 1/4"   2 7/8 yards

Backing   7 7/8 yards
If Fabric II is used for backing, you will need
a total of 12 yards

Total osnaburg needed if double layer is used:
Need 511 3/4"   14 5/8 yards

Eighteen 1 3/8" wooden buttons for duvet flap
Eighteen large snaps

CUTTING FOR DUVET COVER

*To achieve a thick chenille look, we used osnaburg **under** every cut, and sewed the extra layer into the blocks. When washed, this gave the desired effect. This is strictly optional. 1/2" seam allowance is included in every cut.*

FROM FABRIC I, CUT: (OSNABURG)
- **Four 5 1/2" wide strips. From these, cut:**
  - Four - 5 1/2" x 15 1/4" (A15)
  - Four - 5 1/2" x 10 3/4" (A12)
  - Four - 5 1/2" x 8 1/2" (A9)
  - Four - 4" x 5 1/2" (A6)
- **One 4" wide strip. From this, cut:**
  - Four - 4" squares (A1)
- **Two 3 1/4" wide strips for Strip Set 2.**

FROM FABRIC II, CUT: (LT. GOLD HOMESPUN CHECK)
- **Three 16" wide strips. From these, cut:**
  - One - 16" x 40" (Q2)
  - Two - 16" x 26" (Q2) Join these to opposite sides of the 40" strip to = 90".
- **One 6 5/8" wide strip. From this, cut:**
  - Four - 6 5/8" x 8 1/2" (D11, E11)
- **Nine 5 1/2" wide strips. From these, cut:**
  - Four - 5 1/2" x 15 1/4" (B15, C15)
  - Four - 5 1/2" x 14" (F15, G15)
  - Four - 5 1/2" x 13 1/2" (B13, C13)
  - Four - 5 1/2" x 10 3/4" (F13, G13)
  - Four - 5 1/2" x 8 1/2" (B8, C8)
  - Four - 5 1/2" x 7 1/4" (F9, G9)
  - Four - 5 1/2" x 6 3/4" (B7, C7)
  - Four - 5 1/2" x 6 5/8" (D7, E7)
  - Four - 4" x 5 1/2" (F7, G7)
- **Two 4 1/2" wide strips. From these, cut:**
  - Four - 4 1/2" x 14" (D21, E21)
  - Four - 3 1/4" x 5 1/8" (D9, E9)
- **Two 4 1/4" wide strips. From these, cut:**
  - Four - 4 1/4" x 14 1/2" (D17, E17)
  - Four - 2 3/4" x 4" (F1, G1)
- **Four 4" wide strips. Two for Strip Set 3. From remainder, cut:**
  - Four - 4" x 6 3/4" (B1, C1)
  - Four - 4" x 6 5/8" (D1, E1)
  - Four - 3" x 3 1/4" (D19, E19)
  - Four - 2 3/4" x 3 1/4" (D15, E15)
- **Two 3 1/4" wide strips for Strip Set 1.**

FROM FABRIC III, CUT: (NAVY HOMESPUN CHECK)
- **Three 10 1/8" wide strips. From these, cut:**
  - One - 10 1/8" x 40" (Q1)
  - Two - 10 1/8" x 27 1/2" (Q1) Join these to opposite sides of the 40" strip to = 93".

Cut remainder into 2 1/2" wide strips. From these, cut:
  - Four - 2 1/2" x 4 1/2" (D20, E20)
  - Four - 2 1/2" x 4 1/4" (D16, E16)
  - Four - 2 1/2" x 4" (A2)
- **Fifty-three 2 1/2" wide strips. Six strips for Strip Sets 1, 2, and 3. From remainder, cut:**
  - One - 2 1/2" x 40" (Q4)
  - Two - 2 1/2" x 27 1/2" (Q4) Join these to opposite sides of the 40" strip to = 93".
  - Eight - 2 1/2" x 26 1/2" (A23, B20, C20)
  - Four - 2 1/2" x 25 1/2" (D25, E25)
  - Eight - 2 1/2" x 25" (A22, F20, G20)
  - Eight - 2 1/2" x 24" (B18, C18)
  - Four - 2 1/2" x 22 3/4" (A19)
  - Four - 2 1/2" x 21 1/2" (F21, G21)
  - Four - 2 1/2" x 21 1/4" (A18)
  - Eight - 2 1/2" x 20" (D24, E24, F18, G18)
  - Two - 2 1/2" x 16" (Q3)
  - Four - 2 1/2" x 6 3/4" (B2, C2)
  - Eight - 2 1/2" x 6 5/8" (D2, D10, E2, E10)
  - Thirty-six - 2 1/2" x 5 1/2" (A3, B3, C3, D3, D6, E3, E6, F3, F6, F8, F12, F14, G3, G6, G8, G12, G14)
  - Thirty-two - 2 1/2" x 4 3/4" (A7, A8, A13, A14, B6, B9, B12, B14, C6, C9, C12, C14)
  - Twelve - 2 1/2" x 3 1/4" (D8, D14, D18, E8, E14, E18)
  - Four - 2 1/2" x 2 3/4" (F2, G2)

FROM FABRIC IV, CUT: (GREEN HOMESPUN CHECK)
- **Eighteen 3 1/4" wide strips. From these, cut:**
  - Four - 3 1/4" x 25" (A21)
  - Two - 3 1/4" x 24" (B19)
  - Two - 3 1/4" x 20" (G19)
  - Four - 3 1/4" x 16" (D12, E12)
  - Four - 3 1/4" x 15" (B10, C10)
  - Sixteen - 3 1/4" x 14 1/2" (A11, B11, C11, D13, E13, F11, G11)
  - Four - 3 1/4" x 12 1/4" (A10)
  - Four - 3 1/4" x 11" (F10, G10)

FROM FABRIC V, CUT: (RED HOMESPUN CHECK)
- **Six 3 1/4" wide strips. From these, cut:**
  - Four - 3 1/4" x 8 1/4" (B4, C4)
  - Four - 3 1/4" x 8 1/8" (D4, E4)
  - Sixteen - 3 1/4" x 7 3/4" (A5, B5, C5, D5, E5, F5, G5)
  - Four - 3 1/4" x 5 1/2" (A4)
  - Four - 3 1/4" x 4 1/4" (F4, G4)

FROM FABRIC VI, CUT: (DK. GOLD HOMESPUN CHECK)
- **Twenty-nine 3 1/4" wide strips. From these, cut:**
  - Two - 3 1/4" x 24" (C19)
  - Four - 3 1/4" x 22 3/4" (A20)
  - Eight - 3 1/4" x 21 3/4" (B16, C16, D22, E22)
  - Twelve - 3 1/4" x 21 1/4" (A17, B17, C17, F17, G17)
  - Six - 3 1/4" x 20" (D23, E23, F19)
  - Four - 3 1/4" x 19" (A16)
  - Four - 3 1/4" x 17 3/4" (F16, G16)

All seams (including strip sets) are to be sewn wrong sides together. It does not matter in which direction the seams are pressed, as they will be clipped later to form the chenille. Again, 1/2" seams are used throughout this project.

STRIP SETS

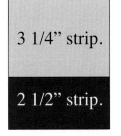

| 3 1/4" strip. |
| 2 1/2" strip. |

Strip Set 1. Make 2. Cut into 16 - 4" wide segments.

| 3 1/4" strip. |
| 2 1/2" strip. |

Strip Set 2. Make 2. Cut into 16 - 4" wide segments.

| 4" strip. |
| 2 1/2" strip. |

Strip Set 3. Make 2. Cut into 20 - 3 1/4" wide segments.

1. Each block uses at least one of the strip sets shown above. Refer to page 6 for Strip Piecing, and make the number of strip sets designated. Cut into the required amount of segments. We suggest putting each strip set into its own bag, and marking the bag with the strip set number to avoid confusion later.

BLOCK A ASSEMBLY

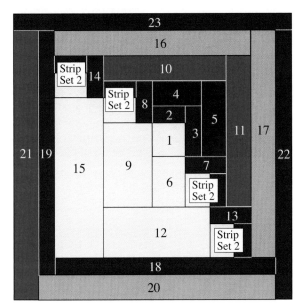

Block A. Make 4. When completed, block should measure 26 1/2" square.

1. Assembly for each block is similar, as they are pieced in numerical order. For Block A, begin by joining units 1 and 2; then add Unit 3 to right side. Join Unit 4 to the top; then add Unit 5 to the right side. Join Unit 7 and one Strip Set 2 segment; then add Unit 6 to the left side of this combination. Join these combined units to the bottom of 1-5 combined units, matching seams.

2. Join Unit 8 and one Strip Set 2 segment; then add Unit 9 to the bottom of these combined units. Join these units to the left side of combined units 1-7. Join Unit 10 to the top of the combined units; then add Unit 11 to the right side as shown.

3. Join Unit 13, and one Strip Set 2 segment; then add Unit 12 to left side of these combined units. Join these units to the bottom of other combined units. Join Unit 14 and a Strip Set 2 segment; then add Unit 15 to the bottom of these combined units. Add these units to the left side of other combined units. Join Unit 16 to the top of the block; then join Unit 17 to the right side. Join Unit 18 to the bottom; then join Unit 19 to the left side. Join Unit 20 to the bottom of the block; then add Unit 21 to the left side and Unit 22 to the right side as shown. Join Unit 23 to the top to complete the block. Make 4.

BLOCK B ASSEMBLY

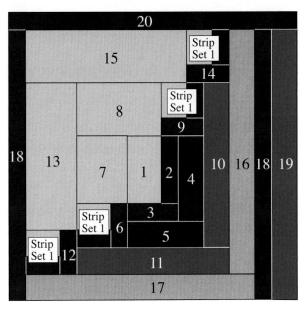

Block B. Make 2. When completed, block should measure 25 1/2" x 26 1/2".

1. For Block B, begin by joining units 1 and 2; then add Unit 3 to the bottom. Join Unit 4 to the right side; then add Unit 5 to the bottom. Join Unit 6 and one Strip Set 1 segment; then add Unit 7 to the top of this combination. Join these combined units to the left side of 1-5 combined units, matching seams.

2. Join Unit 9 and one Strip Set 1 segment; then add Unit 8 to the left side of these combined units. Join these units to the top of combined units 1-7. Join Unit 10 to the right side of the combined units; then add Unit 11 to the bottom as shown.

3. Join Unit 12, and one Strip Set 1 segment; then add Unit 13 to the top of these combined units. Join these units to the left side of the other combined units. Join Unit 14 and a Strip Set 1 segment; then add Unit 15 to the left side of these combined units. Add these units to the top of the other combined units. Join Unit 16 to the right of the block; then join Unit 17 to the bottom. Join Unit 18 to opposite sides of the block; then join Unit 19 to the right side. Join Unit 20 to the top to complete the block. Make 2.

BLOCK C ASSEMBLY

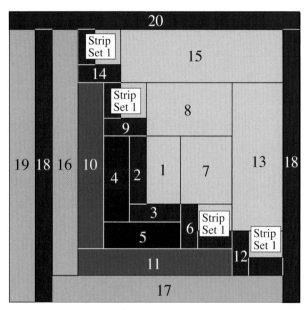

Block C. Make 2. When completed, block should measure 25 1/2" x 26 1/2".

1. Block C, is a mirror image of Block B, except for Unit 19, which is green in Block B, and dark gold in Block C. Refer to the instructions for Block B, keeping in mind that it is a mirror image, so refer to Block C diagram frequently for correct positioning of the units.

BLOCKS D AND E ASSEMBLY

1. Blocks D and E, are mirror images. These instructions for positioning of the units are for Block D. Refer to Block E diagram for correct placement of the units.

2. To begin, join units 1 and 2; then add Unit 3 to the top of these combined units. Join Unit 4 to the left side of the 1-3 combined units, and Unit 5 to the top. Join Unit 6 and one Strip Set 3 segment; then add Unit 7 to the bottom of

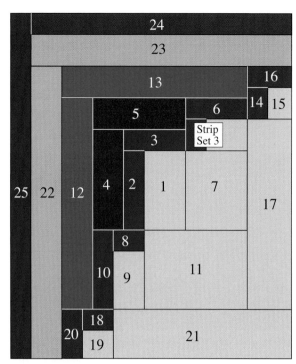

Block D. Make 2. When completed, block should measure 21 1/2" x 25 1/2".

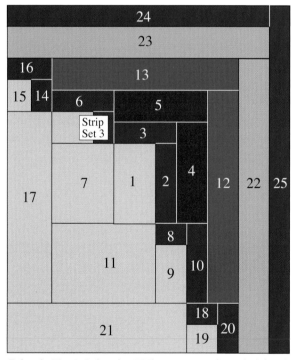

Block E. Make 2. When completed, block should measure 21 1/2" x 25 1/2".

these combined units. Join these units to the right side of combined units 1-5. Join units 8 and 9; then add Unit 10 to the left side of the 8-9 combination, and Unit 11 to the right side. Add to the bottom of other combined units, matching seams. Join Unit 12 to the left side of the combined units; then add Unit 13 to the top.

3. Join units 14 and 15; then add Unit 16 to the top of the

14-15 combination. Join Unit 17 to the bottom; then add these combined units to the right side of the block. Join units 18 and 19; then join Unit 20 to the left side of the 18-19 combination, and Unit 21 to the right side. Join these units to the bottom of the block.

4. Join Unit 22 to the left side of the block; then add Unit 23 to the top. Join Unit 24 to the top of the block; then add Unit 25 to the left side to complete the block. Make 2 of Block D, and 2 of Block E.

BLOCKS F AND G ASSEMBLY

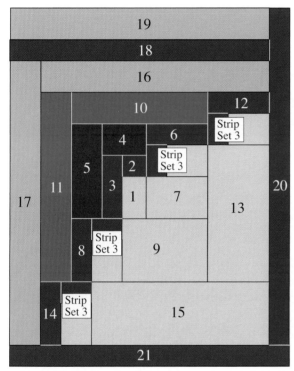

Block F. Make 2. When completed, block should measure 21 1/2" x 26 1/2".

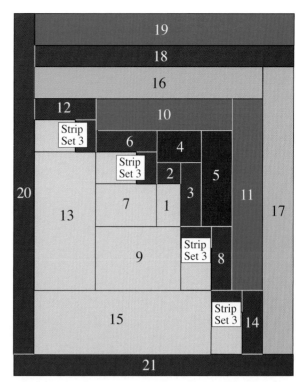

Block G. Make 2. When completed, block should measure 21 1/2" x 26 1/2".

1. Blocks F and G, are mirror images. The only difference is in Unit 19, which is dark gold in Block F, and green in Block G. These instructions for positioning of the units are for Block F. Refer to Block G diagram for correct placement of the units for that block.

2. To begin, join units 1 and 2; then add Unit 3 to the left side of these combined units. Join Unit 4 to the top of the 1-3 combined units, and Unit 5 to the left side. Join Unit 6 and one Strip Set 3 segment; then add Unit 7 to the bottom of these combined units. Join these units to the right side of combined units 1-5. Join Unit 8 and one Strip Set 3 segment; then add Unit 9 to the right side of these combined units. Join these units to the bottom of other combined units, matching seams. Join Unit 10 to the top of the combined units; then add Unit 11 to the left side.

3. Join Unit 12 and one Strip Set 3 segment; then add Unit 13 to the bottom of this combination. Join these combined

units to the right side of the block. Join Unit 14 and one Strip Set 3 segment; then add Unit 15 to the right side of these combined units. Join these units to the bottom of the block.

4. Join Unit 16 to the top of the block; then add Unit 17 to the left side. Join units 18 and 19; then add them to the top of the block. Join Unit 20 to the right side; then add Unit 21 to the bottom to complete the block. Make 2 of Block F, and 2 of Block G.

DUVET COVER TOP ASSEMBLY

If you are making the Duvet Cover using osnaburg behind each piece, DO NOT use it on any of the "Q" units,

We clipped the seams on the individual blocks before sewing the blocks into the duvet cover. To do so, clip seams approximately 1/4" from the seams, and 1/4" apart, including where seams are matched and overlap. DO NOT clip outside edges.

1. Beginning with the top row, join blocks D, B, C and E as shown in quilt diagram on page 96. For Row 2, join blocks F, A, A, and G. Join the two rows together, matching seams.

2. For Row 3, join blocks G, A, A, and F, again referring to quilt diagram for correct placement of blocks. For the

Q3 ←   Q4 ↑   Q2   Q3 →

Q2 Fold line.

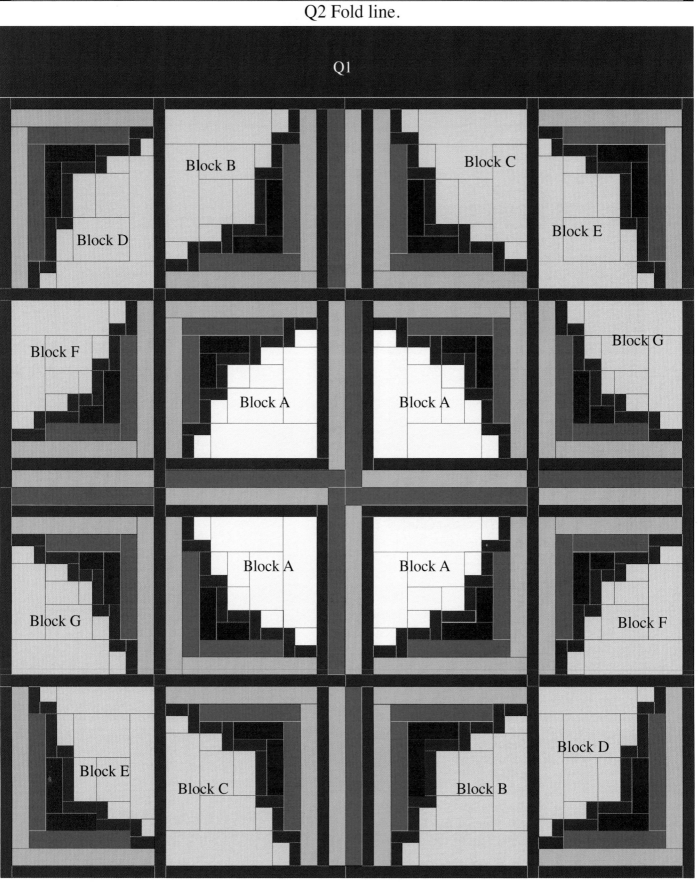

bottom row, join blocks E, C, B and D as shown. Join the bottom row to Row 3, matching all seams; then join the top section to the bottom section, again matching seams.

3. When piecing Unit Q1, seams are sewn right sides together. We serged these seams to keep them from raveling, as they are on the inside. Before joining this unit to the top of the blocks, make a hem on one long side by turning under 1/4"; then another 1/4" and top stitch on right side. Join Unit Q1 across the top of the pieced blocks, *wrong sides together,* again using 1/2" seam. Clip this seam as you would for the blocks.

DUVET COVER FLAP ASSEMBLY

1. To piece the flap, join the Q2 units right sides together as in Step 3 above. Join Unit Q3 (right sides together) to opposite ends of Unit Q2.
2. Fold the flap in half lengthwise (see diagram on page 96 for fold line) wrong sides together, and raw edges matching. Press the fold line. Join Unit Q4, right sides together, raw edges matching, and press seam towards Q4.
3. Refer to diagram below, and place completed flap as shown to complete the Duvet Cover top.

DUVET COVER BACKING

1. For the backing, cut one 40" x 93" strip, and two 34 1/2" x 93" strips. Join the 34 1/2" strips to top and bottom of the 40" strip, right sides together. As the backing seams will be on the inside, to prevent raveling, serge the seams.
2. With right sides facing, place backing on Duvet Cover top. PIN! PIN! PIN! Stitch around all four sides, being careful not to catch hemmed edge of Unit Q1 in stitching. Serge the seams to keep them from raveling.
3. Turn right side out. Now it's time to wash. We recommend washing and drying at a laundromat with COLD water. We also suggest not drying fully to prevent any shrinkage.
4. Sew snaps on under side of flap, and along Unit Q1, evenly spaced. Sew on decorative wooden buttons.

A Great Tip From Susan......

Do not be afraid to wash! Take a devoted friend with you for moral support, and make certain that you sweep the strings from the floor, so bring a broom! Don't worry, it will turn out great!

CUTTING FOR PILLOWCASES

Finished size: 20" x 32". Use 1/2" seams.

From Fabric V, cut:
     * Two - 28" x 41" (pillowcase body)
From Fabric II, cut:
     * Two - 12" x 41" (pillowcase border)

Assembly instructions for one pillowcase:
1. Place short ends of 12" x 41" strip of Fabric II right sides together and stitch the ends, forming a circle. Fold the 12" circle in half lengthwise, wrong sides together, matching raw edges, and press.
2. Fold the 28" x 41" piece of Fabric V right sides together for a measurement of 20 1/2" x 28". Stitch raw edges together as shown in diagram on page 23. Serge the seam. Turn right side out.
3. Place 6" circular border around raw edge of pillowcase. Stitch around the circle using 1/2" seam. Serge the seam. Fold out and press. Decorate with six 7/8" wooden buttons sewn on the border.

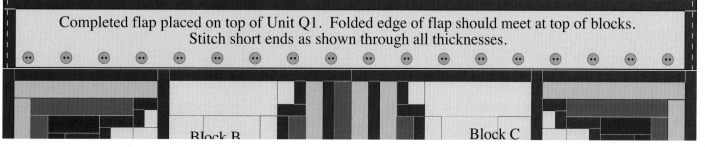

Completed flap placed on top of Unit Q1. Folded edge of flap should meet at top of blocks. Stitch short ends as shown through all thicknesses.

Block B   Block C

Circling Tulips

This is a beautiful quilt when completed, but not suggested for beginners. The blocks are not difficult, and are repetitive, however, a lot of concentration is involved regarding color changes in the blocks, as the dark against light was carefully planned. The decorative quilted shams add a lot to the look, and are easy to make.

Quilt Finishes To: 97 3/4" x 103"

Techniques Used: Diagonal corners, diagonal ends, strip sets used as diagonal corners and diagonal ends.

MATERIALS

Fabric I (burgundy print)
Need 101 5/8"   3 yards

Fabric II (dusty rose print)
Need 175 3/8"   5 yards

Fabric III (pink print)
Need 130 3/8"   3 3/4 yards

Fabric IV (white on ivory print)
Need 54 7/8"   1 5/8 yards

Fabric V (bright yellow print)
Need 54 7/8"   1 5/8 yards

Fabric VI (light green print)
Need 43 1/4"   1 3/8 yards

Fabric VII (medium green print)
Need 67 3/8"   2 yards

Fabric VIII (dark green print)
Need 23 7/8"   7/8 yard

Backing   9 yards

CUTTING

 FROM FABRIC I, CUT: (BURGUNDY PRINT)
- **One 9 3/8" wide strip. From this, cut:**
  * Eight - 4 7/8" x 9 3/8" (7)
- **One 8 3/8" wide strip From this, cut:**
  * Sixteen - 1 1/2" x 8 3/8" (N25, O25)
  Stack this cut:
  * Sixteen - 1 3/4" x 4" (P7, Q7, R7, S7)
- **One 8 1/4" wide strip. From this, cut:**
  * Eight - 4 3/4" x 8 1/4" (8)
- **One 7 5/8" wide strip. From this, cut:**
  * Eight - 3 3/4" x 7 5/8" (V13)
  Stack this cut:
  * Thirty- 1 1/2" squares ((P1a, P2a, P3a, Q1a, Q2a, Q3a, R1a, R2a, R3a, S1a, S2a, S3a)
- **One 4 3/4" wide strip. From this, cut:**
  * Sixteen - 1 1/2" x 4 3/4" (N15, O15)
- **One 4 1/2" wide strip. From this and scrap, cut:**
  * Sixteen - 1 3/8" x 4 1/2" (P5, Q5, R5, S5)
  Stack these cuts:
  * Eight - 2 1/4" squares (T10, U10, W10, X10)
  * Sixteen - 1 1/2" sq. (add to 1 1/2" sq. above)
- **One 4 3/8" wide strip. From this, cut:**
  * Eight - 1 1/4" x 4 3/8" (V3, V9)
  Stack this cut:
  * Sixteen - 1 5/8" squares (P4, Q4, R4, S4)
- **Two 3 7/8" strips. From these, cut:**
  * Forty - 2" x 3 7/8" (N12, N20, O12, O20, V2, V8)
- **One 3 3/4" wide strip. From this, cut:**
  * Sixteen - 1 1/2" x 3 3/4" (N10, O10)
  Stack this cut:
  * Sixteen - 1 3/4" x 1 7/8" (N2, O2)
- **Two 3 3/8" wide strips. From these, cut:**
  * Sixteen - 3" x 3 3/8" (N19, O19)
  * Eight - 1 3/4" x 3 3/8" (T6, U6, W6, X6)
  * Sixteen - 7/8" x 3" (N14, O14)
- **Three 2 3/8" wide strips. From these, cut:**
  * Forty - 2 3/8" sq. (N18, N24, O18, O24, V6, V12)
- **Two 2 1/8" wide strips. From these, cut:**
  * Thirty-two - 2 1/8" squares (N17, O17, P12, Q12, R12, S12)
- **Three 2" wide strips. From these, cut:**
  * Sixteen - 2" x 3 1/2" (P8, Q8, R8, S8)
  * Sixteen - 2" squares (P11, Q11, R11, S11)
  * Eight - 1 7/8" x 2" (T4, U4, W4, X4)
  * Eight - 1 3/4" squares (A9, B9, G9, H9, N9, N23, O9, O23, T9, U9, V5, V11, W9, X9)
- **Six 1 3/4" wide strips. From these, cut:**
  * Sixteen - 1 3/4" x 3 1/8" (N3, O3)
  * Seventy-two - 1 3/4" sq. (add to 1 3/4" sq. above)
  * Eight - 1 1/8" x 2 1/2" (T1a, U1a, W1a, X1a)
- **Four 1 1/2" wide strips. From these, cut:**
  * Four - 1 1/2" x 24 3/4" (V14)
  * Eighteen - 1 1/2" sq. (add to 1 1/2" sq. above)
- **Two 1 1/8" wide strip. From these, cut:**
  * Thirty-two - 1 1/8" x 2 1/4" (N8, O8)

 FROM FABRIC II, CUT: (DUSTY ROSE PRINT)
- **One 9 3/4" wide strip. From this, cut:**
  * Two 9 3/4" squares (9) Cut in half diagonally.
  * Thirty-two - 2 3/8" squares (G17, G18, G24, H17, H18, H24)
- **Five 8 1/8" wide strips. From these, cut:**
  * Sixteen - 7 3/4" x 8 1/8" (2)
  * Sixteen - 4" x 8 1/8" (3)
  * Twenty-five - 1 1/2" sq. (J1a, J2a, J3a, K1a, K2a, K3a, L1a, L2a, L3a, M1a, M2a, M3a)
- **One 5" wide strip. From this, cut:**
  * Sixteen - 1 3/4" x 5" (G15, H15)
  * Twenty-four - 1 1/2" sq. (add to 1 1/2" sq. above)
- **Four 4 3/4" wide strips. From these, cut:**
  * Thirty-two - 4 3/4" squares (1)
- **Two 4 1/2" wide strips. From these and scrap, cut:**
  * Thirty-two - 1 3/8" x 4 1/2" (J5, K5, L5, M5)
  * Sixteen - 1 3/4" squares (G23, H23)
- **Two 4" wide strips. From these, cut:**
  * Thirty-two - 1 5/8" x 4" (J7, K7, L7, M7)
  * Twenty-six - 2" squares (J11, K11, L11, M11)
- **Two 3 7/8" wide strips. From these, cut:**
  * Thirty-two - 2" x 3 7/8" (G12, G20, H12, H20)
  * Twenty - 1 1/2" sq. (add to 1 1/2" sq. above)
- **One 3 3/4" wide strip. From this, cut:**
  * Sixteen - 1 3/4" x 3 3/4" (G10, H10)
  * Sixteen- 1 1/2" sq. (add to 1 1/2" sq. above)
- **Two 3 5/8" wide strips. From these, cut:**
  * Sixteen - 3" x 3 5/8" (G19, H19)
  * Twenty-four - 1 1/2" sq. (add to 1 1/2" sq. above)
- **Six 3 1/2" wide strips. From these, cut:**
  * Four - 3 1/2" x 40 1/2" (10) Piece two together to equal two 80 1/2" lengths.
  * Thirty-two - 2" x 3 1/2" (J8, K8, L8, M8)
  * Nineteen - 1 1/2" sq. (add to 1 1/2" sq. above)
- **One 2 3/8" wide strip. From this, cut:**
  * Sixteen - 2 3/8" sq,. (add to 2 3/8" sq. above)
- **Eleven 2 1/2" wide strips for straight-grain binding**
- **Two 2 1/8" wide strips. From these, cut:**
  * Thirty-two - 2 1/8" squares (J12, K12, L12, M12)
  * Six - 2" squares (add to 2" squares above)
- **Two 1 3/4" wide strips. From these, cut:**
  * Sixteen - 1 3/4" x 3 1/8" (G3, H3)
  * Sixteen - 1 3/4" x 1 7/8" (G2, H2)
- **Two 1 5/8" wide strips. From these, cut:**
  * Thirty-two - 1 5/8" squares (J4, K4, L4, M4)
  * Nine - 1 1/8" x 3" (G14, H14)
- **Three 1 1/8" wide strips. From these, cut:**
  * Seven - 1 1/8" x 3" (add to G14, H14 above)
  * Thirty-two - 1 1/8" x 2 1/4" (G8, H8)

 FROM FABRIC III, CUT: (PINK PRINT)
- **Five 8 1/8" wide strips. From these, cut:**
  * Sixteen - 7 3/4" x 8 1/8" (5)
  * Sixteen - 4" x 8 1/8" (6)
  * Twenty-five- 1 1/2" squares (C1a,C2a,C3a, D1a, D2a, D3a, E1a, E2a, E3a, F1a, F2a, F3a)
- **One 5" wide strip. From this, cut:**
  * Sixteen - 1 3/4" x 5" (A15, B15)

100

* Twenty-four - 1 1/2" sq. (add to 1 1/2" sq. above)
- **Four 4 3/4" wide strips. From these, cut:**
  * Thirty-two - 4 3/4" squares (4)
- **Two 4 1/2" wide strips. From these and scrap, cut:**
  * Thirty-two - 1 3/8" x 4 1/2" (C5, D5, E5, F5)
  Stack these cuts:
  * Sixteen - 1 3/4" squares (A23, B23)
  * Forty-two - 1 1/2" sq. (add to 1 1/2" sq. above)
- **Two 4" wide strips. From these, cut:**
  * Thirty-two - 1 5/8" x 4" (C7, D7, E7, F7)
  * Twenty-six - 2" squares (C11, D11, E11, F11)
- **Two 3 7/8" wide strips. From these, cut:**
  * Thirty-two - 2" x 3 7/8" (A12, A20, B12, B20)
  * Twenty - 1 1/2" sq. (add to 1 1/2" sq. above)
- **One 3 3/4" wide strip. From this, cut:**
  * Sixteen - 1 3/4" x 3 3/4" (A10, B10)
  * Four - 1 1/2" squares (add to 1 1/2" sq. above)
- **Two 3 5/8" wide strips. From these, cut:**
  * Sixteen - 3" x 3 5/8" (A19, B19)
  * Sixteen - 1 3/4" x 3 1/8" (A3, B3)
- **Two 3 1/2" wide strips. From these, cut:**
  * Thirty-two - 2" x 3 1/2" (C8, D8, E8, F8)
  * Six - 2" squares (add to 2" sq. above)
- **Three 2 3/8" wide strips. From these, cut:**
  * Forty-eight - 2 3/8" squares (A17, A18, A24, B17, B18, B24)
- **Two 2 1/8" wide strips. From these, cut:**
  * Thirty-two - 2 1/8" squares (C12, D12, E12, F12)
- **Two 1 3/4" wide strips. From these, cut:**
  * Sixteen - 1 3/4" x 1 7/8" (A2, B2)
- **Two 1 5/8" wide strips. From these, cut:**
  * Thirty-two - 1 5/8" squares (C4, D4, E4, F4)
  * Nine - 1 1/8" x 3" (A14, B14)
- **One 1 1/2" wide strips. From this, cut:**
  * Thirteen - 1 1/2" sq. (add to 1 1/2" sq. above)
- **Three 1 1/8" wide strips. From these, cut:**
  * Seven - 1 1/8" x 3" (add to A14, B14 above)
  * Thirty-two - 1 1/8" x 2 1/4" (A8, B8)

◻ **FROM FABRIC IV, CUT: (WHITE ON IVORY PRINT)**
- **One 4 7/8" wide strip. From this, cut:**
  * Twenty-eight - 1 1/8" x 4 7/8" (B7, H7, O7, U8, W8)
  * Fifteen - 1 1/2" squares (C1b, D1b, L1b, M1b, P1b, Q1b)
- **Seven 4 1/4" wide strips. From these, cut:**
  * Forty - 2 1/2" x 4 1/4" (E1, F1, J1, K1, R1, S1)
  * Eighty - 1 1/2" x 4 1/4" (C2, C3, D2, D3, L2, L3, M2, M3, P2, P3, Q2, Q3)
  * Twenty-four - 1 1/8" x 4 1/4" (B6, H6, O6)
  * Thirty-two - 1 1/2" sq. (add to 1 1/2" sq. above)
- **One 3" wide strip. From this, cut:**
  * Twenty-four - 1 5/8" x 3" (A5, G5, N5)
- **Three 2 7/8" wide strips. From these, cut:**
  * Four - 2 1/4" x 2 7/8" (U1, W1)
  * Fifty-two - 1 5/8" x 2 7/8" (B4, B5a, H4, H5a, O4, O5a, U7, W7)
  * Four - 1 5/8" squares (T1b, X1b)
  * Four - 1 1/8" x 1 7/8" (U3, W3)
- **Three 1 7/8" wide strips. From these, cut:**

* Twenty-eight - 1 7/8" sq. (A1, G1, N1, T5, X5)
* Thirty-two - 1 5/8" x 1 7/8" (A4a, G4a, N4a, T2, T7a, X2, X7a)
- **Two 1 1/2" wide strips. From these, cut:**
  * Thirty-three - 1 1/2" sq. (add to 1 1/2" sq. above)

◻ **FROM FABRIC V, CUT: (BRIGHT YELLOW PRINT)**
- **One 4 7/8" wide strip. From this, cut:**
  * Twenty-eight - 1 1/8" x 4 7/8" (A7, G7, N7, T8, X8)
  * Fifteen - 1 1/2" squares (E1b, F1b, J1b, K1b, R1b, S1b)
- **Seven 4 1/4" wide strips. From these, cut:**
  * Forty - 2 1/2" x 4 1/4" (C1, D1, L1, M1, P1, Q1)
  * Eighty - 1 1/2" x 4 1/4" (E2, E3, F2, F3, J2, J3, K2, K3, R2, R3, S2, S3)
  * Twenty-four - 1 1/8" x 4 1/4" (A6, G6, N6)
  * Thirty-two - 1 1/2" sq. (add to 1 1/2" sq. above)
- **One 3" wide strip. From this, cut:**
  * Twenty-four - 1 5/8" x 3" (B5, H5, O5)
- **Three 2 7/8" wide strips. From these, cut:**
  * Four - 2 1/4" x 2 7/8" (T1, X1)
  * Fifty-two - 1 5/8" x 2 7/8" (A4, A5a, G4, G5a, N4, N5a, T7, X7)
- **Three 1 7/8" wide strips. From these, cut:**
  * Twenty-eight - 1 7/8" sq. (B1, H1, O1, U5, W5)
  * Thirty-two - 1 5/8" x 1 7/8" (B4a, H4a, O4a, U2, U7a, W2, W7a)
  * Four - 1 1/8" x 1 7/8" (T3, X3)
  * Four - 1 5/8" squares (U1b, W1b)
- **Two 1 1/2" wide strips. From these, cut:**
  * Thirty-three - 1 1/2" sq. (add to 1 1/2" sq. above)

▦ **FROM FABRIC VI, CUT: (LT. GREEN PRINT)**
- **Two 4 3/8" wide strips. From these, cut:**
  * Forty-four - 1 1/2" x 4 3/8" (H13, H21, N13, N21, V1)
  * Eight - 1 5/8" x 4 1/8" (L10, M10)
- **One 4 1/4" wide strip. From this, cut:**
  * Four - 1 5/8" x 4 1/4" (G16)
  * Eight - 1 5/8" x 4" (O16)
  * Four - 1 5/8" x 3 3/4" (V10)
  * Four - 1 5/8" x 2 1/2" (U1a, X1a)
  From scrap cut:
  * Eight - 1 5/8" squares (L6, M6)
- **Two 4" wide strips. From these, cut:**
  * Forty - 1 1/2" x 4" (J9, K9, P9, Q9, R9, S9)
  * Eighteen - 2" squares (H12b, H20b, J8b, K8b, N12b, N20b, P8b, Q8b, R8b, S8b, V2b)
- **One 3" wide strip. From this, cut:**
  * Twelve - 1 5/8" x 3" (G22, O22)
  Stack this cut:
  * Twenty-six - 1 1/2" sq. (H12c, H20c, J8c, K8c, N12c, N20c, P8c, Q8c, R8c, S8c, V2c)
- **Two 2 1/2" wide strips. From these, cut:**
  * Thirty-six - 2" x 2 1/2" (G12a, G20a, L8a, M8a, O12a, O20a, V8a)
- **Four 2" wide strips. From these, cut:**
  * Sixty-six - 2" squares (add to 2" sq. above)
  * Eighteen - 1 1/2" sq. (add to 1 1/2" sq. above)

- **Two 1 5/8" wide strip. From these, cut:**
  * Twenty-four - 1 5/8" x 2 1/4" (G8, O8)
  * Four - 1 5/8" x 1 3/4" (G11)
  * Eight - 1 1/2" x 1 5/8" (O11)
- **Two 1 1/2" wide strips. From these, cut:**
  * Forty - 1 1/2" squares (add to 1 1/2" sq. above)

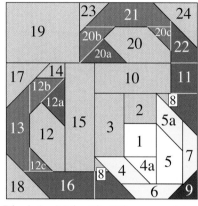 FROM FABRIC VII, CUT: (MED. GREEN PRINT)

- **Eleven 2" wide strips. From these, cut:**
  * 100 - 2" x 2 1/2" (B12a, B20a, E8a, F8a, H12a, H20a, J8a, K8a, N12a, N20a, P8a, Q8a, R8a, S8a, V2a)
  * Eighty-four - 2" squares (A12b, A20b, C8b, D8b, G12b, G20b, L8b, M8b, O12b, O20b, V8b)
  * Four - 1 5/8" x 3 3/4" (V4)
- **Fifteen 1 5/8" wide strips. From these, cut:**
  * Thirty-two - 1 5/8" x 4 1/4" (B16, H16, P10, Q10, R10, S10)
  * Thirty-two - 1 5/8" x 4 1/8" (E10, F10, J10, K10)
  * Eight - 1 5/8" x 4" (N16)
  * Twenty-four - 1 5/8" x 3" (B22, H22, N22)
  * Four - 1 5/8" x 2 1/2" (T1a, W1a)
  * Forty-eight - 1 5/8" x 2 1/4" (B8, H8, N8)
  * Sixteen - 1 5/8" x 1 3/4" (B11, H11)
  * Forty-eight - 1 5/8" squares (E6, F6, J6, K6, P6, Q6, R6, S6)
  * Eight - 1 1/2" x 1 5/8" (N11)
- **Fourteen 1 1/2" wide strips. From these, cut:**
  * Fifty-two - 1 1/2" x 4 3/8" (A13, A21, G13, G21, O13, O21, V7)
  * Thirty-two - 1 1/2" x 4" (C9, D9, L9, M9)
  * Eighty-four - 1 1/2" squares (A12c, A20c, C8c, D8c, G12c, G20c, L8c, M8c, O12c, O20c, V8c)

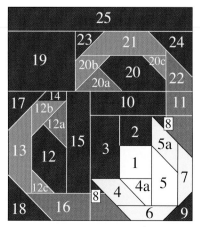 FROM FABRIC VIII, CUT: (DK. GREEN PRINT)

- **Four 2" wide strips. From these, cut:**
  * Forty-eight - 2" x 2 1/2" (A12a, A20a, C8a, D8a)
  * Sixteen - 2" squares (B12b, B20b E8b, F8b)
- **Seven 1 5/8" wide strips. From these, cut:**
  * Twelve - 1 5/8" x 4 1/4" (A16)
  * Twenty-four - 1 5/8" x 4 1/8" (C10, D10)
  * Twelve - 1 5/8" x 3" (A22)
  * Twenty-four - 1 5/8" x 2 1/4" (A8)
  * Twelve - 1 5/8" x 1 3/4" (A11)
  * Twenty-four - 1 5/8" squares (C6, D6)
- **Three 1 1/2" wide strips. From these, cut:**
  * Eight - 1 1/2" x 4 3/8" (B13, B21)
  * Eight - 1 1/2" x 4" (E9, F9)
  * Sixteen - 1 1/2" squares (B12c, B20c, E8c, F8c)

ASSEMBLY OF BLOCKS A, G, and N

Although there are many blocks in this quilt, most are assembled in the same way, and are represented with graphics. The major differences are color changes in the flowers and leaves. Refer to the graphics frequently for these changes. It is essential that your pieces are organized in a logical manner as they are cut. Refer to page 10 for the best way to organize your cut pieces.

When making this quilt, we discovered that placing the individual blocks into their own bag, marked with their block letter avoids confusion at the end when it is time to assemble the quilt top.

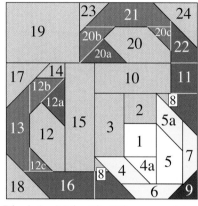

Block A. Make 12. When completed, block should measure 8 5/8" square.

1. Refer to the block diagrams, and the illustrations on page 103. Follow the diagrams and instructions for assembly the three sections.
2. Join combined units 1-11 to combined units 12-18, matching leaf seam. Join combined units 19-24

to the top of the tulip section, again matching leaf seams. For Block N, join Unit 25 to the top.
3. Make 12 of Block A, 4 of Block G, and 8 of Block N.

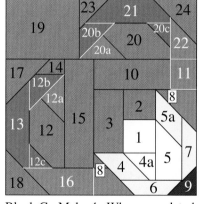

Block G. Make 4. When completed, block should measure 8 5/8" square.

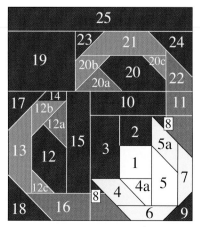

Block N. Make 8. When completed, block should measure 8 3/8" x 9 3/8".

Making units 1 thru 11 for Blocks A, G, and N.
Refer to block diagrams for color changes.

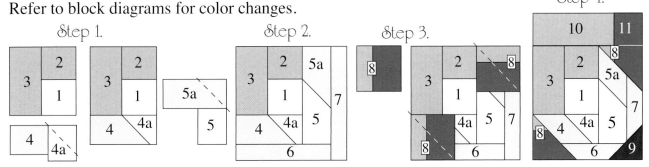

This diagram is for Block A. Assembly of these units, for all three blocks is the same. Refer to the block diagrams for unit color changes.

Step 1. Use diagonal end technique to make one of units 4 and 5. Join units 1 and 2; then add Unit 3 as shown. Join Unit 4 to bottom, matching seams.
Step 2. Join Unit 5 to side of the 1-4 units; then join Unit 6 to the bottom. Join Unit 7 to the right side.
Step 3. For block A, Unit 8, join 1 1/8" x 2 1/4" strip of Fabric III with 1 5/8" x 2 1/4" strip of Fabric VIII.
For Block G, Unit 8, join 1 1/8" x 2 1/4" strip of Fabric II with 1 5/8" x 2 1/4" strip of Fabric VI.
For Block N, Unit 8, join 1 1/8" x 2 1/4" strip of Fabric I with 1 5/8" x 2 1/4" strip of Fabric VII.
These units now become diagonal corners. Refer to "Strip sets used as diagonal corners" on page 7, and the diagrams above.
Place the strip set diagonal corners as shown above with raw edges matching. Stitch diagonal, trim seam and press.
Step 4. Join units 10 and 11. Join these combined units to the top of the tulip, matching leaf seam.

Making units 12 thru 18 for Blocks A, G, and N. Refer to block diagrams for color changes.

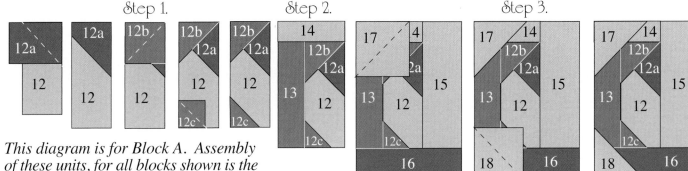

This diagram is for Block A. Assembly of these units, for all blocks shown is the same. Refer to the block diagrams for unit color changes.

Step 1. Use diagonal end technique to make one of unit 12. Join diagonal corners in alphabetical order as shown.
Step 2. Join Unit 13 to the left side of Unit 12; then join Unit 14 to the top.
Step 3. Join Unit 15 to side of combined units 12-14; then add Unit 16 to the bottom. Join diagonal corner, Unit 17 to top corner as shown, raw edges matching. Trim center seam and press. Join diagonal corner, Unit 18 to bottom corner. Trim seam and press.

Making units 19 thru 24 for Blocks A, G, and N. Refer to block diagrams for color changes.

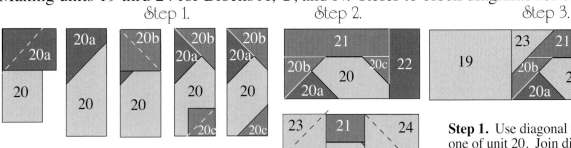

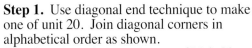

This diagram is for Block A. Assembly of these units, for all blocks shown is the same. Refer to the block diagrams for unit color changes.

Step 1. Use diagonal end technique to make one of unit 20. Join diagonal corners in alphabetical order as shown.
Step 2. Join Unit 21 to the top of Unit 20; then join Unit 22 to the side. Join diagonal corners 23 and 24. Trim seams and press
Step 3. Join Unit 19 to the side as shown.

ASSEMBLY OF BLOCKS B, H, and O

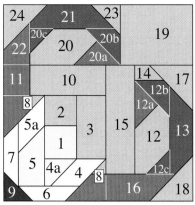
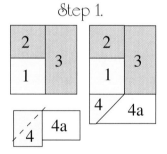

Block B. Make 4. When completed, block should measure 8 5/8" square.

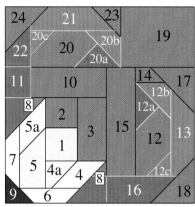
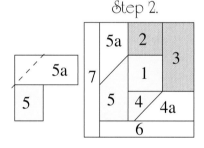

Block H. Make 12. When completed, block should measure 8 5/8" square.

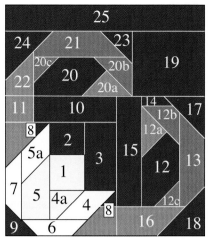
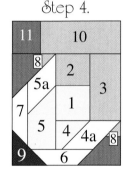

Block O. Make 8. When completed, block should measure 8 3/8" x 9 3/8".

1. Refer to the block diagrams, and the illustrations below and on the following page. Follow the diagrams and instructions to assemble the three sections. The assembly is the same as for blocks A, G, and N, except that they are mirror images.
2. Join combined units 1-11 to combined units 12-18, matching leaf seam. Join combined units 19-24 to the top of the tulip section, again matching leaf seams. For Block O , join Unit 25 to the top.
3. Make 4 of Block B, 12 of Block H, and 8 of Block N.

Making units 1 thru 11 for Blocks B, H, and O.

Step 1.   Step 2.   Step 3.   Step 4.

Assembly of these units, for all three blocks is the same. Refer to the block diagrams for unit color changes.

Steps 1, 2, and 4 assembly is the same as on page 103, except they are mirror images. Step 3 below gives correct fabrics for Unit 8.
Step 3. For block B, Unit 8, join 1 1/8" x 2 1/4" strip of Fabric III with 1 5/8" x 2 1/4" strip of Fabric VII.
For Block H, Unit 8, join 1 1/8" x 2 1/4" strip of Fabric II with 1 5/8" x 2 1/4" strip of Fabric VII.
For Block O, Unit 8, join 1 1/8" x 2 1/4" strip of Fabric I with 1 5/8" x 2 1/4" strip of Fabric VI.
These units now become diagonal corners. Refer to "Strip sets used as diagonal corners" on page 7, and the diagrams above.

Making units 12 thru 18 for Blocks B, H, and O. Refer to block diagrams for color changes.

Step 1.   Step 2.   Step 3.

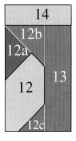
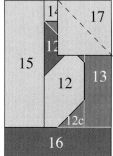
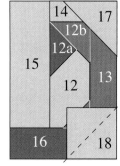
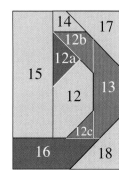
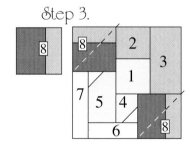

Making units 19 thru 24 for Blocks B, H, and O. Refer to block diagrams for color changes.

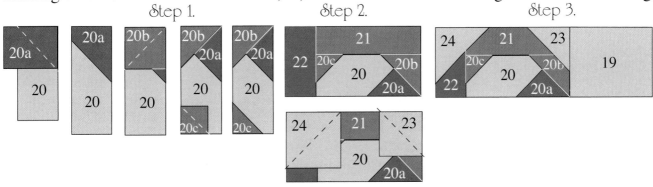

ASSEMBLY OF BLOCKS C, D, E, F, J, K, L, M, P, Q, R, AND S.

Please note: The blocks on this page, and the following page, are mirror images. Refer to the diagram for leaf assembly and the block diagrams frequently for correct placement of all units and colors.

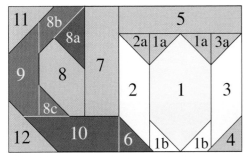

Block C. Make 12. When completed, block should measure 5 1/8" x 8 1/8".

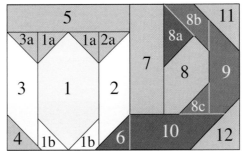

Block D. Make 12. When completed, block should measure 5 1/8" x 8 1/8".

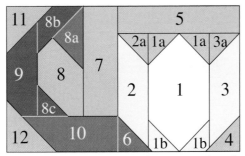

Block E. Make 4. When completed, block should measure 5 1/8" x 8 1/8".

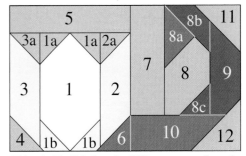

Block F. Make 4. When completed, block should measure 5 1/8" x 8 1/8".

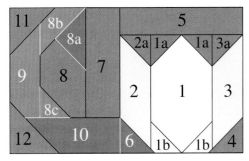

Block J. Make 12. When completed, block should measure 5 1/8" x 8 1/8".

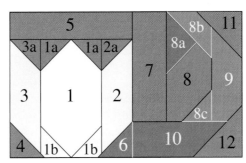

Block K. Make 12. When completed, block should measure 5 1/8" x 8 1/8".

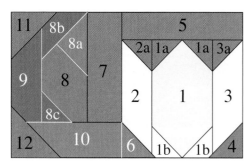

Block L. Make 4. When completed, block should measure 5 1/8" x 8 1/8".

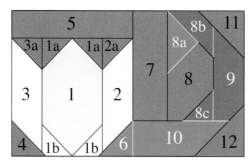

Block M. Make 4. When completed, block should measure 5 1/8" x 8 1/8".

1. To assemble the tulip for all blocks, use diagonal corner technique to make one each of units 1, 2, and 3. Join these units in a row as shown. Join Unit 5 to the top.

2. Referring to mirror image diagrams, place diagonal corners 4 and 6 in the bottom corners, right sides together, raw edges matching. Stitch the diagonals, trim seam and press.

3. Refer to diagrams and instructions below and on the following page to assemble the leaf sections.

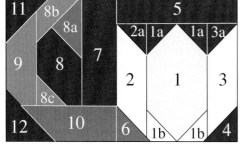

Block P. Make 4. When completed, block should measure 5 1/8" x 8 1/4".

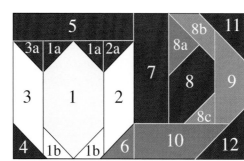

Block Q. Make 4. When completed, block should measure 5 1/8" x 8 1/4".

Join the tulip section to the leaf section to complete the blocks.

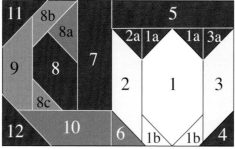

Block R. Make 4. When completed, block should measure 5 1/8" x 8 1/4".

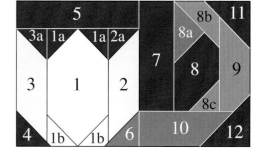

Block S. Make 4. When completed, block should measure 5 1/8" x 8 1/4".

Making units 7 thru 12 For Blocks C, E, J, L, P, and R. Refer to block diagrams for color changes.

Step 1.   *Step 2.*   *Step 3.*

This diagram is for Block C. Diagram on following page is for Block D. Assembly of these units, for all blocks shown is the same. Refer to the block diagrams for unit color changes for background, flowers and leaves.

Step 1. Use diagonal end technique to make one of unit 8. Join diagonal corners in alphabetical order as shown.
Step 2. Join Unit 9 to side of Unit 8; then join diagonal corner, Unit 11 to the top. Join Unit 10 to the bottom.
Step 3. Join diagonal corner, Unit 12 to the bottom corner. Stitch diagonal, trim seam and press.

Making units 7 thru 12 For Blocks D, F, K, M, Q, and S. Refer to block diagrams for color changes.

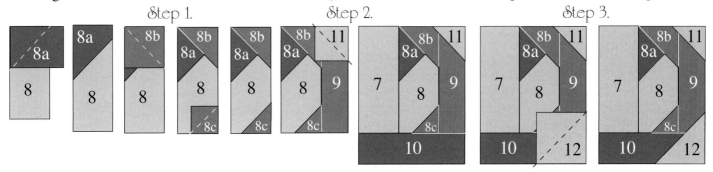

Step 1.   Step 2.   Step 3.

ASSEMBLY OF BLOCKS T, U, W, X

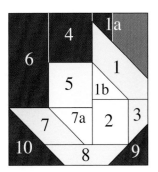 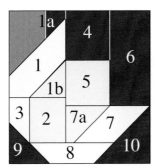 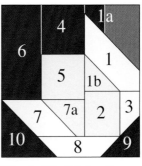 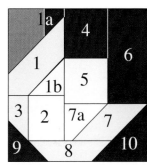

Block T. Make 2.
When completed, block
should measure
4 7/8" x 5 1/8".

Block U. Make 2.
When completed, block
should measure
4 7/8" x 5 1/8".

Block W. Make 2.
When completed, block
should measure
4 7/8" x 5 1/8".

Block X. Make 2.
When completed, block
should measure
4 7/8" x 5 1/8".

Making Blocks T and W

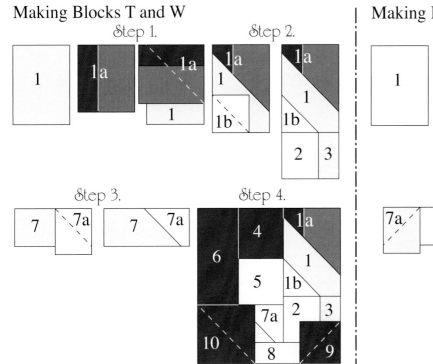

Making Blocks U and X.

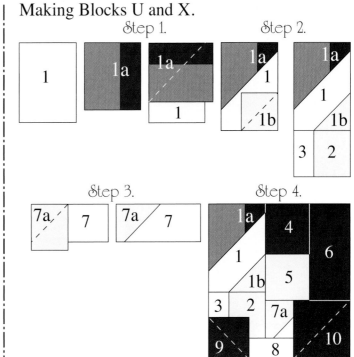

These four blocks have color changes in the flowers and leaves. They are also mirror images. Refer to these diagrams frequently for correct position of all units, and for color changes.

ASSEMBLY OF BLOCKS T, U, W, X CONTINUED

Step 1. For Block T and W, join 1 1/8" x 2 1/2" strip of Fabric I with 1 5/8" x 2 1/2" strip of Fabric VII for strip set 1a.
For Block U and X, join 1 1/8" x 2 1/2" strip of Fabric I with 1 5/8" x 2 1/2" strip of Fabric VI for strip set 1a.
For both blocks, The small strip set will now be used as a diagonal end. Place the strip set as shown, right sides facing and raw edges matching. Stitch diagonal, trim seam and press.
Step 2. Join diagonal corner, Unit 1b as shown. Trim seam and press. Join units 2 and 3; then join them to the bottom of Unit 1, matching seams.
Step 3. Use diagonal end technique to make one of Unit 7.
Step 4. Join units 4 and 5; then add Unit 6 to the side of these units as shown. Join Unit 7 to the bottom. Join the 1-3 combined units and the 4-7 combined units, matching seams. Join Unit 8 to the bottom. Join diagonal corner, Unit 9. Trim seam and press. Join diagonal corner, Unit 10 in the same manner to complete the blocks.

ASSEMBLY OF BLOCK V

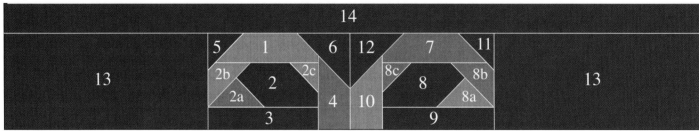

Block V. Make 4. When completed, block should measure 4 3/4" x 24 3/4".

Making the two sections of Block V.

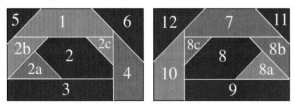

1. Leaf assembly for Block V is the same as for blocks A, B, G, H, N, and O. Refer to the mirror image diagrams on pages 103 and 105.
2. Use diagonal end technique to make units 2 and 8. Join diagonal corners in alphabetical order. For the left side leaves, join units 1, 2, and 3 in a row; then add Unit 4 to the right side. Join diagonal corners 5 and 6 to the top corners. Trim seams and press.

3. For the right side leaves, join units 7, 8, and 9 in a row; then add Unit 10 to left side. Join diagonal corners 11 and 12 as shown. Trim seams and press. Join the two leaf sections, matching seams; then add Unit 13 to opposite sides and Unit 14 to the top.

TRIANGLE ASSEMBLY FOR THE QUILT TOP

Make 4 of each. White dashed line is seam line. Black dot/dash line is cut line, and is 1/4" out from seam line.

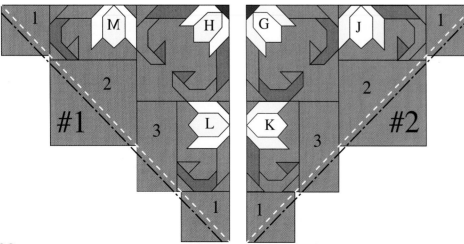

1. The center section of the quilt top is made up of large triangles. The triangles assembled on this page and on page 110 make up the quilt top center.
2. To begin, refer to triangle diagram #1. Join Unit 1 and Block M; then add Unit 2 to the bottom of Block M. Join Unit 3 and Block L. Join Block H to the top of the Unit 3-Block L combination, and Unit 1 to the bottom, lining it up along the outside edge of the block as shown. Refer to triangle dia-

gram, and join the two sections together.

3. Draw a line with water erasable pen from the top corner of Unit 1 to the bottom corner of remaining Unit 1. This is your seam line. Place your ruler on this line, and cut 1/4" away from the seam line as shown to form the triangle. Accuracy is essential here.

4. Refer to triangle diagram #2. Join Block J and Unit 1 as shown. Join Unit 2 to the bottom of Block J. Join Unit 3 and Block K; then add Block G to the top of this combination, and Unit 1 to the bottom, lining it up along the outside edge of the block as Refer to the triangle diagram, and join the two sections together. Follow Step 3 for cutting the triangle.

5. For triangle diagram #3, follow Step 2, substituting blocks K, H, and J, instead of blocks M, H, and L.

Make 8. White dashed line is seam line. Black dot/dash line is cut line, and is 1/4" out from seam line.

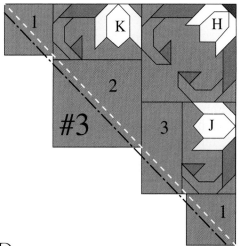

Helpful Tip: When all triangles are completed, label each one with the number shown for quick assembly of the quilt top.

TRIANGLE ASSEMBLY FOR THE QUILT TOP CONTINUED

White dashed line is seam line. Black dot/dash line is cut line, and is 1/4" out from seam line.

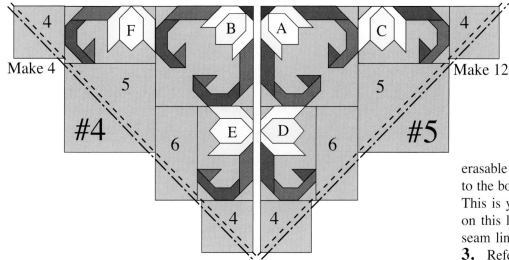

1. Refer to triangle diagram #4. Join Unit 4 and Block F; then add Unit 5 to the bottom of Block F. Join Unit 6 and Block E. Join Block B to the top of the Unit 6-Block E combination, and Unit 4 to the bottom, lining it up along the outside edge of the block as shown.

2. Draw a line with water erasable pen from the top corner of Unit 4 to the bottom corner of remaining Unit 4. This is your seam line. Place your ruler on this line, and cut 1/4" away from the seam line as shown to form the triangle.

3. Refer to triangle diagram #5. Join Unit 4 and Block C; then add Unit 5 to the bottom of Block C. Join Unit 6 and Block D. Join Block A to the top of the Unit 6-Block D combination, and Unit 4 to the bottom, lining it up along the outside edge of the block as shown. Refer to the triangle diagram, and join the two sections together. Follow Step 2 for cutting the triangle.

JOINING THE TRIANGLES FOR THE QUILT TOP

1. Refer to quilt top diagram on page 111. Note that any blocks that must be matched are on the straight, not on the bias. When joining the bias part of the triangles, be careful not to stretch the fabric, and pin these triangles together. Find the center and pin. Pin the ends; then begin pinning from the center to the outer edges making certain that the edges are flat.

2. Beginning in the top left corner, join triangles 3 and 5 along the bias edge, forming a square. Make two. Join triangles 3 and 4 along the bias edge, again forming a square. Make two. You will now join the large squares together. Careful pinning is necessary as leaf and flower seams must be matched. Refer to the quilt diagram for correct placement of each large square. Join a combination of 3/5 triangles with 3/4 triangles. Make two. Join the two sets together, forming a large square. Match seams carefully. Make two of these large squares. One for the top left corner, and one for the bottom right corner.

3. For the top right corner, and the bottom left corner, to make the large square, join triangle #5 and triangle #2 on the bias edge. Make two. Join triangle #5 and triangle #1 together along the bias edge. Make 2. Join the squares together as in Step 2. Make two of these large squares.

4. Refer to the quilt diagram for correct placement, and join the large squares together. Join the two top squares, carefully matching all seams; then join the two bottom squares together, again matching seams. Join the top and bottom square sections together to form the center of the quilt top.

PIECING THE BORDERS

1. Refer to quilt top diagram on page 111. To piece the side borders, begin in the top left corner and join Block Q and Unit 8. Join Unit 7 to the top of this combination, and Block O to the bottom. Join blocks P, X, W, and S in a row as shown, carefully matching seams. Join Block V to the top of the row, matching leaf seams. Join Block N to the top of this section, and Block O to the bottom. Join this section to the bottom of the Block Q and Block O combination.

2. Join Block R and Unit 8; then add Unit 7 to the bottom of this combination, and Block N to the top as shown. Join this combination to the bottom of the other combined blocks to complete the side border. Make 2. Refer to the quilt diagram for correct placement of the rows and join them to the quilt sides, matching flower seams.

3. To piece the top and bottom borders, begin in the top left corner and join Block P and Unit 8. Join Unit 7 to the left side of this combination, and Block N to the right side. Join blocks Q, T, U, and R in a row as shown, carefully matching seams. Join Block V to the top of the row, matching leaf seams. Join Block O to the left side of this section, and Block N to the right side. Join this section to the right side of the Block P and Block N combination.

4. Join Block S and Unit 8; then add Unit 7 to the right side of this combination, and Block O to the left side. Join this combination to the right side of the other combined blocks to complete the top and bottom borders. Join Unit 9 to opposite short ends of the border; then add previously pieced Unit 10 to the top. Make 2. Join these borders to the top and bottom of the quilt, matching seams. Line your ruler up with Unit 9 diagonal and trim Unit 10 to complete the quilt top.

QUILTING AND FINISHING

Mary quilted beautiful feather swirls in the open areas of the quilt that extend into the flower and leaf sections. She always quilts lovely finishing touches inside the flowers to make them stand out.
Use the eleven 2 1/2" wide strips of Fabric II to make straight-grain binding, and bind your quilt.

MAKING TWO KING SIZE QUILTED SHAMS

Shams finish to: 21" x 38"

From Fabric II, cut:
      * Eight - 2" x 18" for sham ties.
From Fabric III, cut:
      * Two - 42" x 39 3/4" pieces for sham body.
From muslin and batting, cut:
      * Two - 42" x 39"

1. Lay the batting out on a table, and place the muslin on top of it. Place the Fabric III sham body piece on top of the muslin, right sides together.
2. Using 1/4" seam, sew through all the layers on the 42" side with raw edges matching. Trim excess from batting and muslin, leaving your 1/4" seam allowance.
3. Refer to diagram at right and open Fabric III out as shown. Press seam towards Fabric III.
4. Turn Fabric III over batting and muslin, wrong sides together and raw edges matching. Batting will be in the middle. Press finished edge and top stitch, forming your finished edge.

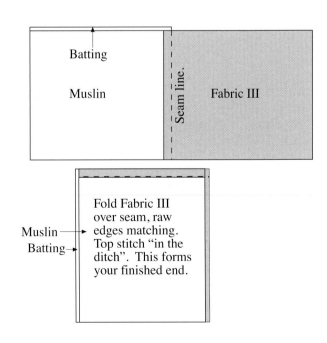

5. Pin the layers together so that they do not slip. We used a double lattice pattern for the quilting that is 1" apart. The double lattice is quilted 3 1/2" apart, leaving a 3 1/2" square between each double lattice.

6. Fold the quilted sham in half, right sides together, raw edges matching and stitch the unfinished end and side. If you have a serger, you may want to serge these seams. Turn right side out.

7. Fold the ties right sides together lengthwise, making certain that raw edges are together. Stitch around the raw edges, leaving an opening to turn. Clip corners, and turn right side out. Slip stitch the opening. Press the ties so that the seam is along one edge.

8. Find the center of the sham opening, and mark it with a pin.

Space two ties 4 1/2" on either side of the center. They will be 9" apart. Stitch in place along the top stitched seam line, securing your stitching. Repeat for the other side of the sham. There will be four ties.

9. Place your pillow inside the shams and tie in a bow with the ties.

For those of you who dream of the Orient, and reflect those dreams in the decor of your home, this design offers an added bonus. Check your stash before beginning for that oriental print that you have forgotten about!

Quilt Finishes To: 35 3/4" x 49 1/2". Techniques Used: Diagonal corners, diagonal ends, and strip sets used as diagonal corners.

**Backing needed:
2 1/4 yards.**

MATERIALS

Fabric I (ivory textured solid)
Need 35 5/8"   1 1/8 yards

Fabric II (light green print)
Need 2 3/8"   1/8 yard

Fabric III (med. green textured solid)
Need 5 3/4"   1/4 yard

Fabric IV (dark green print)
Need 6 1/4"   1/4 yard

Fabric V (med. rose textured print)
Need 2 3/8"   1/8 yard

Fabric VI (dark rose textured print)
Need 4"   1/4 yard

Fabric VII (rose oriental print)
Need 5 3/8"   1/4 yard

Fabric VIII (bamboo print)
Need 6 1/2"   1/4 yard

Fabric IX (dark gold solid)
Need 4 1/4"   1/4 yard

Fabric X (metallic gold print)
Need 2"   1/8 yard

Fabric XI (dark gold textured print)
Need 1 5/8"   1/8 yard

Fabric XII (dark brown print)
Need 3 1/2"   1/4 yard

Fabric XIII (dk. brown oriental print)
Need 31 7/8"   1 yard

Fabric XIV (medium rust print)
Need 2 3/4"   1/8 yard

Oriental Palm

CUTTING

□ **FROM FABRIC I, CUT: (IVORY TEXTURED SOLID)**
- One 10 7/8" wide strip. From this, cut:
  * One - 8 5/8" x 10 7/8" (Q11)
  * One - 3 1/4" x 10 1/2" (Q45)
  * One - 8 5/8" x 9 3/4" (Q12)
  * One - 7 5/8" x 8 7/8" (Q71)
  * One - 7 1/4" x 8 3/8" (Q22)
  * Two - 1" x 8" (Q77)
  * One - 1 5/8" x 7 5/8" (Q48)
  * One - 1 1/4" x 7 5/8" (Q60)
- One 7 1/2" wide strip. From this, cut:
  * Eight - 1" x 7 1/2" (Q78)
  * One - 3 3/4" x 7 1/4" (Q23)
  * Six - 1" x 6 1/2" (Q74, A6, A23)
  * One - 6 1/8" x 12 5/8" (Q46)
  * One - 1 7/8" x 6 1/8" (Q10)
  * One - 1 5/8" x 5 3/4" (Q8)
  * Two - 1" x 5 5/8" (Q75)
  * Two - 1 7/8" x 5" (B2, B28)
- One 5 1/4" wide strip. From this, cut:
  * Two - 1" x 5 1/4" (Q73)
  * One - 2" x 5" (Q41)
  * Two - 1 5/8" x 5" (B4, B35)
  * One - 1 5/8" x 4 5/8" (Q70)
  * Two - 4 1/4" squares (A10, A16)
  * One - 1 1/4" x 4 1/4" (Q47b)
  * Two - 1 5/8" x 3 7/8" (B6, B36)
  * Two - 2" x 3 1/2" (Q15, Q16)
  * Five - 1 1/4" x 3 1/2" (Q18, Q47, Q52, B16, B29)
  * Two - 3 1/8" squares (B17, B32)
  * One - 2 3/8" x 2 3/4" (Q65)
- Two 3" wide strips. From these, cut:
  * One - 3" x 31 3/8" (Q72)
  * One - 3" x 12 1/2" (Q13)
  * One - 2" x 2 7/8" (Q63)
  * Two - 2 3/4" squares (B5a, B34a)
  * Five - 1 5/8" x 2 3/4" (Q43, Q57a, A9a, A13a)
  * Three - 1 1/4" x 2 3/4" (Q20, B14, B31)
  * Two - 1 1/4" x 2 3/8" (B3, B26)
  * Seven - 2" squares (Q9b, Q24a, Q29, A2a, A22a, B5b, B34b)
- One 2 3/8" wide strip. From this, cut:
  * Nine - 2 3/8" squares (Q3, Q6, Q24b, Q30, Q49a, Q58, Q59, B7a, B33a)
  * Two - 2" x 3 1/8" (Q5a, Q9a)
  * Five - 1 5/8" x 2" (Q31, Q35, Q64, A5a, A20a)
  * Two - 1 1/4" x 2" (Q42a)
  * Two - 1" x 2" (B1a, B27a)
- One 2" wide strip. From this, cut:
  * Two - 2" x 8" (B8, B37)
  * Two - 1" x 1 3/4" (B1b, B27b)
  * Two - 1 1/2" x 1 5/8" (Q36, Q40)
  * Four - 1 1/4" x 1 5/8" (Q54, Q56, B12a, B21a)
  * One - 1 1/2" x 9 7/8" (Q44)
  * Two - 1 1/2" x 3 1/8" (A1, A21)
- One 1 5/8" wide strip. From this, cut:
  * Eleven - 1 5/8" squares (Q1a, A2b, A3a, A18a, A22b, B9, B13, B15a, B23, B24, B30a)
  * One - 1 1/8" x 1 1/2" (Q61)
  * Six - 1 1/4" squares (Q21a, Q49b, Q51, Q69a, A5b, A20b)

▪ **FROM FABRIC II, CUT: (LT. GREEN PRINT)**
- One 2 3/8" wide strip. From this, cut:
  * One - 2 3/8" x 6 1/8" (B33)
  * Two - 1 5/8" x 2 3/8" (A9, A9b)
  * One - 1 1/4" x 2 3/8" (B22)
  * Two - 1 1/4" x 2" (B21, B31a)
  * One - 1 5/8" x 4 1/4" (A8)
  * One - 1 5/8" x 3 7/8" (A4)
  * Two - 1 5/8" x 3 1/2" (A5, B30)
  * One - 1 1/4" x 1 5/8" (B25)
  * Three - 1 1/4" squares (B3a, B18c, B26b)
  * One - 1" x 3 1/4" (B1)

▪ **FROM FABRIC III CUT: (MED. GREEN TEXTURED SOLID**
- One 5 3/4" wide strip. From this, cut:
  * One - 1 5/8" x 5 3/4" (Q1)
  * One - 1 1/4" x 5 3/4" (Q2)
  * One - 2 3/4" x 5" (B5)
  * One - 2" x 5" (Q9)
  * One - 1 5/8" x 4 1/4" (A14)
  * One - 1 5/8" x 3 7/8" (A19)
  * One - 1 5/8" x 3 1/2" (A20)
  * One - 1" x 3 1/4" (B27)
  * One - 2 3/4" square (Q7)
  * Two - 1 5/8" x 2 3/8" (A13, A13b)
  * Two - 1 5/8" squares (B4a, B7b)
  * One - 1 1/4" square (B26a)

▪ **FROM FABRIC IV, CUT: (DK. GREEN PRINT)**
- One 4 1/4" wide strip. From this, cut:
  * Two - 2 3/4" x 4 1/4" (A7, A15)
  * Two - 2 1/4" x 3 7/8" (A3, A18)
  * Two - 3 1/8" x 3 1/2" (A2, A22)
  * One - 1 5/8" x 3 1/2" (B15)
  * Two - 2 3/4" squares (A11, A17)
  * One - 2 3/4" x 5" (B34)
  * One - 2 3/8" x 6 1/8" (B7)
  * One - 1 1/4" x 2 3/8" (B11)
  * Two - 2" squares (B8a, B37a)
- One 2" wide strip. From this, cut:
  * One - 2" x 4 5/8" (Q5)
  * Two - 1 1/4" x 2" (B12, B14a)
  * One - 1 5/8" x 5 3/4" (Q4)
  * Four - 1 5/8" squares (A4a, A19a, B33b, B35a)
  * One - 1 1/4" x 1 5/8" (B10)
  * Two - 1 1/2" squares (A1a, A21a)
  * One - 1 1/4" x 5" (A12)
  * Three - 1 1/4" squares (A9c, B3b, B18b)

▪ **FROM FABRIC V, CUT: (MED. ROSE TEXTURED PRINT)**
- One 2 3/8" wide strip. From this, cut:
  * One - 2 3/8" square (Q24d)

114

* One - 2" square (Q24c)
* One - 1 5/8" x 5 3/8" (Q25)
* One - 1 5/8" square (Q38)

 FROM FABRIC VI, CUT: (DK. ROSE TEX-TURED PRINT)
- **One 2 3/8" wide strip. From this, cut:**
  * One - 2 3/8" x 2 3/4" (Q49)
  * One - 1 7/8" x 2 3/8" (Q67)
  * One - 1 3/8" x 2 3/8" (Q66)
  * One - 1 1/4" x 2 3/8" (Q47a)
  * Two - 1 5/8" x 5" (Q68, Q69)
  * One - 1 5/8" x 4 5/8" (Q57)
  * One - 1 5/8" x 3 1/8" (Q53)
  * Four - 1 5/8" x 2 5/8" (Q94)
  * One - 1 1/4" x 1 5/8" (Q50)
  * One - 1" x 1 1/8" (Q62)
- **One 1 5/8" wide strip. From this, cut:**
  * Five - 1 5/8" squares (Q55, Q58a, Q59a, Q64a, Q70a)
  * Seventeen - 1" squares (Q63a, Q80a, Q83a, Q85a, Q87b, Q97b, Q98b, Q102a)

 FROM FABRIC VII, CUT: (ROSE ORIENTAL PRINT)
- **One 5 3/8" wide strip. From this, cut:**
  * One - 5 3/8" x 7 1/4" (Q24)
  * One - 1 5/8" x 5 3/8" (Q28)
  * One - 1 5/8" x 4 3/4" (Q39)
  * One - 2 3/8" square (Q27)
  * One 1 5/8" x 2 1/8" (Q37)
  * One - 2" square (Q26)

 FROM FABRIC VIII, CUT: (BAMBOO PRINT)
- **Four 1 5/8" wide strips. From these, cut:**
  * Eight - 1 5/8" x 7 1/4" (Q91, Q92)
  * Two - 1 5/8" x 7" (Q90)
  * Four - 1 5/8" x 6 1/4" (Q81, Q82)
  * Two - 1 5/8" x 6" (Q80)
  * Two - 1 5/8" x 5 5/8" (Q83)
  * Four - 1 5/8" x 2 3/8" (Q102)
  * Four - 1 5/8" x 1 7/8" (Q95)
  * Eight - 1 5/8" squares (Q94a)

FROM FABRIC IX, CUT: (DK. GOLD PRINT)
- **Two 1 5/8" wide strips. From these, cut:**
  * Fourteen - 1 5/8" x 1 7/8" (Q84, Q93)
  * Twenty-eight - 1" x 1 5/8" (Q76, Q79, Q88, Q99)
  * Twenty-five - 1" squares (Q73a, Q74a, Q75a, Q77a, Q78a, Q78b, Q85a, Q86a, Q87a, Q97b, Q98a)
- **One 1" wide strip. From this, cut:**
  * Thirty-one - 1" squares (add to 1" sq. above)

FROM FABRIC X, CUT: (METALLIC GOLD PRINT)
- **One 2" wide strip. From this, cut:**
  * Two - 2" x 2 3/8" (Q41a)
  * Two - 1 1/4" x 2" (Q42)
  * One - 1 5/8" square (Q33)

 FROM FABRIC XI, CUT: (DARK GOLD TEXTURED PRINT)
- **One 1 5/8" wide strip. From this, cut:**
  * One - 1 5/8" x 4 1/4" (Q34)
  * One - 1 5/8" square (Q32)
  * One - 1 1/4" x 5 3/4" (Q41b)

 FROM FABRIC XII, CUT: (DK. BROWN PRINT)
- **One 3 1/2" wide strip. From this, cut:**
  * One - 3 1/2" x 4 1/4" (Q17)
  * One - 1 1/4" x 2 3/4" (Q19)
  * One - 2" x 3 5/8" (B18)
  * One - 2" x 2 7/8" (B20)
  * Two - 2" squares (Q14a, Q21)
  * One - 1 1/4" square (Q16a)

FROM FABRIC XIII, CUT: (DK. BROWN ORIENTAL PRINT)
- **One 3 7/8" wide strip. From this, cut:**
  * Four - 3 7/8" squares (Q103)
  Stack these cuts:
  * Eight - 1 5/8" x 2" (Q96, Q101)
  * Two - 1" x 8" (Q97)
  * Four - 1" x 6 1/2" (Q86)
- **Four 3 3/8" wide strips. From these, cut:**
  * Two - 3 3/8" x 40 1/2" (Q100)
  * Two - 3 3/8" x 26 3/4" (Q89)
  Stack these cuts:
  * Two - 1" x 6 1/8" (Q87)
  * Two - 1" x 5 3/4" (Q85)
- **Five 2 1/2" wide strips for straight-grain binding1**
- **Two 1" wide strips. From these, cut:**
  * Eight - 1" x 7 1/2" (Q98)

 FROM FABRIC XIV, CUT: (MED. RUST PRINT)
- **One 2 3/4" wide strip. From this, cut:**
  * One - 2 3/4" x 3 1/2" (Q18)
  * One - 2" x 3 1/2" (Q14)
  * One - 2" x 2 1/2" (B19)
  * Two - 2" squares (B18a, B20a)
  * One - 1 1/4" square (Q15a)

BLOCK A ASSEMBLY

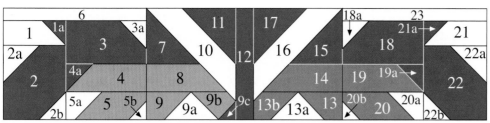

Block A. Make One. When completed, block should measure 5" x 20 3/4"

1. Use diagonal corner technique to make one each of units 1, 2, 3, 4, 18, 19, 21, and 22. Use diagonal end technique to make one each of units 5, 9, 13, and 20, shown below.

2. To assemble the block, begin by joining units 1 and 2. Join units 3, 4, and 5 in a row as shown. Join this row to the right side of the 1-2 combination; then add

Unit 6 to the top as shown. Refer to the diagram below for assembly of units 7-12. Combined units 13-17 are made the same way, only they are mirror images. Refer to the diagram below.

3. Join Unit 12 to the right side of combined units 7-11; then add this combination to the right side of the 1-6 combined units. Join combined units 13-17 to right side of Unit 12.

4. Join units 18, 19 and 20 in a vertical row. Join units 21 and 22; then join the 21-22 combination to the right side of combined units 18-20. Join Unit 23 to the top. Add this section to the right side of the other combined units to complete Block A. Make 1.

Making units A5 and A20

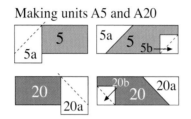

Making units A9, and A13

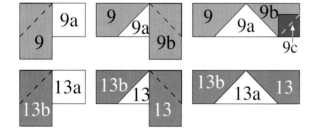

Making combined units A13-A17

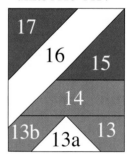

Making combined units A7-A12

Step 1   Step 2

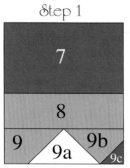 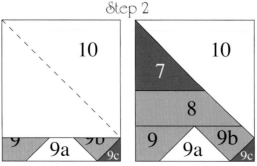 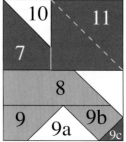 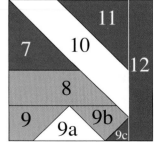

Join units 7, 8, and 9.

Place diagonal corner, Unit 10 as shown. Right sides facing and raw edges matching. Stitch diagonal. We suggest not trimming the center seam on Unit 10 as it is a light fabric on dark.

Join diagonal corner, Unit 11. Stitch diagonal, trim seam and press; then join Unit 12 to right side.

116

BLOCK B ASSEMBLY

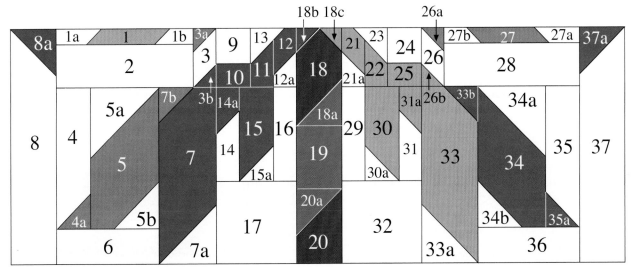

Block B. Make One. When completed, block should measure 8" x 20 3/4"

1. Use diagonal corner technique to make one each of units 3, 4, 5, 7, 8, 15, 18, 20, 26, 30, 33, 34, 35, and 37. Use diagonal end technique to make one each of units 1, 12, 14, 21, 27, and 31, shown below.

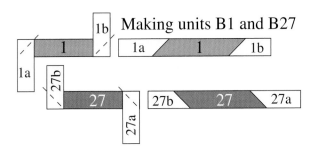

Making units B1 and B27

Making units B12 and B21

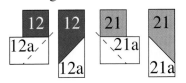

Making units B14 and B31

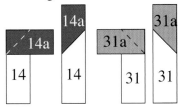

2. To assemble the block, begin by joining units 1 and 2; then add Unit 3 to the right side. Join units 4 and 5; then join Unit 6 to the bottom of these combined units. Join Unit 7 to the right side of the combined 4-6 units; then add these units to the bottom of combined units 1-3, matching leaf seam. Join Unit 8 to the right side.

3. Join units 9 and 10. Join units 11 and 12; then add diagonal corner, Unit 13 to the top left corner of the 11-12 combined units. Join these units to the right side of combined 9-10 units, matching leaf seam. Join units 14, 15, and 16 in a row; then add Unit 17 to the bottom of the row.

Join these units to the bottom of combined units 9-13, matching leaf seam. Join this section to the right side of combined units 1-8, matching leaf seam.

4. For the trunk of the tree, join units 18, 19, and 20 in a vertical row; then join this row to other combined units, again matching top leaf seam.

5. For the right section of the block, join units 21 and 22; then add diagonal corner, Unit 23 to the top right corner of the combined units. Join units 24 and 25; then add Unit 26 to the right side of these combined units, matching the leaf seam. Join units 27 and 28; then join them to the right side of combined units 21-26.

6. Join units 29, 30, and 31 in a row; then add Unit 32 to the bottom and Unit 33 to the right side. Join units 34 and 35; then join Unit 36 to the bottom of these combined units. Join the 34-36 combined units to the right side of Unit 33. Join the top section of the leaves to the top of combined units 29-36, matching leaf seams; then add Unit 37 to the right side.

7. Join the right side of the Palm to the right side of the trunk, matching the top leaf seam to complete the block. Make 1.

8. Join blocks A and B together, as shown in quilt diagram. Be careful to match the leaf seams. When the two blocks are joined, join Unit Q13 to the right side of the combined blocks.

ASSEMBLY OF SECTION 1

1. Use diagonal corner technique to make one of Unit Q1. Use diagonal end technique to make one each of units Q5 and Q9.

Making mirror image Unit Q42

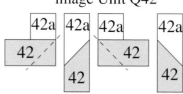

Making combined units Q1-Q9 for Section 1

Step 1

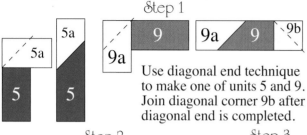

Use diagonal end technique to make one of units 5 and 9. Join diagonal corner 9b after diagonal end is completed.

Step 2

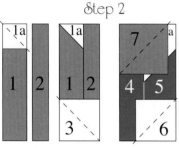

Use diagonal corner technique to make Unit 1. Join units 1 and 2; then add diagonal corner, Unit 3. Join units 4 and 5; then add diagonal corners 6 and 7 as shown.

Step 3

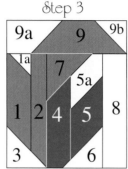

Join combined units 1-3 to left side of combined units 4-7; then add Unit 8 to right side. Join Unit 9 to the top, matching seams.

Making combined units Q17-Q18.

Join 1 1/4" x 3 1/2" strip of Fabric I with 2 3/4" x 3 1/2" piece of Fabric XIV. This will now be used as a diagonal corner.

Place Unit Q18 as shown on top of Unit Q17, raw edges matching. Stitch diagonal, trim seam, and press.

2. Refer to diagram and instructions above for making combined units Q1-Q9. We do not suggest trimming the Q3 and Q6 as they are light fabric on top of dark fabric.
3. Refer to the quilt diagram, and join Unit Q10 to the top of Unit Q9; then add Unit Q11 to the left side and Unit Q12 to the right side to complete Section 1.

3. To assemble Section 2, begin by joining units Q15, Q14, and Q16 in a row as shown. Join units Q19 and Q20; then add Unit Q21 to bottom of these combined units, matching seams. Join Unit Q18 to the left side as shown. Join the row of combined units Q14-Q16 to the top, matching seams; then add Unit Q22 to the left side and Unit Q23 to the right side.

ASSEMBLY OF SECTION 2

1. Use diagonal corner technique to make one of units Q14, Q15, Q16, Q21, and Q24. Use diagonal end technique to make two of mirror image Unit Q42 and one of Unit Q41, as shown on this page.
2. To assemble combined units Q17-Q18, refer to the diagram and instructions above right. Combined units Q24-Q30 are shown on the following page. This unit is made with a series of diagonal corners. Follow the diagram and instructions to complete this unit.

Making Unit Q41

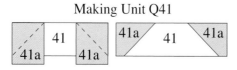

SECTION 2

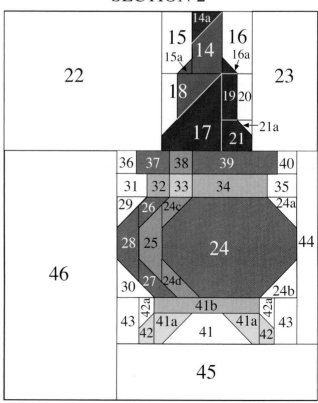

Making combined units Q24-Q30

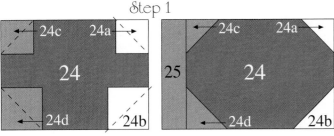

Step 1

Use diagonal corner technique to make Unit 24. Join the diagonal corners in alphabetical order. Join Unit 25 to left side as shown, and press.

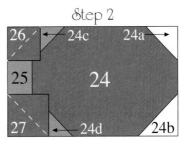

Step 2

Join diagonal corners 26 and 27. Trim seams and press.

Step 3

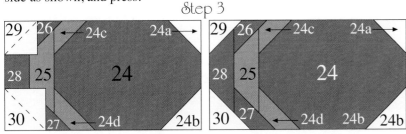

Join Unit 28 to left side of the pot; then add diagonal corners 29 and 30 as shown.

4. To complete the bottom section, join units Q36, Q37, Q38, Q39, and Q40 in a horizontal row. Join units Q31, Q32, Q33, Q34, and Q35 in a horizontal row. Join the two rows together as shown, matching seams. Join combined units Q24-Q30 to the bottom of the two rows, matching seams. Join units Q41 and Q41b together. Join mirror image units Q43 and Q42 together, referring to Section diagram for correct placement of mirror image units. Join the combined Q42-Q43 units to opposite sides of combined Q41-Q41b units. Join these units to the bottom of the bowl. Join Unit Q44 to the right side of the bowl; then add Unit Q45 to the bottom. Complete the section by joining Unit Q46 to the left side. Join the top and bottom sections together to complete Section 2.

ASSEMBLY OF SECTION 3

1. Use diagonal corner technique to make one of units Q49, Q58, Q59 Q63, Q64, and Q70. Use diagonal end technique to make one each of units Q47, and Q57, shown below.

Making Unit Q47

Making Unit Q57

2. To assemble Section 3, begin by joining units Q47 and Q48 as shown in section diagram below. Join units Q50 and Q51; then add Unit Q49 to the left side of these combined units. Join Unit Q52 to the bottom; then add Unit Q53 to the right side. Join units Q54, Q55, and Q56 in a vertical row. Join this row to the right side of Unit Q53. Join Unit Q57 to the bottom as shown. Join units Q58 and Q59. Add these units to the right side of combined units Q49-Q57, matching seams. Join Unit Q60 to the bottom. Join combined units Q47-Q48 to the top of the combined units, matching seams.

3. Join units Q61 and Q62. Join units Q63 and Q64. Join these two combined units together as shown. Join units Q66, Q65, and Q67. Join Unit Q68 to the top and Unit Q69 to the bottom. Join combined units Q61-Q64 to the right side; then add Unit Q70 to the left side. Join the top combined units to the bottom combined units; then add Unit Q71 to the bottom to complete Section 3.

4. Join Section 2 and Section 3 together as shown on quilt diagram. Join combined blocks A and B to the top of combined sections 2 and 3; then add Unit Q72 to the left side. Join Section 1 to the top as shown, matching the tree trunk seams to complete the center of the quilt.

SECTION 3

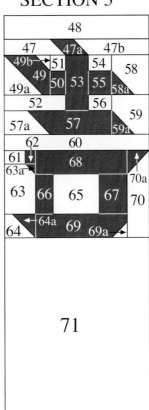

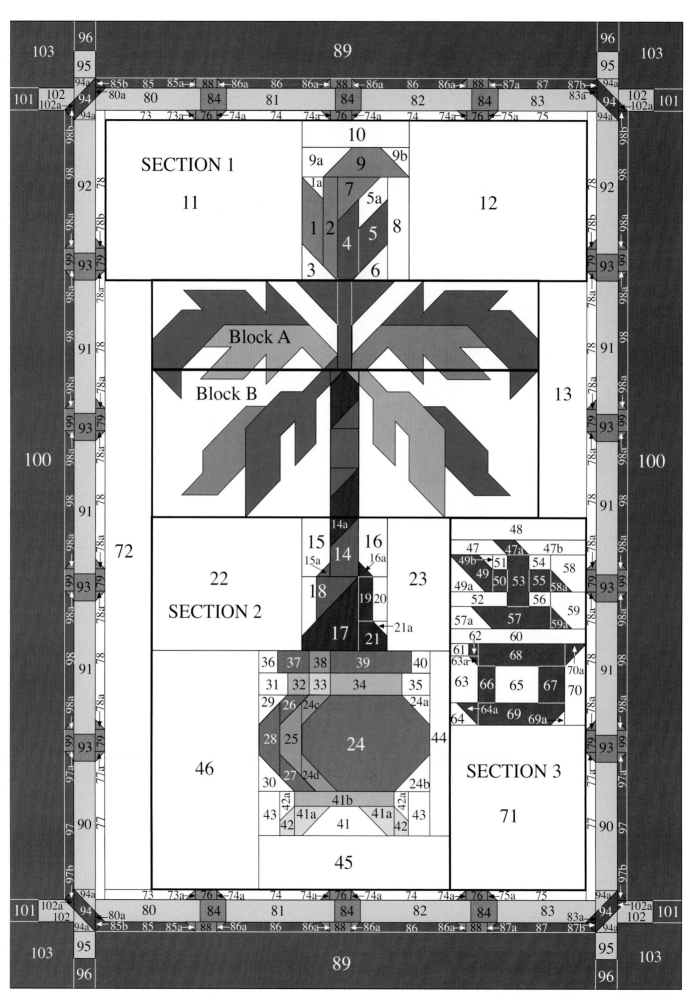

120

INNER BORDER ASSEMBLY

1. For top and bottom inner borders, use diagonal corner technique to make four of Unit Q74, and two each of mirror image units Q73 and Q75.

2. Beginning with the top row, refer to the quilt diagram on the preceding page for correct placement of mirror image units. Join Unit Q73, Q76, Q74, Q76, Q74, Q76, and Q75. Join the units in this order for the bottom row noting that the main difference is the placement of the mirror image diagonal corners on units Q73 and Q75.

3. Join these borders to the top and bottom of the quilt top.

4. For the side inner borders, use diagonal corner technique and make eight of Unit Q78 (two are mirror imaged) and two of mirror image Unit Q77.

5. Both borders are pieced the same way except for the position of the mirror image units. To piece them, beginning at the top, join units Q78 (one diagonal corner), Q79, Q78, Q79, Q78, Q79, and Q77. Join these borders to opposite sides of the quilt top.

TOP AND BOTTOM BORDER ASSEMBLY

1. For the top and bottom bamboo borders, use diagonal corner technique to make two each of mirror image units 80 and 83. To piece these borders, refer to quilt diagram for correct placement of mirror image diagonal corners. Join units Q80, Q84, Q81, Q84, Q82, Q84, and Q83 in a horizontal row. Join the borders to the top and bottom of the quilt top, matching seams.

2. For the top and bottom Fabric XIII borders, refer to quilt diagram for correct placement of mirror image units. Working from left to right, join units Q85, Q88, Q86, Q88, Q86, Q88, and Q87. Join these borders to the top and bottom of the quilt top, matching seams. Join Unit Q89 to top and bottom of quilt.

SIDE BORDER ASSEMBLY

1. For the side bamboo borders, use diagonal corner technique to make four of Unit Q94. To piece the borders, beginning at the top, join units Q96, Q95, Q94, Q92, Q93, Q91, Q93, Q91, Q93, Q91, Q93, Q90, Q94, Q95, and Q96. Make two. Join these borders to opposite sides of the quilt top.

2. For the side Fabric XIII borders, use diagonal corner technique to make eight of Unit Q98, and two of mirror image Unit Q97. For the corner bamboo, use this technique to make four of mirror image Unit 102. To piece the border, beginning at the top, join units Q98, Q99, Q98, Q99, Q98, Q99, Q98, Q99, and Q97. Make two.

3. Join Unit Q100 to sides of Fabric XIII border as shown. Join units Q101 and Q102, checking quilt diagram for correct placement of mirror image units. Join corner Unit Q103 to combined units Q101-Q102 as shown. Join the corners to opposite short ends of the other combined border units. Make 2. Join these combined borders to opposite sides of the quilt top to complete it.

QUILTING AND FINISHING

Mary ditched the patchwork, and quilted an oriental shell background. She quilted straight lines in the outer borders approximately 1 1/2" apart.

Use the five strips of Fabric XIII for straight-grain binding, and bind your quilt.

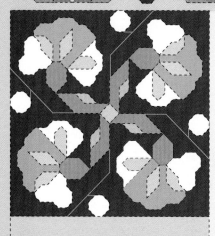

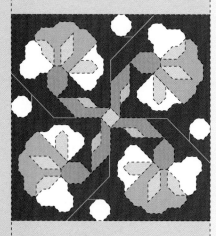

Folk Flowers

This charming table runner was photographed for our last book, "Pieces Of Baltimore...The Ultimate Collection." Unfortunately there was not enough room for it in the book. I loved the design and vowed to use it in the next book. It enhances any table, no matter what the time of year, but is especially appealing at any holiday gathering. It's easy piecing with hand or machine embroidery for the stems.

Table runner finishes to: 24" x 61"
Techniques used: Diagonal corners, diagonal ends and triangle-squares.

MATERIALS

Fabric I (barn red print)
Need 44 5/8"   1 3/8 yards

Fabric II (leafy tan print)
Need 28 1/2"   1 yard

Fabric III (ivory print)
Need 15"   1/2 yard

Fabric IV (gold marble print)
Need 10 1/2"   3/8 yard

Fabric V (dark green print)
Need 8 1/2"   3/8 yard

Fabric VI (medium green print)
Need 11 1/2"   1/2 yard

Fabric VII (light green print)
Need 1 3/8"   1/8 yard

Backing   2 yards

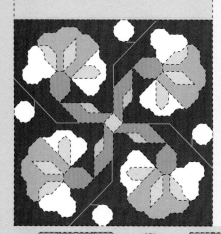

CUTTING

◼ FROM FABRIC I, CUT: (BARN RED PRINT)
- **One 3 7/8" wide strip. From this, cut:**
    * Twelve - 1 7/8" x 3 7/8" (A27)
    * Fifty-seven - 1" squares (A1b, A11b, A20a, A32a)
- **One 3 3/4" wide strip. From this, cut:**
    * Twelve - 1 3/4" x 3 3/4" (A6)
    * Four - 1 5/8" x 3 1/2" (D11)
    * Twelve - 1 1/8" x 2 5/8" (A5)
- **One 3 1/8" wide strip. From this, cut:**
    * Twelve - 3 1/8" squares (A26)
- **One 2 5/8" wide strip. From this, cut:**
    * Twelve - 2 1/8" x 2 5/8" (A9)
    * Twelve - 1 3/8" x 2 1/2" (A23)
- **Five 2 1/2" wide strips for straight-grain binding.**
- **Two 2 3/8" wide strips. From these, cut:**
    * Eight - 2 3/8" squares (C1)
    * Twelve - 2" x 2 3/8" (A28)
    * Four - 1 5/8" x 2 3/8" (D10)
    * Twelve - 1 1/4" x 2 1/4" (A33)
    * Fourteen - 1" squares (add to 1" squares above)
- **One 2 1/4" wide strip. From this, cut:**
    * Twelve - 1" x 2 1/4" (A8)
    * Twelve - 2" squares (A20b)
    Stack this cut:
    * Twelve - 1" x 1 1/8" (A31)
- **Two 1 3/4" wide strips. From these, cut:**
    * Twelve - 1 3/4" x 2 1/8" (A12)
    * Twelve - 1 3/4" x 2" (A21)
    * Twelve - 1 1/8" 1 3/4" (A19)
- **One 1 1/2" wide strip. From this, cut:**
    * Twenty-four - 1 1/2" squares (A4a, A14a)
    * One - 1" square (add to 1" squares above)
- **Six 1 1/8" wide strips. From these, cut:**
    * Twelve - 1 1/8" x 9 1/2" (A13)
    * Twelve - 1 1/8" x 4 3/8" (A22)
    * Seventy-six - 1 1/8" squares (A7a, A29a, D9a)

◼ FROM FABRIC II, CUT; (LEAFY TAN PRINT)
- **One 10 1/2" wide strip. From this, cut:**
    * Two - 1 3/8" x 10 1/2" (F7)
    * Four - 1 3/8" x 10 1/4" (E7)
    * Eight - 1 3/8" x 9 1/2" (B7)
    * Two - 1" x 10 1/2" (F8)
    * Four - 1" x 10 1/4" (E8)
    * Eight - 1" x 9 1/2" (B8)
    * Four - 1 1/4" x 2 5/8" (F4a)
    * Eight - 1 1/4" x 2 1/2" (E4a)
    * Sixteen - 1 1/4" x 2 3/8" (B4a)
- **One 3 3/4" wide strip. From this, cut:**
    * Twelve - 1 3/4" x 3 3/4" (A18)
    Stack this cut:
    * Twelve - 1 5/8" x 2 1/8" (A10)

- **One 2 3/8" wide strip. From this, cut:**
    * Eight - 1 1/8" x 2 3/8" (C2)
    * Eight - 1" x 2 3/8" (C3)
- **Two 2 1/8" wide strips. From these, cut:**
    * Twenty-eight - 2 1/8" squares (B6a, E6a, F6a)
- **One 1 5/8" wide strip. From this, cut:**
    * Twenty-four - 1 5/8" sq. (A1a, A2)
- **Two 1 3/8" wide strips. From these, cut:**
    * Forty - 1 3/8" squares (A24a, B5a, E5a, F5a)
- **Two 1 1/8" wide strips. From these, cut:**
    * Sixty-eight - 1 1/8" squares (A11a, A16, A17, C1a)
- **One 1" wide strip. From this, cut:**
    * Two - 1" x 18 1/2" (Q1)

◻ FROM FABRIC III, CUT: (IVORY PRINT)
- **Three 2 3/8" wide strips. From these, cut:**
    * Sixteen - 2 3/8" squares (A29, D9)
    * Twelve - 2 1/4" x 2 3/8" (A32)
    * Twelve - 2" x 2 1/8" (A11)
- **One 2" wide strip. From this, cut:**
    * Twelve - 2" x 3 1/8" (A20)
- **One 1 7/8" wide strip. From this, cut:**
    * Twelve - 1 7/8" squares (A4b)
    * Twelve - 1 1/2" squares (A18b)
- **One 1 3/4" wide strip. From this, cut:**
    * Twelve - 1 3/4" squares (A18c)
    * Twelve - 1 1/8" x 1 3/4" (A30)
- **Two 1 1/8" wide strips. From these, cut:**
    * Forty-eight - 1 1/8" squares (A6a, A14c, A17, A21a)
    * Twelve - 1" squares (A10a)

◼ FROM FABRIC IV, CUT: (GOLD MARBLE PRINT)
- **One 2 5/8" wide strip. From this, cut:**
    * Twelve - 2 5/8" x 3 1/8" (A4)
- **One 2 1/4" wide strip. From this, cut:**
    * Twelve - 2 1/4" x 2 5/8" (A1)
- **One 1 3/4" wide strip. From this, cut:**
    * Twelve - 1 3/4" squares (A18a)
    * Twelve - 1 1/4" squares (A10b)
- **One 1 5/8" wide strip. From this, cut:**
    * Twelve - 1 5/8" x 2 1/4" (A7)
    * Twelve - 1 1/8" x 1 5/8" (A3)
- **Two 1 1/8" wide strips. From these, cut:**
    * Forty-eight - 1 1/8" squares (A5a, A14b, A15, A16)
    * Twelve - 1" squares (A2a)

◼ FROM FABRIC V, CUT: (DK. GREEN PRINT)
- **One 3 1/2" wide strip. From this, cut:**
    * Four - 1 3/8" x 3 1/2" (F5)
    * Eight - 1 3/8" x 3 3/8" (E5)
    * Sixteen - 1 3/8" x 3" (B5)
- **Two 2 1/2" wide strips. From these, cut:**
    * Twenty-eight - 2 1/8" x 2 1/2" (B6, E6, F6)

FROM FABRIC VI, CUT: (MED. GREEN PRINT)

- **One 4" wide strip. From this, cut:**
  - * Twelve - 2 1/4" x 4" (A25)
- **One 2 3/8" wide strip. From this, cut:**
  - * Twelve - 2 3/8" x 3 1/4" (A14)
- **One 1 3/8" wide strip. From this, cut:**
  - * Twelve - 1 3/8" x 2 3/4" (A24)
- **Three 1 1/4" wide strips. From these, cut:**
  - * Twelve - 1 1/4" x 2 1/8" (E4, F4)
  - * Sixteen - 1 1/4" x 1 7/8" (B4)
  - * Twenty-eight 1 1/4" squares (B6b, E6b, F6b)

FROM FABRIC VII, CUT: (LT. GREEN PRINT)

- **One 1 3/8" wide strip. From this, cut:**
  - * Twelve - 1 3/8" x 1 5/8" (A23a)
  - * Twelve - 1 3/8" squares (A25a)

BLOCK A ASSEMBLY

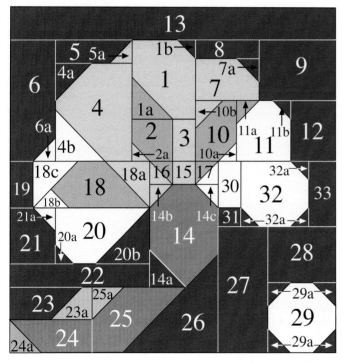

Block A. Make 12. When completed, block should measure 9 1/2" square.

These instructions are for one block.

1. Use diagonal corner technique to make one each of units 1, 2, 4, 5, 6, 7, 10, 11, 14, 18, 20, 21, 24, 25, and 29. Use diagonal

Making Unit A23

Place 1 1/8" squares of fabrics II and IV right sides together. Stitch diagonal down the center, trim seam and press.

Place 1 1/8" squares of fabrics II and III right sides together. Stitch diagonal down the center, trim seam and press.

Making Unit A18

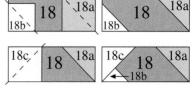

end technique to make one of Unit 23. Use triangle-square technique to make one each of units 16 and 17, as shown above.

2. To piece the block, begin by joining units 2 and 3; then join Unit 1 to the top of these combined units, matching seams. Join units 4 and 5; then add them to the left side of the 1-3 combined units. Join Unit 6 to the left side as shown.

3. Join units 7 and 8; then add Unit 9 to the right side of the 7-8 units. Join units 10, 11, and 12 in a row. Join this row to the bottom of combined 7-9 units. Join the left side of the flower to the right side; then add Unit 13 across the top.

Step 4

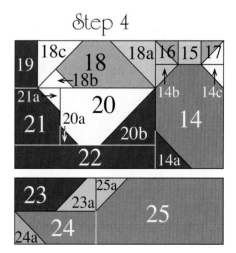

4. Refer to the diagram above, and join units 16, 15, and 17 in a horizontal row as shown. Join Unit 14 to the bottom of this row, matching seams. Join units 18 and 19. Join units 21 and 20; then add Unit 22 to the bottom of the 20-21 combined units. Join these units to the bottom of combined units 18-19, again matching seams. Join combined units 18-22 to combined units 14-17. Join units 23 and 24; then add Unit 25 to the right side of these combined units as shown, matching seams.

Step 5

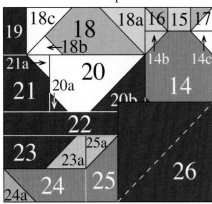

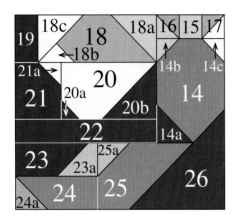

Block C. Make 8. When completed, block should measure 2 3/8" x 3 1/2".

Block D. Make 4. When completed, block should measure 3 1/2" sq.

BLOCKS B, E and F ASSEMBLY

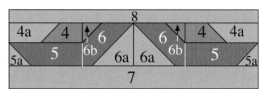

Block B. Make 8. When completed, block should measure 3 1/2" x 9 1/2"

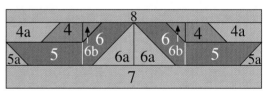

Block E. Make 4. When completed, block should measure 3 1/2" x 10 1/4"

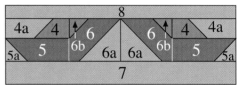

Block F. Make 2. When completed, block should measure 3 1/2" x 10 1/2"

5. Join combined units 23-25 to the bottom of combined units 14-22. Join diagonal corner, Unit 26 to bottom right side of the block. Stitch diagonal, trim seam and press.

6. Referring to Block A diagram, join units 30 and 31. Join units 32 and 33; then add these combined units to the right side of the 30-31 combined units. Join units 28 and 29; then add Unit 27 to the left side of the 28-29 units. Join these combined units to the bottom of combined units 30-33.

7. Join combined units 27-33 to the right side of combined units 14-26, matching seams. Join the top flower section to the bottom flower section, matching seams to complete Block A. Make 12.

BLOCKS C AND D ASSEMBLY

1. Refer to the diagram above right. Use diagonal corner technique to make one of Unit 1. To assemble the block, join units 2, 1, and 3 in a vertical row as shown. Make 8.

2. For Block D, use diagonal corner technique to make one of Unit 9. To assemble the block, join units 9 and 10; then add Unit 11 to the bottom to complete the block. Make 4.

1. Assembly for all three blocks is the same. The only difference in the blocks is their size. For each block, use diagonal corner technique to make two each of mirror image units 5 and 6. Use diagonal end technique to make two of mirror image Unit 4, shown below.

2. To assemble the blocks, begin by joining mirror image Units 6. Join mirror image units 4 and 5, referring to the block diagrams for correct placement of these units. Join these combined units to opposite sides of combined Unit 6's; then join Unit 7 to the bottom and Unit 8 to the top to complete the blocks.

Making mirror image units B4, E4, and F4

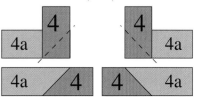

TABLE RUNNER ASSEMBLY

1. Join Block A's together in a series of four as shown at left. Match center seams, and make 3 sets. We worked the stems by hand with six strands of gold embroidery floss to match the gold in the flowers. A chain stitch was used. Refer to page 11 for this stitch. If you prefer, the stems can be worked with a machine satin stitch with stabilizer on the back. You will find it much easier to work the embroidery of the three sets of four, before they are pieced together.

2. To join the three sets of A blocks together, join Unit Q1 between the sets as shown below. For the top border, join Block B, Block C, Block E, Block C, Block F, Block C, Block E, Block C, and Block B in a horizontal row. Make 2. Join these border rows to the top and bottom of the table runner.

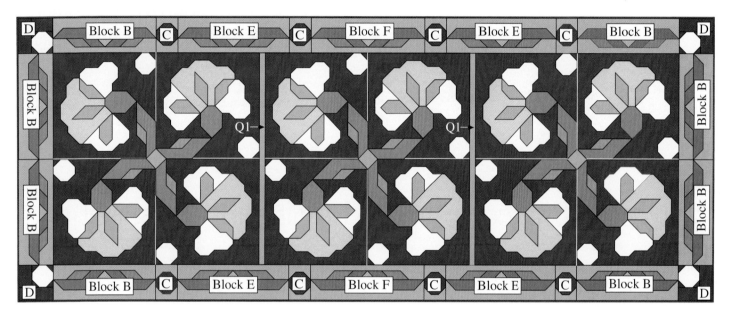

3. For the side borders, refer to diagram above and join two of Block B, matching leaf tips. Join Block D to opposite short ends of the side borders. Make 2. Join to opposite sides of the table runner to complete it.

QUILTING AND FINISHING

Mary used a large stipple stitch in the dark red background and a small stipple on the borders. The patchwork was "ditched".

Join the five 2 1/2" wide strips of Fabric I. Refer to page 12 for making straight-grain binding, and bind the table runner.

Why don't-cha come up and quilt with me sometime!

Ask for more Leisure Arts/Pam Bono Designs
books where ever quilting books are sold.

The Big Book Of Rotary Cutter Quilts
Quilts a la Carte
Dear Pam....Teach ME Your Quick Quilting Techniques.
Pieces Of Baltimore....The Ultimate Collection.

www.leisurearts.com and www.pambonodesigns.com

For more of the joy to be shared with this gorgeous
model, visit her on the internet at: www.zeldawisdom.com

128